Turn eBay® Data Into Dollars:

Tools and Techniques to Make More Money on Every Transaction

Ina Steiner

McGraw-Hill

New York   Chicago   San Francisco   Lisbon
London   Madrid   Mexico City   Milan   New Delhi
San Juan   Seoul   Singapore   Sydney   Toronto

The McGraw·Hill Companies

McGraw-Hill books are available at special quantity discounts to use as premiums and sales promotions, or for use in corporate training programs. For more information, please write to the Director of Special Sales, Professional Publishing, McGraw-Hill, Two Penn Plaza, New York, NY 10121-2298. Or contact your local bookstore.

**Turn eBay® Data Into Dollars: Tools and Techniques
to Make More Money on Every Transaction**

1234567890 FGR FGR 0198765

ISBN 0-07-226236-2

The sponsoring editor for this book was Marjorie McAneny and the project editor was LeeAnn Pickrell. The copy editor was Lisa Theobald, the proofreader was Susie Elkind, and the indexer was Ted Laux. Composition and illustration by ITC. Cover design by Pattie Lee.

This book was composed with Adobe® InDesign®.

Information contained in this work has been obtained by The McGraw-Hill Companies, Inc. from sources believed to be reliable. However, because of the possibility of human or mechanical error by our sources, McGraw-Hill, or others, McGraw-Hill does not guarantee the accuracy, adequacy, or completeness of any information and is not responsible for any errors or omissions or the results obtained from the use of such information.

Library of Congress Cataloging-in-Publication Data

Steiner, Ina.
   Turn eBay data into dollars : tools and techniques to make
more money on every transaction / by Ina Steiner.
      p. cm.

  ISBN 0-07-226236-2
  1. eBay (Firm) 2. Internet auctions. 3.
Auctions--Computer network resources. I. Title.
  HF5478.S74 2006
  658.8'7--dc22
                    2005033669

*To my husband and best friend,
David, and to Maggie the Auction Hound,
who kept me company while I wrote.*

About the Author

Ina Steiner, M.B.A., is Editor of AuctionBytes.com, publisher of content for the online-auction industry. She has been quoted as an eBay authority in *The New York Times, Wall Street Journal, USA Today, Smart Money* magazine, *Fortune Small Business*, CNET.com, *San Jose Mercury News*, and the *Boston Globe*. She has also appeared on TV and radio, including Public Radio's "Marketplace" and Bloomberg Radio's "Tomorrow Tonight." Ina is a weekly guest on the syndicated radio show "Calling All Collectors," which reaches nearly 10,000 listeners each week, and she appeared on eBay Radio last July in a segment about AuctionBytes called "A great resource for the SERIOUS eBay Seller." Ina also writes "The Web Page" column for *New England Antiques Journal*. Prior to founding AuctionBytes, Ina worked for more than a decade in market research and product management; her research has been published by International Data Corporation. She is a member of the Online News Association.

About the Technical Reviewer

Dave Taylor is recognized as a leading guru in the technology industry and has been involved with the Internet since 1980. Author of 20 business and computer books, he is also a prolific blogger, primarily at www.AskDaveTaylor.com and Blog.Intuitive.com, and a frequent public speaker and workshop leader. He has been involved with the online auction space since the mid 1990s when he launched an auction-related startup of his own called iTrack.com. Dave can be reached any time at taylor@intuitive.com.

Contents

Acknowledgments xi

Introduction xiii

PART I **The Joys and Pitfalls of eBay Data**

CHAPTER 1 **What Is eBay Data?** **3**

No Magic Pills or Secret Formulas 4

Background and Definitions 5

eBay Data Paints a Picture 8

Applying eBay Data to Your Business 8

Why You Need to Analyze eBay Data 9

Using Data to List Smarter 11

Using Data to Market Smarter 12

Research and Analysis Tools 12

Market-Data Tools 13

Sales Performance Reporting and Analysis Tools 13

Analytics (Traffic-Tracking) Tools 13

Competitive Intelligence Tools 13

The Cost of Data Analysis Tools 13

eBay: An Ever-Changing Marketplace 14

Multi-Channel Seller Tools 15

Wrapping Up 16

CHAPTER 2 **What eBay Data Can and Can't Tell You** **17**

Use eBay Data Wisely 18

Be Careful How You Test 18

Know What You Don't Know 19

Caveats and Pitfalls 19

Items for Sale vs. Completed Listings 20

Comparing Apples to Oranges 20

Phantom Items 21

Shill Bidding 21

Issues of Rarity—Lack of Data Points 22
Fads—Timing Is Everything 23
Seasonality and Retail Cycles (Mittens in July) 24
Free Listing Days and Other Promotions 24
Dominant Players 25
Misleading and Irrelevant Keywords 25
Typos 25
Listing Quality and Feedback 25
Unstructured Data 27
Fixed-Price vs. Auction Listings 27
eBay Category Changes 27
Limitations of eBay's Market Data License 28
Wrapping Up 29

PART II   **Using eBay Data Tools**

CHAPTER 3   **eBay Data Mining Basics** **33**
Basic Strategies 35
eBay Search: How Many Items Are Listed? 36
Conducting an eBay Search 36
Using eBay Pulse to Uncover Popular Searches 39
Completed Listings Search: How Many People Want My Item? 41
Conducting an eBay Completed Listings Search 43
Basic eBay Sales Reports 47
How to Access Sales Reports and Sales Reports Plus 47
eBay Sales Reports Plus 48
Sales Summary 48
Sales By Format 48
Sales By Category 50
eBay Marketplace Research 52
Archived Reports 52
eBay Stores Traffic Reports 54
How to Access eBay Store Traffic Reports 55
Types of Store Traffic Reports 56
Individual Traffic Reports 58
Selecting a Date Range 63
Downloading eBay Store Traffic Reports 64
Featured and Anchor Store Traffic Reports 64
eBay Developers Program 68
eBay Market Data Program 70
Licensing Options 71
Wrapping Up 73

CHAPTER 4	**Evaluating Research Tools, and All About Andale**	**75**
	Evaluating eBay Market-Data Tools	77
	How the Tools Work: Hosted vs. Desktop Systems	77
	Relevance: Excluding Auctions from Results Lists	78
	Comprehensive Coverage: Categories Included	78
	Special Features	78
	Currency and Lag Time	78
	Dates of Coverage	78
	Saving and Exporting Reports	78
	Andale Research Tools	79
	What's Hot	80
	Andale Research	82
	Counters	86
	Sales Analyzer and Sales Analyzer Pro	87
	Wrapping Up	88
CHAPTER 5	**Taking the Guesswork out of eBay Selling with Terapeak**	**91**
	Understanding Terapeak Navigation	93
	Terapeak Main Tools	93
	Category "Trails"	95
	Viewing and Comparing Subcategories	96
	Jumping Categories	96
	Viewing by Date or Range	97
	Hot List	97
	Item Specifics Provides More Research Options	99
	Report Tool	100
	Key Ratios	101
	Listing Features	101
	Pricing	102
	Listing Type Usage vs. Success Rate	104
	Hourly Analysis (PST)	105
	Price Ranges	106
	Successful Listing Duration Lengths	107
	Subcategory Revenue and Seller Breakdown	108
	Listings Tool	109
	Sellers Tool	110
	Trends Tool—Browsing Categories	112
	Trends Tool—Searching Listings	115
	Features Tool	117
	Save Report	118
	Wrapping Up	119

CHAPTER 6   **Digging Into Data with DeepAnalysis** **121**

     DeepAnalysis Navigation   124

         Findings Tab   127

         Report Tab   127

         Auction Tab   135

         Seller Tab   137

         Keyword Tab   138

     How to Search   139

         eBay Auction (Keyword and Category Searching)   139

         eBay Category   140

         eBay Seller (Analyzing Your Own Sales)   140

     Wrapping Up   140

CHAPTER 7   **Tracking Shoppers' Movement with Sellathon** **141**

     Nonapproved eBay Tools   142

     Traffic Data: An Introduction to "Analytics"   144

         Study Traffic to Increase Your Sales   144

         Conversion Rates vs. Sell-through Rates   145

         Measuring eBay Conversion Rates   145

         Pitfalls to Analyzing Traffic Data   146

     Sellathon ViewTracker   148

         How Sellathon Works   148

         Sellathon ViewTracker Navigation   149

         First Things First: Create Tracking Codes   151

         ViewTracker Reports: Highlights Page   153

         ViewTracker Reports: Detailed Visitors Log Pages   159

         For Advanced Users: Managing Custom Folders   162

         Using Folders to Manage Multiple eBay User IDs   164

         Understanding ViewTracker's Tracking Methodology   164

         Downloading Data   164

     Wrapping Up   166

PART III   **Putting eBay Data to Work**

CHAPTER 8   **Basic Listing Strategies: Make More Money**
               on Every Transaction **169**

     #1 Find the Best Time to End an Auction   171

         Study the Ending-Time Data   174

     #2 Determine Optimal Auction Duration   176

         Some Background on Auction Duration   176

         Practicals vs. Collectibles   177

         The Case for 1-Day Auctions   177

         Currency (and Lag) of eBay's Search Index   178

         Study the Duration Data   178

     #3 Choose the Most Profitable Starting Price   179

         Pricing Low to Attract Bids   179

Starting Prices: Auction vs. Fixed Price Format 180
When Cost Doesn't Matter: eBay as a Marketing Campaign . . . 181
The 99-cent/NR Starting Price Strategy 181
Study the Price Data 181
#4 Locate the Best Category 183
eBay's Item Specifics and Product Finder 183
eBay Search Expansions: Saved by the Category 184
Study the Category Data 185
#5 Uncover the Most Effective Keywords 186
Why Keywords Are Critical 187
Searching Title vs. Title and Description 187
Study the Keyword Data 189
How the Tools Stack Up 189
eBay's Completed Item Search 190
eBay Sales Reports Plus & Traffic Reports 190
Andale 190
Terapeak 190
DeepAnalysis 191
Sellathon 192
Wrapping Up 193

CHAPTER 9   Advanced Listing Strategies: Grow Your Business **195**
#1 Research What to Sell 196
Finding Out What's Hot 197
Factors to Consider When Evaluating Products 201
Study the Research Data 201
#2 Choose Auction-Style Listings vs. Fixed Price Format 201
Rare vs. Common Items 203
The Stores Effect: Auctions as a Marketing Tool 204
Study the Format Data 206
#3 Analyze Effectiveness of Reserve Price 207
Study Reserve Price Data 207
#4 Evaluate Optional Features and Upgrades 208
What the Experts Say 208
Study the Features Data 208
#5 Refine Your Offer and Policies 210
Components of an eBay Listing 210
Test, Test, Test 211
Keeping Up with the Joneses 212
Shipping and Handling Policies 212
Study the Policies Data 213
How the Tools Stack Up 213
eBay's Completed Listings Search 213
eBay Sales Reports Plus and Traffic Reports 213
Andale 214

	Terapeak	215
	DeepAnalysis	215
	Sellathon	215
	Wrapping Up	215
CHAPTER 10	**Marketing Strategies: Market Like a PowerSeller**	**217**
	#1 Cross-Promote Your Listings	218
	eBay's Cross-Promotions Tool	219
	Other Cross-Promotional Tools	219
	PowerSellers Do It Their Way (Cross-Promote, That Is)	220
	Study the Cross-Promotions Data	222
	#2 Increase Repeat Sales	223
	Tracking Repeat-Purchase Campaigns	224
	Study Repeat Sales Data	225
	#3 Improve Your Advertising and Publicity	226
	To Advertise, or Not to Advertise: That Is the Question	226
	Advertise Auctions or Websites?	227
	Types of Advertising	227
	Study the Advertising-Generated Traffic Data	232
	#4 Enhance Your Reputation and Credibility	234
	eBay Feedback	234
	Third-Party Services	235
	Study the Test Data	235
	#5 Expand Your Presence	237
	Test the Waters	237
	Study the Marketplace Traffic Data	238
	How the Tools Stack Up	239
	eBay Reports and Sellathon ViewTracker	239
	Wrapping Up	241
CHAPTER 11	**Staying One Step Ahead of the Competition**	**243**
	Reasons to Monitor Your Competitors	244
	Know Your Market Share	245
	Data Tools: Know Your Category	246
	How to Monitor Your Competitors	246
	Think Like a Buyer	246
	Use Data Tools to Identify Competitors	246
	Monitor Competitors' Activities	248
	eBay's Biggest Sellers	251
	Wrapping Up	252
APPENDIX A	**Data Reports from Auction Management Services**	**253**
APPENDIX B	**eBay MarketPlace Research**	**261**
	Index	**265**

Acknowledgments

Thanks to my husband and business partner, David Steiner, and our families, especially my mom and dad, Hannah and Joseph Champ, for all their support (and patience) while I was writing this book.

I am indebted to my friends and colleagues Franci Neale, Jane Magee, Julia Wilkinson, and Phil Davies for their knowledge and advice given throughout this project, and to all of the AuctionBytes writers who are so generous and talented. My heartfelt thanks to Edith Reynolds, Janelle Elms, Michele Alice, Nikki Ballard, Barbara Shaughnessy, Gary Sohmers, Jim and Maryrose Whittaker, Ranson Johnson, Helen and John Fleming, Mark O'Neill, and so many others for their support and friendship. Thanks also to my friends in the Franco Club, Ruth Orenstein, Sue Feldman, and Ruth Winett, who have influenced my professional life over the last 20 years.

My thanks to Marjorie McAneny, acquisitions editor at McGraw-Hill, who inspired me to write this book and gave me the guidance and confidence to see it through, to Agatha Kim for keeping things on track, and LeeAnn Pickrell, Senior Project Editor Extraordinaire. Thanks to Dave Taylor who pushed me to do better with his insightful and brilliant technical editing, and Lisa Theobald whose input went well beyond copy editing.

Thanks to the eBay sellers who gave of their time to talk to me about their listing and marketing strategies and to the companies in the online-auction industry who provide services to buyers and sellers, including the ones featured in this book, and to the eBay Public Relations department.

But most of all, thanks to AuctionBytes readers who support my writing and publishing in this industry through their readership, forum participation, article contributions, and wonderful and helpful letters! When I sit behind the keyboard, I do my best to do right by you. I'm appreciative of your many years of support.

Introduction

"Knowledge is happiness, because to have knowledge—broad, deep knowledge—is to know true ends from false, and lofty things from low."

—*Helen Keller (1880–1968)*

If you've been selling on eBay for any length of time, you've probably asked yourself these questions: where are my buyers coming from, how are they searching to find my items, and what can I do to drive new traffic to my listings? In fact, a recent survey conducted by eBay found that 70 percent of the community's most active sellers believe that more access to marketplace data would help increase their sales. Most serious sellers are thirsty for more details about how shoppers search and browse eBay, but this information was not readily available to eBay sellers until fairly recently. The emergence of data-analysis tools has opened up a world of information. And as the tools become more robust, the data that sellers can access is becoming more abundant. Applying that knowledge to your own listings can help you increase your sales, and your eBay-selling experience—not an MBA—is all you need to get started.

NOTE
Have no fear—you don't need an MBA or specific technical knowledge to use eBay data. All that's required is some experience selling items on eBay. The eBay data tools covered in this book are software programs just like the ones you're already using in your day-to-day work.

With this book, you'll learn how to research new products and determine if they will bring you attractive prices in the competitive eBay marketplace. You will learn how you can increase your sales and profits by using tools and techniques that help you *sell smarter*, not work harder. You'll get a first-hand look at the kinds of eBay data tools that are available, how to use them, and how to apply them to your selling activity for great results.

This is the first book to educate eBay sellers about online auction data and marketplace research. This book is not about theory—it offers practical techniques you can apply right away to your everyday eBay sales activities.

Who Should Read This Book

This book assumes you know the basics of selling on eBay and uses terms and concepts familiar to intermediate-level sellers. Part-time sellers will benefit as much as full-time and high-volume sellers.

Companies that don't sell on eBay but wish to learn more about how eBay data can be mined for sales data, market information, and competitive intelligence will also find this book useful.

How This Book Is Organized

The two chapters in Part I, "The Joys and Pitfalls of eBay Data," introduce readers to the concept of data analysis and why it's important to make informed decisions about eBay listing strategies. They also explain what eBay data can and can't tell you, and show you the imperfections and pitfalls of data analysis so you will know how to identify them and avoid falling into the trap of using bad data to make decisions.

In Part II, "Using eBay Data Tools, you'll learn about data tools from eBay and other companies, including some resources and techniques that are free to use. You'll learn the basics of eBay data-mining and how to use search, completed-item search, eBay Sales Reports, and eBay Traffic Reports to help you improve your sales.

Part II will also teach you how to evaluate data tools from companies that operate independently of eBay. I introduce three such tools—Andale Research, Terapeak, and HammerTap DeepAnalysis—and show you how they work. You'll also learn about the concept of traffic-tracking, also called analytics, and you'll learn how to use Sellathon ViewTracker to track visitor traffic to your listings and eBay Store.

In Part III, "Putting eBay Data to Work," you'll learn how to apply the data you've mined to your listing and marketing activities. In Chapter 8, I examine five basic listing strategies; in Chapter 9, five advanced listing strategies; and in Chapter 10, five marketing strategies. You will learn in each chapter how to apply data to increase your sales and will be introduced to some PowerSellers who are doing just that. Chapter 11 will show why it's important to keep an eye on your competitors and how doing so can help your sales.

In Appendix A, you'll see some examples of reports from auction-management services that provide useful data about your sales. There are many tools to help you manage your eBay sales activity, and you should find out if the one you use provides these kinds of reports.

As this book was going to press, eBay announced its eBay Marketplace Research service. This is a very useful tool and is complementary to the market-data tools profiled in this book. Appendix B explains the basics of eBay's new market-data tool.

Staying Up-to-Date

I welcome you to subscribe to my company's newsletters at AuctionBytes.com to keep apprised of new information about eBay data tools. AuctionBytes has been providing information, news, and product reviews to online-auction sellers since 1999, and it's one of the best ways to keep abreast of news and trends in the eBay world.

Lastly, please visit the website supporting this book at www.TurnEbayDataIntoDollars.com. This site provides an online forum where readers can ask questions, discuss strategies, and keep up-to-date on new features and products being introduced to the market. Vendors are also welcome to participate by answering questions and announcing new features, workshops, and promotions. I'll see you there!

Part I

The Joys and Pitfalls
of eBay Data

Chapter 1

What Is eBay Data?

Most eBay sellers enjoy the independent lifestyle of online selling and being their own boss. But if you sell on eBay, you know how time-consuming it can be. If you sell part-time, you've probably realized that listing even ten items a week can take a lot of hard work and test your organizational skills. Sometimes you can feel like a hamster on an exercise wheel. You don't dare stop moving—the e-mails keep coming, the orders keep coming, and there's no time to stop and smell the roses (or pop the bubblewrap).

This book is not about helping you move faster so you can process more orders. It's about investing some time in research so you can learn to sell *smarter*. That investment in time will help you make more money, and if you do it right, you'll also have more time to do enjoy the fringe benefits of working for yourself. This book will show you how to use tools to help you make more money—more profit—from each sale you make on eBay and get greater satisfaction from your selling activities.

No Magic Pills or Secret Formulas

No magic pills or secret formulas can help you sell more on eBay, and none are available when it comes to doing eBay data research. Studying your sales and researching other eBay information takes time and common sense. However, the good news is that it's a fun process, and with just a little bit of time invested, you'll begin selling smarter right away and making more money on every transaction.

You need to find out for yourself what works best for the kind of seller you are and the types of items you are listing. Sellers who work on improving listing and marketing strategies by studying their performance on eBay generally enjoy the process, and all are enthusiastic about how the process increases their profits. They learn that doing homework and putting what they learn into action gives them more control over their business.

We'll review such tools as eBay sales and traffic reports, Andale Research Tools, Terapeak, and DeepAnalysis, and Sellathon ViewTracker, and you'll learn how to use data from these tools to make key decisions like the following about your eBay business:

- When to use a Reserve Price
- When to hold 10-day auctions and when to make them 7-day auctions
- How to find the most effective keywords for your listing titles
- How to improve your marketing strategies
- How to keep an eye on what your competitors are doing

You probably already do some research. Have you ever checked eBay's Completed Listings search to see what an item sold for, or to help you decide which category might be best for listing your product? Advanced tools are available today, and they allow sellers to apply what they learn immediately to their operations so they can increase profits.

eBay is a dynamic marketplace. What works for you today might not work as well next year. That's why learning how to read the marketplace by studying your competitors and your own sales can pay off with big dividends. Every seller can improve his or her sales, but each seller is different. It's up to you to find out what works best for you, and the tools and techniques outlined in this book will help you do that.

Background and Definitions

If you're reading this book, you probably have a working knowledge of eBay and some experience listing items on the site. Throughout the book, I'll help you identify critical information about eBay data and your own sales performance to help you understand how to sell better. If you *are* brand new to eBay, this book will help you determine whether you want to continue, and it may help you avoid some costly mistakes.

The principles covered here will help you no matter what new tools may come on the scene and which features may change. You'll learn about tools and techniques that can help you determine useful information, such as traffic data, historic pricing data, and even which products on eBay are hot sellers.

Following are definitions of some terms that frequently appear in this book. Don't worry about remembering these terms; they will be explained clearly to you as you read the book, and you can always come back and refer to these definitions.

Data Tools, or Data-Analysis Tools   Refers to all of the tools included in the book:

- eBay Sales Reports
- eBay Traffic Reports
- Andale Research Tools
- Terapeak
- Bright Builders DeepAnalysis (formerly known as HammerTap)
- Sellathon ViewTracker

Market-Data Tools   Refers specifically to tools included in this book that license eBay's market data:

- Andale Research Tools
- Terapeak
- Bright Builders DeepAnalysis

We'll learn more about eBay's Market Data Program in Chapter 3, and we'll begin to profile the market-data tools in Chapter 4.

Analytics Tools, or Traffic-Tracking Tools   *Analytics* may sound like a technical term, but it simply refers to how well your website is doing in terms of attracting shoppers. You can use analytics tools to measure how many people—or *unique visitors*—are coming to your site, which pages they are visiting, how much time they are spending on your site, and other traffic data.

Analytics tools help you determine whether your marketing campaigns are working and how well your site is designed to help people navigate through your listings.

eBay Traffic Reports and Sellathon ViewTracker are two tools specifically designed for eBay sellers based on the principles of web analytics. I also refer to these programs as *traffic-tracking tools*. I'll discuss how you can use these analytics tools to help you improve your eBay sales.

Metric   A standard of measurement. In this book, the term *metrics* refers to measurements such as average selling price and sell-through rates.

Average Selling Price (ASP)   Average selling price is an accounting term (eBay calls this *average sales price*) that refers to the average price your items realize when sold. The higher the ASP, the better. ASP is one of the most important metrics you can track, and it can serve as an early-warning system to alert you if your prices are falling. eBay Sales Reports track your ASPs by month, by format (auction, Fixed Price, and store inventory), or by ending day and ending time. Figure 1-1 shows a graph from an eBay Sales Report that shows how total ASP for one seller fluctuated on a monthly basis (March, April, and May 2005).

The beauty of the tools covered in this book is that they calculate ASPs for you, both your own and category averages. This allows you to compare your current performance with your own past performance as well as those of others.

Sell-through Rate (STR)   Sell-through rate (STR), called *success rate* in eBay, is the percentage of items you list that actually end with a sale. Data tools calculate the STRs for you, so you can track your STR over time and also compare it to those of other sellers and with categories as a whole. As with ASP, the higher the STR, the better.

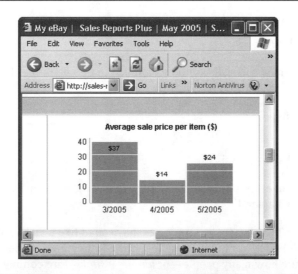

FIGURE 1-1   eBay Sales Reports show your ASP by month. In this three-month period, the ASP for this seller was $37 in March, $14 in April, and $24 in May.

Calculating ASP Manually

If you sell three Barbie dolls on Monday, here's how you manually calculate the ASP for sales of those dolls.

Barbie Doll #1 sold for $16.

Barbie Doll #2 sold for $24.

Barbie Doll #3 sold for $12.

Take the sum of your sales ($16 + $24 + $12 = $52) and divide by the number of items sold (3), to get an ASP of $17.33. Many sellers keep track of ASPs by product and category on a daily, weekly, monthly, and quarterly basis to determine whether they are getting higher or lower selling prices for their products. If the ASP of your Barbie dolls this month is $17, but last month it was $40, you know your ASP is declining. It's up to you to determine why, and I'll cover some of the factors that can affect your sales, such as seasonal demand and competitive factors, in Chapter 2 and throughout the book.

NOTE   *ASPs and STRs are the most important metrics you can track.*

Gross Merchandise Sales (GMS)/Gross Merchandise Volume (GMV)   Gross merchandise sales (GMS), frequently called *gross merchandise volume* (GMV), is how much revenue you are earning on eBay. If you sell $200,000 worth of merchandise in a year, that's your GMS, even if you made only $50,000 in profit (revenue less expenses). GMS is an eBay term—your accountant will call it simply *gross sales* or *gross revenues*.

Mining Data   Mining data (or data-mining) is just a handy way to refer to the activity of using tools to retrieve data. You mine the data with the tool.

Return on Investment (ROI)   Return on investment in accounting terms is the ratio of the amount gained relative to an investment. An eBay seller might ask, "Is using the optional Bold feature

Calculating STRs

Let's say you sell three Barbie dolls on Monday. If you listed ten Barbie doll auctions that ended on Monday, but only three sold, that would equal a 30 percent STR. To calculate this, take the number of items sold in a given time period (3) and divide by the number of items you listed that ended in that time period (10) to get the STR (.30, or 30 percent).

In this scenario, you still have seven unsold dolls that you will have to re-list or put aside. However, if you had listed three Barbie dolls and all three dolls sold, that would be a 100 percent STR. The higher the STR, the better, since you want all of your items to sell.

in my eBay listings going to net me a good return?" I don't have to use a calculator to know that if a $1 investment in using boldface type returns a $20 higher selling price for my eBay items, that is a good return on my investment. Likewise, if the $1 fee for using boldface type has no effect on selling price, then a negative ROI results (or in other words, that's $1 down the drain). I'll show you how the tools in this book can help you gauge whether optional fees are a good investment of your dollars.

eBay Data Paints a Picture

eBay data is nothing mysterious. If you listed 1000 items last month, that is a piece of data. Viewed by itself, however, that data may not mean much to anyone reading this. But if you listed 1000 items on eBay last month, and 500 of those items sold successfully, that data would be a little more interesting. An observer would know you sold 50 percent of your items listed—you had a 50 percent STR.

Data can answer questions such as these:

- Could you have sold more than 50 percent of the items listed, perhaps by using listing upgrades such as Gallery or Bold?

- Could you have saved money with a different listing strategy, such as using 5-day or 7-day auctions instead of 10-day auctions?

- Could you have sold a different product line and increased sales or lowered your costs?

- Are you successful in using eBay auctions to drive traffic to your eBay Store or your own website?

Applying eBay Data to Your Business

This book will help you learn to turn data into useful, actionable information. We'll review the following:

- Which types of data are most useful to eBay sellers

- Which tools and techniques are helpful for mining data from eBay

- How to interpret and analyze data to put it to practical use

Data can be viewed two ways: your own sales, and the sales of a particular product or category as a whole. Different tools and techniques are available to help you accomplish both of these tasks, and they'll be introduced in later chapters.

As mentioned, two of the most useful pieces of data for eBay sellers are ASPs and STRs. Sellers who track these two *metrics* for their own sales over time can recognize early warning signs and can make better decisions about their businesses. Sellers can also use these metrics to take the pulse of a product or category to estimate the market potential.

Sellers can also compare the ASP of a particular item with the ASP of that category as a whole. The same goes for STRs. Table 1-1 shows how this might play out.

Item ASP	Category ASP	What It Might Mean
Going up	Going up	These are good results, likely a case of "the rising tide lifts all boats." Expect competition as other sellers jump in, unless you have a lock on supply.
Going up	Going down	The item you sell may be one of a few popular items in a category, but be wary when selling in a declining category.
Going down	Going up	You have a "dog" in a winning category. Are you selling an unpopular item or the "wrong" brand? See if your competition is doing something different to achieve higher prices for their items.
Going down	Going down	Has supply flooded the marketplace? Or has a new technology or fad replaced your item? It may be time to hold off on selling the item and wait it out, or cut your losses now: consider combining your items in larger lots to sell them off quickly at a discount.

TABLE 1-1   Comparing an Item ASP with Its Category ASP

Table 1-1 provides a quick look at how to analyze pricing performance on eBay, but it demonstrates the kind of questions you should constantly be asking yourself in the course of your business. Ideally, you should compare your listing with the category as a whole and with your own past performance.

You'll learn how to determine ASPs for your sales in Chapter 3 and for specific eBay categories in Chapters 4 through 6, and you'll learn lessons from tracking ASPs throughout the book.

Why You Need to Analyze eBay Data

What if you have an opportunity to purchase a pallet of great widgets to resell on eBay? Suppose the price is too good to be true, and you think you just can't pass on this great deal. What if doing a little research shows those kinds of widgets don't sell well on eBay? That's exactly what happened to one of the most knowledgeable PowerSellers I know—it was garden tools, not widgets, and he learned his lesson the hard way.

Skip McGrath explains in the January 2005 issue of *The eBay Seller's News* newsletter (www.auction-sellers-resource.com/newsletters/jan)

> I once ordered 100 sets of garden tools in plastic cases that I got at such a good price I knew I could make money. After 6 weeks, I was giving them away at my cost. Had I done some research—which I belatedly did, I would have learned that the better quality more expensive garden tools were selling very well on eBay, while the cheaper ones were not.

> I also knew of an eBay consignment store that purchased a lot of wedding gowns to sell on eBay. The price was too good for the seller to pass up, but the wedding gowns were not designer-label, and they failed to sell. Several unfortunate decisions like this put the store out of business in its first year. Such mistakes *might* be avoided by more experienced sellers, but doing research goes a long way to helping *any* seller make a more informed purchasing decision.

If you are an eBay newbie, you are bound to make a few mistakes, even with research. I recommend that new sellers start small so the mistakes you make don't put you out of business in your first year.

While crunching numbers will be useful to help put tips to the test, just reading about the principles of eBay data should give you some great ideas and help you think in new, more creative ways. eBay becomes more competitive each year as new sellers join the site. Selling smarter is more important than ever.

Learn from Others: Market Data Is a Diamond in the Rough

eBay Gold PowerSeller George Wagner (www.auctionisle.com) sells DVDs on eBay under the user ID auctionisle* (the asterisk is part of his user ID). George believes that using market data reports can be helpful in getting a handle on the market, but this is only part of the picture. Sellers need to take a look at their own costs, and George says it's crucial to look at the active sellers in a market as well. Where are they getting their inventory, what are their costs, and what techniques are they using that might make it difficult to compete with them?

George knows firsthand the value of research. He had considered diversifying his business by entering one of the gemstone categories. He thought his eBay expertise, background in jewelry, and knowledge of wholesale sources and contacts could be a winning combination. But he knew some market research was vital to help him decide whether it would be a profitable strategy.

George used market data reports from Terapeak to assess the market for that gemstone on eBay. (I'll talk more about Terapeak's market-data services in Chapter 5.) The Terapeak reports showed detailed data about the gemstone in both category and keyword reports. He brought the reports to a friend who sells those gemstones, who said one of the largest eBay sellers in the category was getting prices that seemed impossibly high. The two used this report, along with their experience of eBay, to identify the seller. They determined the seller was using a certification technique that, while legitimate, made it appear to buyers that they were getting something better than they actually got.

It could just have easily turned out that the seller had a cheaper supplier or some other competitive edge. The important thing was that George's friend concluded that if George were to sell identical gemstones, the other seller would get higher prices because of buyers' perceptions, and George would have a tough time competing.

George used the market data to get an overview of the category and help him identify the top sellers. He concluded that gemstones were not going to be profitable for him given the techniques employed by the competition as well as his own costs of doing business.

When you come across a case like this, it doesn't mean you shouldn't enter the market—only you can decide this, based on many factors. In George's case, he might have tried to find a way around the existing challenges in the market. But the market data he mined from eBay using Terapeak saved him valuable time in reaching an informed decision.

Using Data to List Smarter

eBay data can do more than help you purchase inventory. It can help you move inventory faster by using effective listing and marketing strategies, so you can answer questions like the following:

- Should I run a 1-day auction or a 10-day auction?
- On which day of the week should I end my auction?
- At what price should I start my listing?
- Should I set a Reserve Price?
- Which keywords should I use in my listing title?
- Should I use optional features like Bold?
- Should I list my item as an auction or in a Fixed Price format?

A glance at eBay fees for optional features can help drive home the point. Go to http://pages .ebay.com/help/sell/fees.html for a breakdown of eBay fees (see Figure 1-2). They range from under a dollar to large sums—like the fees for using the Reserve Price feature.

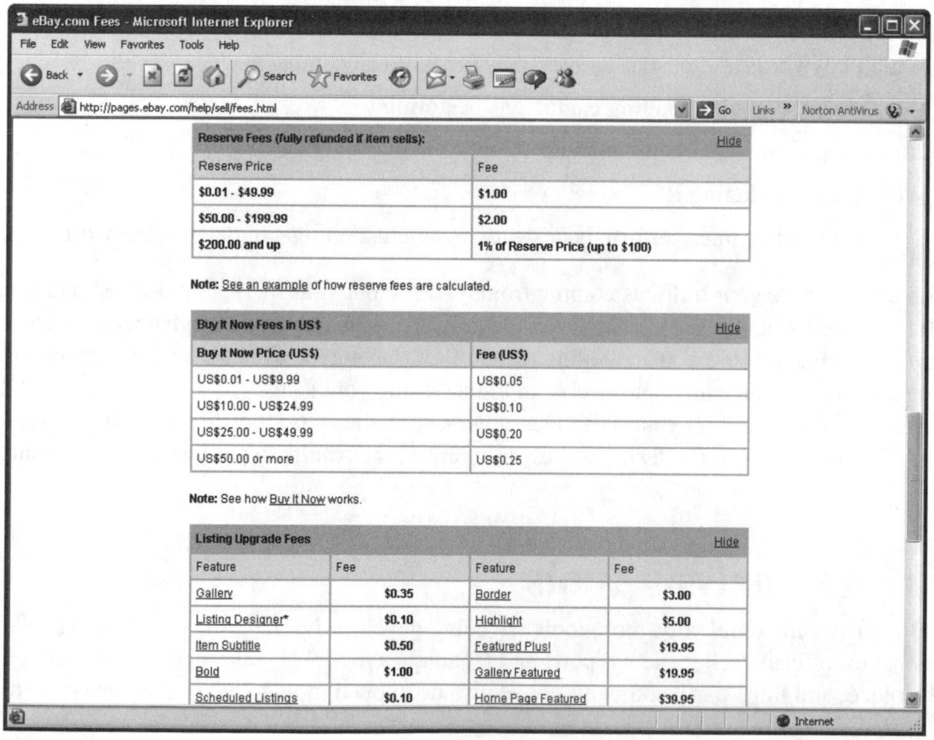

Reserve Fees (fully refunded if item sells):   Hide

Reserve Price	Fee
$0.01 - $49.99	$1.00
$50.00 - $199.99	$2.00
$200.00 and up	1% of Reserve Price (up to $100)

Note: See an example of how reserve fees are calculated.

Buy It Now Fees in US$ Hide

Buy It Now Price (US$)	Fee (US$)
US$0.01 - US$9.99	US$0.05
US$10.00 - US$24.99	US$0.10
US$25.00 - US$49.99	US$0.20
US$50.00 or more	US$0.25

Note: See how Buy It Now works.

Listing Upgrade Fees   Hide

Feature	Fee	Feature	Fee
Gallery	$0.35	Border	$3.00
Listing Designer*	$0.10	Highlight	$5.00
Item Subtitle	$0.50	Featured Plus!	$19.95
Bold	$1.00	Gallery Featured	$19.95
Scheduled Listings	$0.10	Home Page Featured	$39.95

FIGURE 1-2   eBay sellers can choose to add features to their listings to try and attract more bidders.

eBay's Reserve Price feature allows a seller to require a minimum price on a listing. If bidding does not reach the Reserve Price, the seller is not obligated to sell to the highest bidder. The fees for using Reserve Price are tiered. If the item sells, the Reserve Price fee is refunded. But if you run many listings with the Reserve Price and only a portion of them sell, these fees can quickly add up.

It's smart to take the time to research whether these features are a good investment or are likely to cost you money with no return. If you list smart, you can save money on unnecessary features and drive more sales using the features that are effective and give you a good ROI.

Using Data to Market Smarter

Data analysis can also help you market smarter. More and more sellers are advertising and marketing their eBay business. Conducting research using data tools can help you answer questions like these:

- Where is my traffic coming from?
- What are my conversion rates?
- What is my rate of repeat customers?
- Should I use a keyword advertising campaign like eBay Keywords, Google AdWords, or Yahoo! Search Marketing?
- Which keywords are most effective in my keyword ad campaigns?
- How are my e-mail marketing campaigns performing?
- How are my cross-marketing and upselling campaigns performing?
- What is my marketing ROI?
- Do some product lines perform better with certain marketing campaigns than with others?

If you know where your traffic is coming from, you can put your marketing dollars (and time) to good use. Advertising is a big investment, and analyzing data to determine what works best for you is critical to making sure you are getting a good ROI. Taking the time to run the numbers on marketing and advertising campaigns is critical to increasing your sales.

It often requires testing on your part to learn what strategies work best for the items you are listing. We'll review how to run tests and how to interpret the results to put lessons learned into action.

Research and Analysis Tools

While eBay grows in complexity, more tools are being developed to help the professional seller. eBay has begun offering sellers new reports and techniques to look at sales and pricing data on its marketplace, and third-party companies have also developed tools to help sellers even more.

Market-Data Tools

Market-data tools, such as Andale Research Tools, Terapeak, and DeepAnalysis, can help you uncover the sales performance of a particular type of item or an entire category. These tools search a database of eBay's past listings going back many months. By revealing which items sold most successfully, they can help you determine which categories and features to use when listing your items today. They can identify key data points, such as the highest-priced items that sold and the lowest-priced items that sold by keyword or by category.

Sales Performance Reporting and Analysis Tools

Becoming familiar with your own past sales history is important in understanding how you can increase your performance going forward. eBay Sales Reports and some auction-management services provide reporting tools that show you detailed information such as average selling prices and month-to-month sales growth that can help you make good decisions in the future.

Analytics (Traffic-Tracking) Tools

Tools such as eBay Traffic Reports and Sellathon's ViewTracker can tell you where your traffic is coming from and what keywords visitors use to find your listings. These kinds of tools are what most people think of when they hear the term *web analytics*. Analytics tools give you real-time information about who is visiting your listings and how they got there, helpful data to use in measuring the effectiveness of your marketing efforts.

Competitive Intelligence Tools

As in other industries, many eBay sellers find it useful to keep an eye on the competition. No one competitive intelligence tool gives you all these answers. When HammerTap owned DeepAnalysis, it could give you an amazing amount of details about a seller's eBay activity just by entering an eBay user ID. However, eBay had concerns over the privacy issues this raised for its users. When HammerTap sold its tools to Bright Builders, an eBay certified developer that conforms to eBay's privacy policies, Bright Builders instituted a requirement that users enter a password to conduct analysis of a user ID. This limited analyses to your own accounts, since you don't have access to your competitors' passwords. You can, however, use a variety of techniques to try to stay on top of the competition.

The Cost of Data Analysis Tools

eBay and third-party services range in price from a few dollars a month to thousands of dollars for custom reports. We'll review data tools closely in Chapters 3 through 7. This book will also reveal techniques that cost nothing but the time it takes to put them into action. This book is not just about theory, however. Chapters 8 through 10 show you how to put these tools and techniques to best use so you can benefit from them immediately, and Chapter 11 shows you how to analyze and keep an eye on your competitors.

Each seller has unique requirements and business models. This book will expose you to the tools and techniques that are available, so you can decide which ones are best suited for your business.

eBay: An Ever-Changing Marketplace

An important thing to keep in mind when reading this book and applying the lessons is that eBay is not a static marketplace. Every day, new buyers come online, new products are introduced, products go in and out of fashion, and economic forces shift. eBay is a dynamic marketplace and follows the law of supply and demand. You constantly need to monitor your sales, your competitors, and the marketplace.

In eBay's early years, antiques and collectibles dealers were quick to see the value of the auction site. Collectibles made up about 60 percent of gross merchandise sales (GMS) on the U.S. site in 1999. (*Gross merchandise sales*, now called *gross merchandise volume*, is the value of goods sold on the site.)

While collectibles continued to grow, other items grew at a faster pace on eBay. In 2003, eBay estimated that collectibles made up only 13 percent of GMS. The remaining items, which eBay calls *practicals*, comprised items such as consumer goods, electronics, and business equipment.

Over time, antiques dealers began seeing a decrease in the ASPs and STRs of their items. This happened for two reasons: Supply caught up with demand as more sellers flooded the marketplace with goods, and buyers discovered that items they thought were rare were often not quite so rare after all. When lay people could go online and see the prices for which collectibles were selling, they went into their attics and basements and uncovered hidden treasures that they proceeded to list on eBay.

AuctionBytes published a pricing study in May 2001 (www.auctionbytes.com/pr5301/pr5301 .html) that showed how these factors affected the prices of collectibles on eBay (see Table 1-2). The AuctionBytes collectibles price index showed the ASP of a sample of collectible items sold on eBay decreased from $34.85 in 2000 to $26.28 one year later. By 2003, the ASP of the sample items had dropped to $22.60, and the STR had gone from 72 percent in 2000 to 45 percent in 2003, according to the May 18, 2003, issue of the *AuctionBytes-Update* newsletter (http://auctionbytes .com/cab/abu/y203/m05/abu0095/s02).

Year	ASP	Difference	STR	Difference
2000	$34.85	N/A	72 percent	N/A
2001	$26.28	−25 percent	N/A	N/A
2002	$23.30	−11 percent	55 percent	−24 percent
2003	$22.60	−3 percent	45 percent	−18 percent

TABLE 1-2   AuctionBytes Collectibles Price Index

The data was taken from a sample of collectibles, not entire categories. But it confirmed many dealers' beliefs that it was taking more work to make the same amount of money. Of course, in the meantime, other sellers were finding categories on eBay that were just budding—in their eBay "infancy," so to speak—where ASPs and STRs were attractive.

This study shows how eBay can change over time, and how individual categories can perform much different from eBay as a whole. eBay can also fluctuate quite rapidly depending on fads, supply, and other factors. Paying attention to pricing and STRs over time can help you identify trends so you can prepare yourself for changes in the marketplace.

Multi-Channel Seller Tools

If you have your own e-commerce website, you may be surprised to learn of the limitations eBay sellers typically experienced in trying to measure and analyze sales results. You have probably used your log files and tools like WebTrends to measure traffic and conversion rates. Until 2004, eBay users had no analytics tools to measure such information, or they could do so only in the most primitive form.

It's challenging for multi-channel sellers to learn how best to measure sales results and compare data with sales on their own sites and other venues. Third-party services such as ChannelAdvisor, Infopia, Marketworks, and Truition generate sales reports and support international sites and multiple marketplaces, and these auction- and marketplace-management services allow you to export sales data into spreadsheets for further analysis.

You should be aware that tools developed specifically for the eBay marketplace are often expanded over time to include other auction marketplaces. For example, after Overstock.com introduced an online auction marketplace in late 2004, many auction-related services added features to their tools so they would work with Overstock auctions. In 2005, Sellathon reached an agreement with Overstock to have its tool be the default hit-counter on the Overstock auctions marketplace. And while this book focuses on eBay data, you can apply the principles of sales analysis across all the marketplaces in which you sell.

A Note for Non-eBay Sellers

For individuals and businesses who don't sell on eBay, this book may still provide valuable information. The market data mined from eBay can be enormously helpful in understanding the demand for products. Chapter 3 covers eBay's Market Data Program and how organizations can participate in the program.

Terapeak and Bright Builders provide custom reports and consulting services to manufacturers and retailers. They understand the value of eBay market data and how it can be used on an industry level in addition to the individual seller level. Contact these companies directly to get a quote on custom services.

Wrapping Up

In *Turn eBay Data Into Dollars*, I walk you through the various tools and techniques available to mine data from eBay. We'll review what kind of sales data is useful for your business and how you can apply it to make smarter decisions and more money. We'll also look at common pitfalls and caveats to help you avoid making false assumptions.

You'll learn how to apply data to basic eBay listing strategies, such as knowing what to sell and how to determine best starting prices and features to use. You'll also learn how to apply data to your marketing strategy to find out how to improve traffic and conversion rates. Finally, we'll spend some time talking about how to use competitive intelligence techniques to stay one step ahead of your competition.

By applying data to your eBay listing and marketing strategies, you will produce more bids, achieve higher closing prices, and add to your profits.

Chapter 2

What eBay Data Can and Can't Tell You

Even the most experienced seller can get off on the wrong track when looking at reports about eBay average selling prices (ASPs), sell-through rates (STRs), and What's Hot lists. And if you have no experience selling on eBay, the danger of drawing incorrect conclusions is even greater.

This chapter is a summary of some of the data conditions that can lead you astray. If you are aware of the potential pitfalls in analyzing data, you can avoid making bad decisions based on false assumptions. It's crucial that you use good data and analyze the data correctly, being aware of the shortcomings of the information. After all, analyzing eBay data is not an academic exercise—its value lies in the decisions you make about your business as a result.

Whether you are a beginner or a PowerSeller, you learn as you go along. Sometimes mistakes can be costly, so do your homework and remember that the best lessons are learned from experience. If beginners want to brush up on eBay selling basics, I recommend *eBay QuickSteps* by Carole Matthews and *How to Do Everything with Your eBay Business, Second Edition*, by Greg Holden.

Use eBay Data Wisely

Accountants and software programmers have a saying: "Garbage in, garbage out." It refers to the fact that if your data is flawed, so will be your analysis. If your analysis is flawed, most likely you will make flawed business decisions.

The sales data for a product or category during the past 12 months is helpful information to know, but many other factors should go into your eBay decision making. Sales data can help you decide what products to list and for how much, which optional features to use, and what kinds of marketing to undertake, but remember that past performance is only one indicator of sales potential; it's not a guarantee of future sales activity.

Looking at only one aspect of market data or analytics can result in erroneous assumptions. Talking to customers, vendors, service providers, marketplaces, and other sellers about trends, techniques, and approaches to selling practices can help you avoid becoming too narrowly focused.

Be Careful How You Test

Many eBay sellers test various approaches, from trying out new product lines to tweaking the titles of their listings. The trickiest part of testing one aspect of your sales is to make sure other factors aren't influencing the results.

Let's say, for example, that you are researching a brand to see how well it sells on eBay, but you don't realize that a shortage is driving up prices in the short term. Or you don't realize that eBay is running a promotion on its home page, driving traffic to that category for a week or a month. You could make a purchase of inventory at a price that could end up being a costly mistake. Before you commit, you must do research to discover all the factors that could be affecting the results of your tests.

Direct marketers have long believed in testing the response of direct mail pieces, and this belief has carried over into online marketing as well. Marketing directors create materials using various aspects, perhaps to test copy, color, or other factors to determine which materials do best with which aspects. However, they never mix the tests—they know that they can test only one aspect at a time with reliable results. In the case of eBay, you can run two identical listings. The two test listings must include identical products, durations, ending times, titles, features, copy, and photos, with only one of those factors changed—the feature you are testing. For instance, you could see if adding the words *Free Shipping* to your listing title results in a higher ASP. Or you might try using two different—but comparable—user IDs to run tests; however, if the two user IDs do not have the same feedback rating and longevity and if they weren't used to buy and sell similar items, your test results will not be reliable.

The pitfalls discussed later in this chapter in the section "Caveats and Pitfalls" are some of the factors that can influence results of your analysis—being aware of the pitfalls is important so you know what to look out for.

When testing, it's best to do the following:

- Have an objective; make sure you know what problem you are trying to solve or what you are trying to learn.

- Determine what kinds of testing will help you meet your objective.

- Determine how you will measure the results—do this before you begin.

- Have a plan in place for putting your plan into action after the test so it doesn't become merely an academic exercise.

- Continue to test, test, test!

Know What You Don't Know

Knowing what you *don't* know is important to keep in mind while you're analyzing what you *do* know. Many eBay sellers are interested in learning what their competitors are doing. If my competitor is selling more than I am, I should copy my competitor's approach, the thinking goes. Studying competition can reveal useful, actionable information. But remember that what you don't know is a lot: your competitor may have higher costs of doing business than you do. Your competitor may be spending a lot in advertising to drive traffic to their listings, or they may be drop-shipping, spending more on customer service, and so on. No one-strategy-fits-all approach works on eBay, and you can't assume that more *sales* equals more *profits*.

Comparing your business to another can be helpful, but it's important to remember that doing this won't give you all the information you need to do better. It may be worth digging deeper to discover what you don't know—even going so far as to hire a researcher to help.

Caveats and Pitfalls

The adage "A little knowledge can be dangerous" comes to mind when I think about the pitfalls of data analysis. Make sure you understand the following pitfalls before you make assumptions about your eBay business based on the tools and techniques discussed in this book.

Items for Sale vs. Completed Listings

When doing research, it's important that you differentiate between items currently for sale and items that have been sold—completed listings. You should limit your search to *completed* listings to get the true market value of the item. If you are looking at a current listing and assuming the item will sell for a certain price, you may be completely mistaken. Listings can end without the item being sold, and items can be stalled at a certain price for most of the listing period and then suddenly receive bids that drive the ending price much higher. That's why you should never make assumptions based on listings that have not yet ended.

Suppose you do a search for a particular kind of computer memory stick and the results show 100 listings. Seventy of the listings have ended successfully with an average selling price of $50. Thirty of the listings are *active* listings with an average bid of $20. You should not count those 30 active listings in your data, because they may eventually sell for a much higher price than the current bids.

When using data-analysis tools, never assume which type of auctions the tool is drawing upon to make its analysis. The only accurate sales data comes from items that have sold.

Comparing Apples to Oranges

Many, if not all, data-analysis tools allow you to view the actual listings used in the analysis. You should always peruse the listings after doing a search to make sure your data set is truly representative of the items you are analyzing. Lots of variables can influence the analysis.

Used Items vs. New Items

eBay's selling form has traditionally lacked a field to indicate whether an item is new versus used, though the Item Specifics condition field allows sellers to add this type of information. However, sellers are not required to fill in item specifics, and the condition field is available only in some categories. Therefore, data-analysis tools cannot always differentiate between listings for new items versus listings for used items. Yet this information would make a big difference to buyers in many categories and can heavily influence the prices realized by sellers.

Understand when you examine data-analysis results that a mix of used and new items may be included in the analysis. Data tools provide the actual listings that make up the results of their reports, so you should peruse them to make sure they represent items similar to those in which you are interested. Some tools allow you to eliminate listings that aren't relevant to your research and recalculate the numbers to get data that applies more closely to your research needs.

Brands vs. Generics

If you analyze a category as a whole and come up with ASP and STRs, consider the effect of brands on the pricing. Recall the seller in Chapter 1 who discovered that non-designer wedding dresses don't sell on eBay, and the seller who had to sell his cheap gardening tools at cost while branded gardening tools achieved healthy prices. Make sure you understand which brands make up the listings in your category analysis, and generate reports that show which brands sell for what prices.

Reproductions, Fakes, and Counterfeits

While many antique reproductions command high prices and hold their value, they are not equal to genuine antique items. Sometimes sellers don't realize what they have is a reproduction, or they deliberately misrepresent items. Likewise, some items are out-and-out fakes and have little value, but a potential buyer (or researcher) has no way of knowing that from the listing description. Trading in counterfeit designer items is rampant (online and offline). Try to determine whether the results you are viewing contain reproductions or fakes and determine how that may affect the metrics you are reviewing.

Quantity of Items

eBay allows you to sell in *lots*. Your search results may contain some listings offering two or more items, and you want to determine the average selling price of one item. It's up to you to look through the listings for items that may throw off the true average price.

Data-analysis tools often provide average selling price for *item* versus *listing*, but these are provided for *Dutch auctions*, for which the seller specifies the quantity. For example, if a Dutch auction offers ten pens for sale, ten different buyers may each purchase one pen. This is in contrast to one listing of ten pens, where only one buyer gets all ten pens. Data analysis tools see the second listing as a single *auction* and one *item*, despite the fact that ten pens are in the lot.

Phantom Items

Unfortunately, fraud exists online as in the offline world. Some fraudsters put up *phantom items* for sale on eBay, hoping to collect money from buyers but never intending to ship an item (since it may not even exist). I call these phantom items or phantom listings.

Some scammers are sophisticated and will copy a legitimate auction from a real seller, photos and all. But they will list the items under their own user ID and will instruct buyers to send payment to them. High-ticket items such as automobiles or consumer electronics (such as plasma TVs) may be more likely to be targeted for this scam than items in other categories.

Phantom listings can indicate that more supply exists than is actually available, and they usually drive down average selling prices reported by data-analysis tools. This is because scammers have learned that it's easier to trick people with lower prices, because some folks just can't pass up a good deal. (Yes, some people think you can buy a plasma screen TV worth thousands for a few hundred dollars.) By listing phantom items for a fraction of the true value, scammers drive down average selling prices—a misnomer considering the items don't even exist.

Shill Bidding

Some sellers bid on their own items to attract bidders and achieve higher selling prices. This is known as *shill bidding*. Shill bidding is against eBay's policy and is grounds for suspension. Shill bidding skews the data for ASPs, making some listings artificially higher through bid manipulation. It can result in a higher ASP for a category as a whole, but when you list your item, you may not achieve that higher price.

Phantom Playstations: Buyers Left Holding the Bag—er, Box

In 2000 and 2001, some unscrupulous eBay sellers listed auction items as "Playstation 2 Original Box And Receipt." Sellers of these auctions were actually selling empty boxes, and at least one shopper bid $425 on such an auction.

Others have offered "wholesale lists" of places where you can purchase products at wholesale prices. Unfortunately, these unethical sellers didn't make it clear that the buyer would actually acquire a paper list. They intentionally made it look like the buyer was purchasing the product itself at a wholesale price. One unlucky buyer thought he was bidding on a TV when he bid on this auction: "NEW 15" FLAT SCREEN MONITOR FREE SHIP! wholesale list"—with a photo of a television in the auction description.

The rule for buying on eBay is *caveat emptor* (buyer beware), and the rule for readers of this book is researcher beware! Make sure the data you are analyzing represents the items you're researching.

Shill bidding is difficult to detect, but if you study a particular category on a regular basis and study your competitors, you may be able to spot warning signs. The same buyer purchasing regularly from a seller may or may not be a shill bidder, but if the bidder *never* wins the auction, that might be an indication. Some sellers have regular customers who make frequent purchases, so be careful before jumping to any conclusions.

NOTE
I have been told "off the record" that eBay users who report another member are usually investigated themselves by eBay. eBay staff are aware that some users sometimes play dirty and file false reports against their competitors.

Issues of Rarity—Lack of Data Points

Using eBay to place a value on a rare item can be problematic, since not enough transaction data may exist to yield good pricing statistics. Sellers who think they have a rare item may do better by visiting an appraiser or other expert to get a value estimate.

Another challenge in measuring sales of rare items is that the eBay marketplace makes inefficient markets efficient. For example, if someone bids $2000 on an item thought to be rare, sellers will often jump on the bandwagon and list identical items if they can find them. This drives down the price, since it becomes apparent to buyers and collectors that the piece is not as rare as once thought.

On the other hand, items that are truly rare can go for very high prices in the eBay auction format.

2

Shill Bidding on eBay

Here is part of eBay's explanation of shill bidding:

> Because family members, roommates and employees of sellers have a level of access to item information which is not available to the general Community, they are not permitted to bid on items offered by the seller—even if their sole intent is to purchase the item. Family members, roommates, or employees may purchase items from a seller without violating this policy simply by using purchasc options—such as Buy It Now—which do not involve bidding.

You can learn more about shill bidding and eBay's policy against it on the eBay help pages at http://pages.ebay.com/help/policies/seller-shill-bidding.html.

Warning signs of shill bidding can include the following, but they are warning signs only—some shoppers like buying from the same seller, and just because a buyer and seller are located in the same town isn't proof of deceptive practices:

- Many bids on a listing from different users with 0 feedback.

- The first bid is received minutes after the item was listed.

- The seller and high bidder are using the same server, in the same location, using the same language, terms, and registration date.

- An account has won auctions but never received any feedback.

- An account has received feedback only from this seller.

- Both the seller's and bidder's listings include images that are hosted on the same private server (assuming the bidder has items for sale).

- Bidders all sign up for eBay within a short period of time.

- Bid retractions are apparent.

- The high bidder retracts a bid after pumping up the bidding.

Fads—Timing Is Everything

Fads like children's trading cards and Beanie Babies are nothing new, but manufacturers seem to be getting ever better at creating them. The fad phenomenon exists across many categories.

One recent Christmas-holiday season, Ugg boots were hot items but in short supply due to a sheepskin shortage in Australia. Did this mean Ugg boots would sell for the same price next holiday season? Not necessarily! Will the Beanie Baby you bought on eBay in 1999 achieve the same price today? Probably not.

Fads drive up demand for products, but once a fad is on the decline, prices decline as well, and so do STRs. You don't want to be buying pallets of goods based on fad pricing unless you are really good at timing the market and can sell them before they decline in popularity.

Here's a list of some fads:

- Children's toys and games, such as Beanie Babies, Pokemon, and Yu-Gi-Oh cards
- Xbox
- Clothes like Ugg boots and jackets with fringe trim
- Diets books and nutrition bars
- Lance Armstrong "LiveStrong" charity bracelets

Seasonality and Retail Cycles (Mittens in July)

The "seasonality" factor seems obvious but bears mention in this discussion. If you are selling mittens while most of your buyers are experiencing hot weather, your selling prices and STRs are bound to be abysmal. When you look at data analysis, keep the seasonality factor in mind.

Certain times of year are better for retailers than others, and this carries over to the online world as well. From September through December, you usually see an increase in listings on eBay from sellers hoping to capitalize on holiday shopping demand. And June and early July tend to have the lowest number of listings.

Medved tracks the number of eBay listings in graph form at www.medved.net/cgi-bin/cal .exe?EIND. Note that some spikes in the Medved charts may be due to promotions offered by eBay that drive up the number of listings.

Hitwise (www.hitwise.com) provides competitive intelligence services in the online market and tracks shopping and classifieds sites, including traffic to retail websites. On December 28, 2004, Hitwise released some interesting statistics about the 2004 holiday shopping season (www.hitwise.com/info/news/hitwiseHS2004/wrapUp_Issue6.html):

- The peak day for shopping and classifieds websites was November 25, Thanksgiving Day.
- Visits to eBay peaked on November 10, compared to December 9 for Dell and December 11 for Amazon.
- Visits to the largest brick-and-mortar sites tended to peak on November 25, Thanksgiving Day.
- For both the 2003 and 2004 holiday seasons, peaks in traffic to shopping and classified sites occurred on weekends, with Sundays typically stronger than Saturdays. The two exceptions were Thanksgiving Day and Christmas Day.

One of the reasons for analyzing data is to make better inventory acquisition decisions. Use past data as a guideline, but remember the pitfalls in making assumptions about future sales. Always keep in mind retail trends and seasonal factors when analyzing data.

Free Listing Days and Other Promotions

eBay holds sales on some features to promote them to sellers, and occasionally it runs free listing days (FLDs). If, for example, you analyze data during a period in which a particular feature, such as Bold, was on sale for eBay listings, it may skew your data. Try to look out for such anomalies.

eBay has become stingy with FLDs. In the past few years, it had offered only one FLD a year, always on December 26. In 2004, it held no FLDs (on the U.S. site); instead, it held a 10-Cent Listing Day Sale on its U.S. and Canadian sites on December 27, 2004.

Free Listing Days can skew STRs, since they artificially inflate supply. So when you look at your data, keep FLDs and promotions in mind.

Dominant Players

Sometimes a category can be dominated by a few sellers. You can use some of the tools discussed in this book to spot this phenomenon. A major change in their listing behavior could have a dramatic impact on category trends as a whole.

A seller can flood a category with a particular product, lowering prices and STRs for everyone. Or a top seller can withdraw a certain product, leaving an opportunity for competitors to fill the void. Sometimes these changes can be temporary, sometimes permanent. Keep that in mind when analyzing data. Keep an eye on the competition, and track products and categories over time to try to identify these kinds of changes and what they may mean for your business.

Misleading and Irrelevant Keywords

eBay sellers are aware that brand matters. Including a brand name in a listing title and description helps buyers searching the eBay site find sellers' items—even if the items really aren't the brand mentioned in the title. Some sellers will deliberately include brands in titles and descriptions to increase the "findability" of their items or to help convey that their item is similar to a branded item, even if it's a knock-off. eBay calls this practice *keyword spamming,* and doing it violates eBay's policies. A search for *Ugg boots* on eBay shows listings for *Ugg boots* and *boots like Ugg*.

Another instance of misleading or irrelevant keywords is when a term is commonly used to describe two very different products. Rings can be jewelry you wear on your finger, or the word *rings* can be part of a movie or book title (*Lord of the Rings*).

Misleading or irrelevant keywords can skew data analysis when you are doing searches by keyword. If you use a tool like Terapeak, DeepAnalysis, or Andale and conduct a keyword search, it's possible the results will be populated by irrelevant listings that contain the keyword you're searching. Always look through the listings that make up your search results to see if you are on track. Most tools allow you to search using a combination of keywords and categories to help you make your search more precise.

Typos

Be on the lookout for how typos may affect your results. Treat common misspellings as synonyms when doing keyword searches.

Listing Quality and Feedback

You'll find a tremendous difference in the quality of listings on eBay. Some listings include numerous high-quality photographs and a professional template and effective keywords in their titles, which would draw more bids than listings with minimal copy and no photos.

Keyword Spam Leads to Indigestion

eBay prohibits keyword spamming. Its "Search Manipulation and Keyword Spamming" policy is found at http://pages.ebay.com/help/policies/keyword-spam.html.

Keyword spamming means using extra words in your listings so they show up in more searches. For instance, if you are selling a pair of Reebok sneakers, keyword spamming would be including the words *Nike* and *Adidas* in your listing in addition to *Reebok*. eBay says, "Keyword spamming occurs when members place brand names or other inappropriate keywords in a title or description for the purpose of gaining attention or diverting members to a listing. Keyword spamming in listings is not permitted on eBay. The text sellers place in listings must be directly relevant to the item being sold."

Here are some points to keep in mind:

- Keyword spamming is a violation of eBay policy and may result in item removal or suspension of the eBay member.

- Certain uses of brand names may also constitute trademark infringement and could expose sellers to legal liability.

- Only in a description are you allowed to compare the item you are offering to another similar product, so long as your listing is not misleading in any way as to which company made the item offered.

Interestingly, a 2005 study by Sellathon showed keyword spamming is not an effective marketing strategy. According to the findings, reported in the January 17, 2005, issue of the *AuctionBytes Newsflash* newsletter (http://auctionbytes.com/cab/abn/y05/m01/i17/s02), the average time spent looking at an eBay item is about 26 seconds. However, when the search term used to find the item doesn't accurately match the item itself, visitors spend an average of only 2.9 seconds on the listing.

The *AuctionBytes Newsflash* article quoted Sellathon CEO Wayne Yeager, "Anybody who expects to make more money or get more bids by adding 'Britney Spears' or 'Paris Hilton' to their auction description is just deluding themselves. It doesn't work. It might make their hit counter go up, but that's all."

Seller feedback also varies widely, both in quantity of feedback points and in ratings. A seller with 5000 feedback points and a 100 percent positive rating will achieve more bids than a seller with 10 feedback points and a 60 percent negative feedback rating, since potential bidders will be scared off by the negative feedback rating.

Many listings on eBay include inconsistent, incomplete, or incorrect descriptions, sometimes by deliberate intent and sometimes because of a lack of knowledge on the part of the seller. This includes typos and spelling mistakes.

All these factors can influence selling prices and STRs, causing potentially misleading metrics. Review results from your search and factor in these possible influences when you review the data-analysis reports.

Unstructured Data

eBay listings consist of *unstructured data*. In most categories on eBay, sellers put the entire listing information in two main fields: Title and Description. The item's brand, model, make, color, condition, and other descriptive data are thrown into one of the two fields. This can make it very challenging for tools to summarize and analyze eBay data, and irrelevant listings can easily creep into search results.

In some categories, eBay includes Item Specifics fields, which allow for attributes such as brand and color, to be included. As the data going into the analytics engines get more structured— at least in some categories—services will be able to provide even better data analysis.

While unstructured data is problematic, trying to impose structure can be equally challenging. For example, eBay market-data tools discussed in Chapters 4 through 6 allow you to research eBay categories. But it's up to the seller to choose the most appropriate category, and sometimes there is a lot of leeway. Sellers struggle with category selection, trying to figure out how shoppers find items on eBay.

Imagine a seller trying to decide whether a typical vintage clothing shopper looks for the type of clothing (shirts, for example) first, then the era (1950s), or would a shopper prefer to browse all clothing items from the 1950s with different types of clothing (shirts, pants, skirts, jackets, shoes, and so on) mixed in? Two different sellers might put the same type of item in two different categories. In addition, eBay often changes the category structure, adding to the challenge of category selection.

When you do category research using eBay market-data tools, keep in mind that you may be missing relevant items in your results, depending on how sellers categorize their listings.

Fixed-Price vs. Auction Listings

eBay sellers have a choice of running listings in an auction format, a Buy It Now format, or a Fixed Price format. Auction listings are the best indicator of the true market value of an item. Sellers set fixed prices that sometimes have more to do with the sellers' costs than what the market will actually bear. Fixed Price items might be set lower than what consumers are actually willing to spend (sometimes part of a loss-leader strategy by the seller), or they may be set higher, leading to lower number of sales.

Keep this in mind and run several reports isolating auction listings from Fixed Price listings to see if you notice a difference in ASPs. Be on the lookout for other factors at play, however.

eBay Category Changes

eBay frequently fine-tunes its category structure. If you are tracking a category over time, this may lead to changes that have to do with a subcategory being added to or removed from the category, and not to actual sales.

eBay announces category changes on its General Announcements page at www2.ebay.com/aw/marketing.shtml. It also announces the changes on Seller Central under News & Updates (http://pages.ebay.com/sellercentral/).

Limitations of eBay's Market Data License

When you use third-party tools like those discussed in Chapters 4 through 6, you should understand that the data eBay provides can be limited. eBay does this to protect users' privacy and to avoid giving competitors complete financial data. It's a balancing act between giving sellers useful information to help them in their businesses while controlling the flow of information.

It's All "Relative"

eBay restricts vendors who license its market data from revealing counts by category, but it lets vendors report numbers when users are searching by keywords. This means if you are using the Browse Categories view to look at data, you'll see relative numbers and ratios, not absolute numbers (*absolute* numbers means the actual number of listings included in the results). But if you are using the Search Listings view to look at eBay market data, you will see actual counts and percentages. (You can, of course, use both techniques to help you get a handle on your category.)

The Many Levels of Data

eBay has more than 30 main categories. These are called Level 1 categories. Underneath each Level 1 categories are Level 2 categories; Level 2 categories may have subcategories, and so on. eBay allows vendors to analyze only Level 3 categories and lower, but not Level 1 or Level 2.

In some categories, only Level 1 and Level 2 categories exist, so you cannot use market-data tools to analyze these categories.

For example, eBay has a main Level 1 category called Books. Under Books are a number of Level 2 categories, including Children's Books. There are currently no subcategories in Children's Books. This is because eBay "rolled up" the category when it introduced Item Specifics. Therefore, you cannot analyze the Children's Books category as a whole—you must do keyword searches within the category to get information about STRs and ASPs. This sounds very complicated, but it's really not. It just means you will have to do keyword searches in a Level 2 category (such as using a keyword term, like *Nancy Drew,* in the Children's Books category).

Terapeak allows you to refine your research using Item Specifics, which is quite helpful, and DeepAnalysis has plans to offer this ability as well. Figure 2-1 shows the way eBay displays Item Specifics to shoppers in two different categories—Women's Shoes and CDs. Sellers can choose to fill in the Item Specifics fields, but it is not required.

Buy It Now Reporting Complicates Things

eBay treats Buy It Now listings in a perplexing manner. If you run a 7-day Buy It Now listing, and the item sells in the first day with a Buy It Now bid, eBay calls that a 1-day Buy It Now listing. It makes it challenging to evaluate optimal duration for Buy It Now listings, since you don't know how the seller listed it (but you do know how long it took to end with

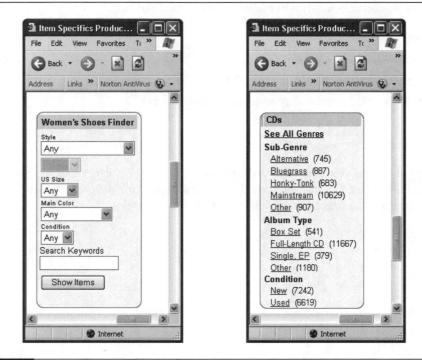

FIGURE 2-1   eBay allows shoppers to narrow their search by attributes called Item Specifics, using a feature called Product Finder.

a Buy It Now bid). Remember that if someone places a regular bid, rather than a Buy It Now bid, that becomes a regular auction listing and would no longer be a Buy It Now listing. Sounds confusing, but if you are already listing items on eBay, you've probably encountered this.

Wrapping Up

Study eBay market data and your own sales performance, as well as your competitors' sales history. Use them as guidelines in the larger context of your business knowledge, and apply what you learn to your day-to-day selling activities. eBay changes rapidly, so keep up-to-date with changes on the eBay platform and with the tool(s) you are using to ensure consistent interpretation and effective application of analysis.

The more familiar you are with eBay, the more likely you will avoid the potential pitfalls of eBay data analysis. The longer you study categories, the better you will be able to notice signals and trends and interpret what they may mean for your business. And the more familiar you are with the kinds of impurities that can taint data, the more effective your use of data-analysis reports will be. Reread this chapter often and peruse the potential pitfalls you can encounter to help you stay on guard.

Using eBay market data *wisely* will enable you to do the following:

- Increase traffic to your listings.
- Increase your average selling prices.
- Increase the percentage of your items that sell.
- Increase the effectiveness of your marketing campaigns.
- Increase your rate of repeat customers.
- Save time and increase your profits.

Applying the lessons you learn after studying market data is the point of data analysis. In future chapters, we'll discuss tools and techniques used for analyzing data, and then we'll take a look at how to apply the data to your listing and marketing strategies.

Part II

Using eBay Data Tools

Chapter 3

eBay Data Mining Basics

When I began selling unusual yard sale finds on eBay in 1999, I discovered the value of data mining on eBay to see how much similar items had previously sold for so I would know if a particular item was worth listing. But at that time, eBay made data available for recently ended auctions only.

Sellers urged eBay to make the pricing data for closed auctions available to them for a longer period of time and in a more structured format so they could make better decisions about how much to pay for inventory and what kinds of inventory to purchase and list on eBay. Sellers have long recognized the value of eBay pricing information and how it could help them in making business decisions. This chapter discusses the ways eBay responded to these requests.

When I started my eBay business, I wanted to know how buyers were finding my listings. This continues to be true now that eBay has gotten more complex—with the addition of eBay Stores, for example—and more competitive. Gone are the days when you could list something on eBay and expect a 90 percent sell-through rate (STR).

Now it's more important than ever to know the right keywords to include in your auction title. Sellers can't simply rely on eBay to drive traffic to their eBay Store listings (plus many sellers operate their own independent websites), so they use various marketing techniques to increase their sales, including the following:

- eBay Cross-Promotions tool and other tools and techniques
- Keyword marketing, such as eBay Keywords, Google AdWords, and Yahoo! Search Marketing
- Multi-channel selling
- Advertising

Knowing which marketing efforts are driving traffic to your listings can help you save money *and* increase your sales:

- You won't spend money on techniques that aren't working.
- You can increase your marketing budget for those marketing activities that do work.
- You can continually fine-tune your marketing techniques and know what is working.

In 2002, eBay began licensing its market data to Andale (which you'll read more about in Chapter 4), and in 2003, eBay opened the floodgates by launching its Market Data Program and by making available sales and traffic reports. You can review eBay sales and traffic reports to help you keep track of your sales, compare listing formats and features, and see where your traffic is coming from.

eBay Sales Report Plus and traffic reports are free to eBay Storeowners, and I'll get to them in more detail later in this chapter. It's vital that you study broader trends in your market or category as well as understanding the specifics of your own sales performance; these reports provide some of the information that can help you do this.

The tools and techniques discussed in this chapter are helpful for gathering and analyzing sales information, and they also give you an understanding of the basic building blocks of eBay data. This will help you evaluate other, often more powerful, tools available and discussed in future chapters.

In this chapter, I'll explain what techniques and tools you can use to get data directly from eBay, including the following:

- eBay search and Completed Listings search to reveal supply and demand
- eBay Sales Reports
- eBay Stores Traffic Reports
- eBay Developers Program
- eBay Market Data Program

In Chapters 4 through 6, we'll look at eBay-approved market-data tools, and in Chapter 7, we'll look at some traffic-tracking tools from companies that work independently of eBay.

Basic Strategies

I'll show you how to use techniques and tools in this and in the next several chapters of this book. In later chapters, you'll learn how to apply 15 basic strategies to your listings and marketing techniques—five basic listing strategies, five advanced listing strategies, and five marketing strategies.

Basic Listing Strategies

- Find the best time to end an auction
- Determine optimal auction duration
- Choose the most profitable starting price
- Locate the best category
- Uncover the most effective keywords

Advanced Listing Strategies

- Research what to sell
- Choose auction-style listings versus Fixed-Price format
- Analyze effectiveness of reserve price
- Evaluate optional features and upgrades
- Refine your offer and policies

Marketing Strategies

- ■ Cross-promote your listings
- ■ Increase repeat sales
- ■ Improve your advertising and publicity
- ■ Enhance your reputation and credibility
- ■ Expand your presence

I will refer to these strategies throughout these early chapters, and they will be explained in detail later in the book. You can use this list as a cross-reference to help you if you want to jump ahead as you read. This list may also help you after you've read the entire book and want to refer back to certain sections later on.

eBay Search: How Many Items Are Listed?

The eBay marketplace is in constant flux, and understanding supply and demand is crucial in helping sellers make decisions about what to list and how to list it most effectively. The best way to get a snapshot of current supply of a particular item is to do a search of current items. But searching eBay for current listings will not help you determine the *demand* for items.

To understand this, consider an example. Let's say you find that 5000 purple ponchos are listed on eBay this week. That is the supply. But what if no one wants to buy a purple poncho on eBay today or this week? *Supply*, or the number of similar items listed on eBay, is only one part of the equation. To assess the likely *demand* for purple ponchos, you can use eBay's Completed Listings search to see how many people have purchased ponchos in the last few weeks.

It's important that you keep in mind that while past demand *is* an indicator, it does not guarantee the level of current and future demand. Chapter 2 covered some of the reasons for this in more depth. It's also important to understand what makes up your search results. If you do a search simply for the word *laptop*, for example, you might end up with a list showing laptop computers, laptop accessories, books about laptops, and even laptop desks that have nothing to do with computers. Knowing how eBay search works will help you understand and use the data tools featured later in this book.

Conducting an eBay Search

Go to eBay (www.ebay.com), and at the top of the page on the right, directly under the Search box, click the Advanced Search link. In the Enter Keyword or Item Number field, type in your search term and click the Search button. Figure 3-1 shows the results for a search for the keyword *laptop*, which returned a total of 30,936 items.

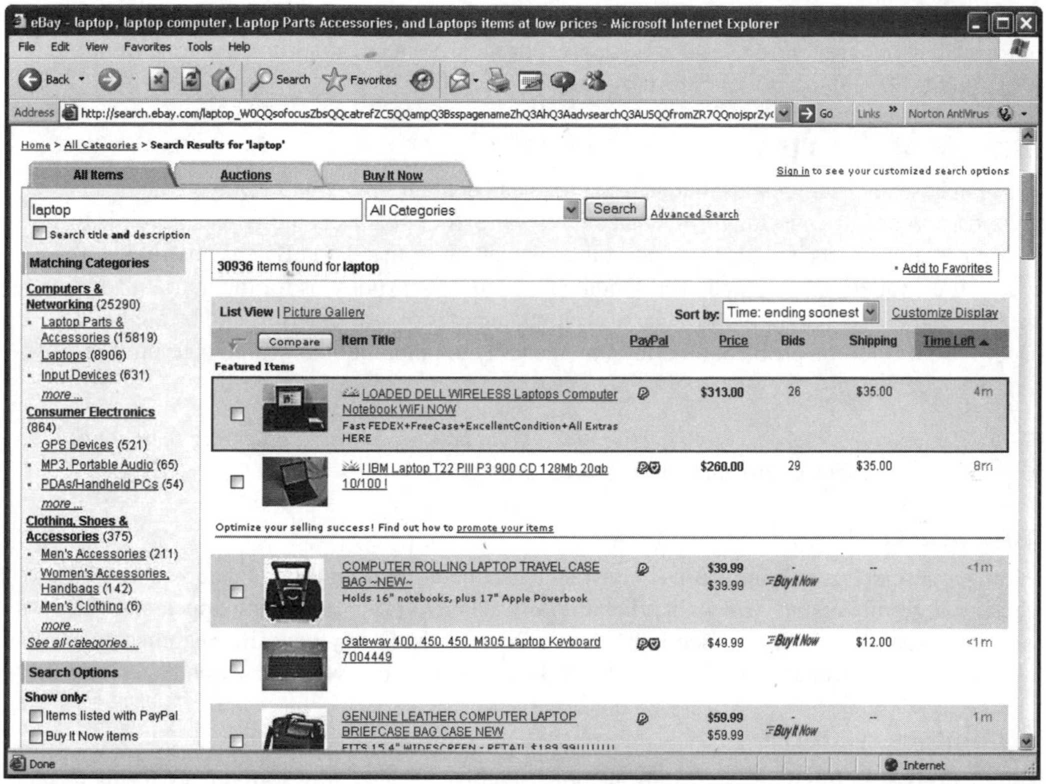

FIGURE 3-1   An eBay search for *laptop* in all categories shows listings currently for sale that include the word *laptop* in the title.

Refining Your Search

On the left side of the results page is a Matching Categories list that shows the variety of items returned by a general, or All Categories, search. Clicking a category will narrow your search. If, for example, you are looking for a laptop computer, and both Computers & Networking and Clothing, Shoes & Accessories categories appear in the Matching Categories list, you can click the Computers & Networking category to exclude Clothing, Shoes & Accessories. (Note that each seller determines the category in which to place a listed item. This can lead to inconsistencies due to inadvertent or deliberate listing decisions on the part of the seller.)

The default search looks for items with the search term in the *title* of the listing only. In Figure 3-1, you'll see that a checkbox for Search Title And Description is located under the search field. You may want to try both kinds of searches and review the items that appear to get a sense for the types of items available on eBay.

Your best research approach is to tinker with the search feature until you think you have narrowed down the right combination of search terms with the category that best represents the item for which you are trying to estimate supply. For items with cross-appeal, generate multiple reports for all relevant categories and study and compare all of them.

Getting Good Results

Some searches can return results that are too broad and contain irrelevant results, while others are two narrow and are missing results that are relevant. Your goal as an eBay data miner is to have your search results include as many of the relevant items listed on eBay as possible, with very few irrelevant items returned. You should also search for synonyms for the item. In addition, make sure you are searching the singular and plural versions of search terms, and be aware of misspellings, a common problem on eBay. Another way to pinpoint your search is to limit results to a relevant category.

> **TIP** *Browsing categories is an effective way to find how sellers are describing their items and can help you formulate your search strategy.*

Saving Searches

You can save searches to help you keep tabs on a particular item on eBay. Once you conduct a search and get the results you want, click the Add To Favorites link, which appears at the upper-right area of the window (see Figure 3-1). On the Add To My Favorite Searches page, type in a name for your search. Click the Save Search button to save your search.

Searching eBay Stores

The main eBay search box searches only auctions and Fixed Price listings. If you are trying to find out how many listings currently offer a particular item, don't forget to search eBay Stores as well. If your regular eBay.com search returns fewer than 21 results, it will also display up to 30 eBay Store items. If you want to search across all eBay Stores, go to Advanced Search, and in the left column, click Items In Stores under the Stores heading. On the next page that appears, you will see a box entitled Search Store Inventory Items Only. Check this box, enter your search term, and click the Search button.

Brush Up Your eBay Search Techniques

eBay's Getting Started tutorial includes a section on searching called "How to Find Items," at http://pages.ebay.com/help/newtoebay/find-items.html. You can see all the available eBay search commands at http://pages.ebay.com/help/find/search_commands.html.

I also recommend that you consult timeBLASTER's eBay search tips, available at www.timeblaster.com/support_top_10_secrets.shtml. Click Download The Idea Manifesto, a PDF file that was written in 2001 but offers timeless principles for searching.

Other Search Tools

You may also find other eBay search tools useful, such as ItemScout.com (www.itemscout .com), AuctionSieve (www.auctionsieve.com), and The Winning Bid (www.the-winning-bid .com). You can even get search results delivered via RSS (Really Simple Syndication) feeds through Pluck's Perch feature (www.pluck.com) or RSS Auction, a service from Lockergnome and BidRobot (www.rssauction.com).

RSS is a format that websites use to send updated content to you via software *readers* or services such as Bloglines (www.bloglines.com) and even My Yahoo!. You can subscribe to RSS feeds from websites, blogs, and marketplaces like eBay. Software readers gather the content you select from a variety of sources and display it for you in one location. If you want to keep track of every new listing for a particular rare comic book, for example, you can subscribe to an RSS feed, and any time someone lists that comic book on eBay, the listing will show up on your newsreader. It's an excellent way to keep an eye on new listings and content across many websites and marketplaces.

Using eBay Pulse to Uncover Popular Searches

Knowing what people are searching for can give you an indication of products that are in high demand. eBay Pulse, introduced in 2004, gives you a taste of what's popular with eBay buyers by providing dynamically generated lists showing popular searches, stores, and products. eBay Pulse can be accessed at www.ebay.com/pulse. The site is updated daily and also lists the highest priced items and most watched items across eBay.

Beware the Conclusions You Draw from Search Results

If you discover in searching eBay that very few listings appear for the item you are researching, it generally means one of two things (assuming you haven't made any spelling mistakes or typos):

- Not many sellers have access to the item and it might do very well on eBay.
- Other sellers have found that there is no demand for the item and don't bother to list it.

Searching eBay current listings gives you only a piece of the information you are seeking. To get more information, do a Completed Listings search, which is covered a bit later in this chapter.

The lists on the main eBay Pulse page provide an overview of the entire eBay marketplace. You can use the drop-down menu at the top of the page to refine and filter the lists to show the top ten searches for specific eBay categories. Figure 3-2 shows a snapshot of popular searches in the Headphones, Headsets category on the eBay Pulse page, showing the brands of headphones a seller might consider researching.

Harry Potter was the number one search term in the Books category on July 16, 2005, which isn't surprising since that was the day the sixth installment of the *Harry Potter* series became available online and in bookstores. These lists can spark some ideas for products and services worth more investigation, since they tell you what search terms buyers are entering into the eBay Search box.

NOTE   *Popular Products in eBay Pulse include only those products that were listed with Pre-Filled Item Information (known as Item Specifics), available in certain categories.*

In addition to top lists and other details, eBay Pulse offers pop culture information, overall buying trends, fun facts about eBay, and other eBay-related news.

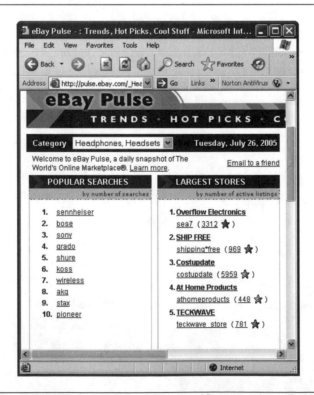

FIGURE 3-2   eBay Pulse lets you drill down into specific categories—in this case, Headphones, Headsets—to see popular search terms.

Completed Listings Search:
How Many People Want My Item?

If I want to list a particular item on eBay, it helps me to know how many other such items are listed on the site (this is the *supply*). But even more important, I'd like to know if anybody will be interested in buying my item—in other words, I'd like to know what the *demand* for my item will be. The more people who want my item, the better.

To get an idea of the demand for an item, you can review listings that have ended over the past 15 days by using eBay's Completed Listings search tool. You can use this tool to determine the total number of items listed in that period (supply) and the number of items that sold successfully (demand). You can figure out average selling prices (ASPs) and STRs, but this is not calculated automatically, and manual calculations can be tedious. On the other hand, the tool is free, and in some cases, a perusal of the listings may tell you all you need to know.

A Completed Listings search is a more effective way to understand demand than using eBay's basic search, and an example will demonstrate why this is so. Suppose an eBay auction ending in two days has a current price of $31. In the last few seconds of the auction, "snipe" bids are placed, and the item closes with a selling price of $75. You won't know the actual price the listing will attain until the auction actually ends.

NOTE   *Snipe bids are placed at the end of an auction, often in the final minute. Buyers snipe because they are hoping to avoid a bidding war that would drive the prices higher.*

Here's another example of the trap inexperienced users can fall into when relying on active-listing pricing: Let's say I am selling a book on the latest fad diet, and I find the same book currently for sale on eBay with a starting price of $19.99 with zero bids. I get really excited, and I list my book right away. But then the first auction closes with no bids at all. Uh-oh. I just spent money (and time) to list my item, and now it appears it may not be popular on eBay after all. Until an auction ends, you have no idea whether anyone will purchase a zero-bid item or not. So assuming that the item is "worth" $19.99, or will sell for $19.99, is a mistake. This is why Completed Listings searches are more reliable than regular searches, since they include only auctions that have ended, and you can see whether items closed with a sale—if they did, you can see how high the bidding went.

You can avoid these false assumptions by using a Completed Listings search instead of the basic search tool on eBay. But you should still be careful in how you use this information. It's important to differentiate between listings that actually sold and listings that ended without a sale. Some listings end without a purchase, making their prices inconclusive. Always remember to check to see how far back the search function covers.

Once you've conducted a Completed Listings search, you should review the results carefully to make sure they don't contain items that will lead you down the wrong path. For example, if you enter *Little Mermaid* in the Search box without selecting a category, you'll find DVDs, clothing, handbags, figurines, iron transfers, View-Masters reels, beach towels, shower curtains, and more. If you wanted results only for the DVD movie *The Little Mermaid*, you'll have to wade through irrelevant items in your search list. You can narrow down your search by selecting a category.

eBay Seller Central's What's Hot Page

On eBay's Seller Central portal page for sellers at http://pages.ebay.com/sellercentral, you'll find a link to What's Hot on the left menu under "Choose a Topic." The What's Hot page offers two tools to help you get ideas on what to list on eBay:

- **Merchandising Calendar** This feature provides advance notice of upcoming seasonal promotions and reveals which types of items will be spotlighted on the eBay homepage.

- **Hot Items By Category** The Hot Categories report lists categories for which demand is growing faster than supply and for which bid-to-item ratios are relatively high. eBay updates this report monthly and delivers it in a PDF file. This list is also called the Hot List.

If you enter *Little Mermaid* in the Search box and select the DVD category, you'll find mostly DVDs of *The Little Mermaid*, which is what you are looking for. But you will also see listings for *The Little Mermaid II*. You may also see listings containing multiple titles (*The Little Mermaid* and *Sleeping Beauty*, for example), as well as a few non-DVD items that sellers may have put into the wrong category. Be aware of this as you scroll through your results looking at ending prices and percentage of items that sold with a winning bid. (Chapter 2 has a lot of information about what to look out for when drawing conclusions about eBay data.)

When you review Completed Listings search results, look at ASPs and the STRs. If items seem to sell in the $50 range, determine whether those items are similar to your item, or if they are of a higher or lower quality than your item. Did one seller get consistently higher prices than other sellers? If so, try to determine why this might be so. If 100 items were listed, how many sold? One person may sell a widget for $100, but that doesn't mean the other 99 widget listings sold successfully.

You can use eBay's Completed Listings search in all of the basic listing strategies outlined in Part III of this book. In fact, before eBay and vendors created specialized tools, many sellers relied on a Completed Listings search to help them determine the best time to end an auction listing, most effective keywords to use in titles, and other information. Reviewing Completed Listings data is a manual process that can be time-consuming, and data tools calculate metrics (key performance indicators) like ASP and STRs for you.

NOTE *Completed Listings searches are helpful, but it takes time to sort through the results and make sense of what you find. In later chapters, we'll look at tools from Andale, Terapeak, and Bright Builders that automatically sort through and analyze completed listing searches for you. It's still important to know how eBay's Completed Listings search feature works, however, to understand the advantages and limitations of eBay data.*

If you are glancing at the pricing data in Completed Listings searches, you need to check the quantity of items in each listing. If, for example, someone sold a *pair* of Dell laptop computers in one listing, the listing may have achieved a higher selling price than if the listing were for a *single* Dell laptop computer. This is a good time to go back to Chapter 2 to review possible pitfalls in using eBay data.

Conducting an eBay Completed Listings Search

eBay requires users to sign in before conducting a Completed Listings search. Go to eBay (www.ebay.com) and at the top of the page on the right, directly under the Search box, click the Advanced Search link. On the Advanced Search page, enter your search term and check the box next to Completed Listings Only. You'll see a secure page where you can log in to eBay if you aren't already logged in. After you are logged in, your search results will appear.

In Figure 3-3, you can see that the Completed Listings search returned 99,582 items found for the term *laptop*. You can click one of the matching categories in the left column to see items listed in that category.

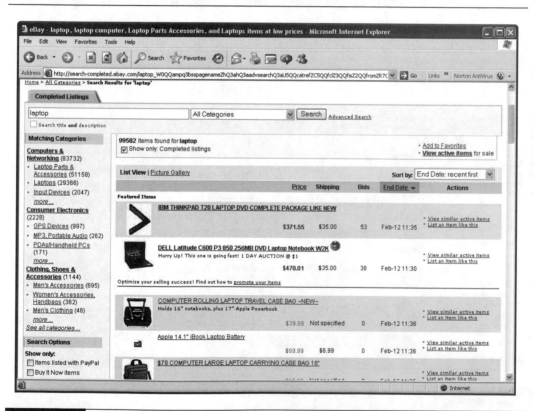

FIGURE 3-3 eBay's Completed Listings search lets you see auction listings that have ended, whether they sold successfully or not.

You'll also notice that the left column may change to reveal terms related to the category you chose, which can help you narrow down your search even more. These are called Item Specifics, and users can use Product Finders to find them. The Item Specifics feature is available only in certain categories on eBay.

eBay created the Item Specifics feature to help sellers better identify their products and the Product Finders feature to help buyers find items according to their specific characteristics. Sellers in certain categories can fill in specific product attributes, which can aid buyers in finding the items more easily. When searching for music, for example, buyers can search by a specific musical *genre*. In clothing, buyers can search for a specific *size* or *color*. When looking up *laptops*, once we selected the category Laptops under Computers & Networking, Item Specifics appeared in the left column; for this search, PC Laptops Finder appeared in the left column.

Figure 3-4 shows a search results page for the search term *laptops* in the Computers & Networking—Laptops category after selecting Dell from the Brand drop-down menu in the PC Laptops Finder tool. It shows 5922 available listings.

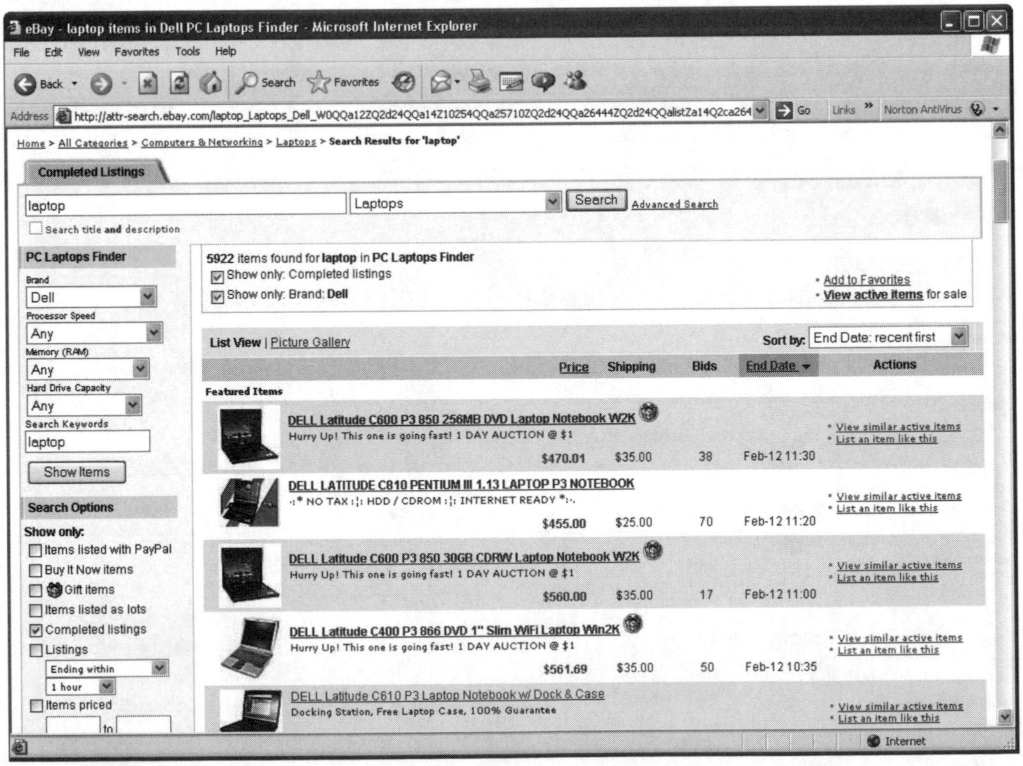

FIGURE 3-4 In some categories, eBay uses a Product Finder to help buyers target their searches according to Item Specifics. In the Laptops category, the feature is called PC Laptops Finder.

NOTE *Because some sellers do not bother to enter the Item Specifics when listing their items, more listings than what shows up in your search may have actually ended on eBay. You may need to be creative when searching for these details.*

To Buy or Not to Buy: That Is the Question

Silver PowerSeller Robert O. Sachs (user ID Rosachs) runs an eBay consignment business selling items for business clients (http://home.midsouth.rr.com/rosachs/RKS). Robert has been selling on eBay since 1997 and also runs an independent user group for eBay's Seller's Assistant software (www173.pair.com/rosachs/SAUG/).

In 2003, Robert faced a challenge: He received an offer to purchase 12,000 pairs of German shoes, brand new and still in their retail boxes, for resale on eBay. Judging from the selling prices of his current shoe inventory, the offer was very generous and could net him two to three times his investment. But Robert was not familiar with this brand of shoes. Should he buy 12,000 pairs of shoes? The decision could help make him a tidy sum, or it could cause him to lose lots of money and waste precious time. He turned to eBay's Completed Listings search to help him figure out what to do.

Robert first searched active eBay listings. Here's a summary of what he discovered and what he believed the data was telling him:

- Lots of listings existed for these shoes, which was a good sign—the brand might be well known. He noted about 60 listings in a two-week period—a decent amount of listings, but not so much that the market was flooded.

- The minimum bid prices were in Robert's target range, which he had calculated based on the acquisition cost, packaging for outbound shipping, and an acceptable markup, with a STR estimate of 25 percent.

- A few items had bids—maybe a half dozen in the seven days' worth of listings noted. Not a lot, but these shoes were not intended to be a mainstay of his sales.

So far, so good: eBay's search of active listings indicated the brand might be well known and some bidding activity was taking place. Then Robert did a search of auctions that had recently ended using eBay's Completed Listings search. Here's what he found:

- Selling prices had not increased beyond the asking prices. This was not necessarily a bad sign, since the asking prices were within Robert's target range. He knew that bidding up would have meant more profit, but if the shoes sold at the asking price, he would still make his target profits.

- Sell-through was low. In the two-week period displayed, 60 listings were posted and only nine sales resulted; that's a 9/60, or 15 percent STR—in this category, that was not good at all.

(continued)

Robert's research into the shoes using a Completed Listings search concerned him, so he did some more digging. He did a search for the shoes on eBay Stores and found no store listings for the shoes or for sellers who had been listing the shoes. In fact, most of the sellers who had sold shoes one week had not listed any more shoes in the two or three weeks following—this told Robert that perhaps these sellers were getting rid of shoes they had tried and did not like, and once the shoes were gone, the sellers moved on to other things. Or, it might indicate that sellers didn't want to flood the market and reduce selling prices even more.

Robert had used the eBay search to estimate the following:

■ Supply (how many items were currently listed)

■ Average starting price

■ Bidding activity on current listings

He had used a Completed Listings search to estimate the following:

■ Average starting and selling prices

■ STR

Robert also searched store listings to determine whether sellers were committed to selling this brand of shoes. Then he scanned some other auction sites and found even fewer listings and fewer sales, so he concluded that using alternate sites would not help.

Since sales were slow and low, and alternative sites' sales were worse, he realized that there was little chance he'd be able to bulk lot these to other sellers. He knew that they'd do the same research he had done and would come to the same conclusions.

So even though the pricing seemed good for the inventory and sales were happening at Robert's target price, the numbers showed him that these 12,000 pairs of shoes would take him a lifetime to unload if he wanted to make a profit. Having carefully mined the data available through eBay search and Completed Listings search, Robert decided to pass on the shoes and stay on the lookout for better opportunities.

Sellers are responsible for properly listing their items in the correct category. Sellers *should* put a Dell laptop power adapter in the Computers & Networking—Laptop Parts & Accessories category, for example, but they *could* list it in the Computers & Networking—Laptops category. In our example, if 50 sellers did that, it would mean 50 fewer Dell laptops would show up in our search. This is just one more reason to look carefully through search results when conducting eBay research.

Basic eBay Sales Reports

eBay makes available reports to its sellers that offer information about sellers' own sales, as opposed to raw numbers of items listed on eBay. You should become familiar with eBay Sales Reports and use them as a stepping stone to more advanced reports, which are covered in later chapters.

eBay Sales Reports are free to all users who have a minimum feedback rating of 10 and who have listed at least one item in the previous four months. Sales reports can be used to gather important performance metrics for your business and sales. The basic sales report has two parts—a Sales Summary and Fees Summary.

The Sales Summary part of the eBay Sales Report provides sales activity trended over a three-month period. It includes total sales, month-to-month sales growth, ended listings, the number and the percentage of successful listings, and average sale price per listing.

The Fees Summary part of the report includes net eBay and PayPal fees listed separately and combined. (The PayPal fees in eBay Sales Reports include only those fees associated with eBay transactions.)

A November 2004 eBay workshop on using sales reports suggested that sellers use the reports to understand which metrics are contributing most to the change in sales. For example, your sales might go up because you added more listings, your average sales prices increased during that time period, your percent of successful listings increased, or any combination of these. Different sellers will have different key performance indicators.

> **NOTE** *We take a look at eBay Sales Reports Plus, which has more features than basic reports, in the next section.*

eBay Sales Reports do have some limitations. You can look at data only at a high-level view; since your metrics are almost certain to vary by category and other criteria, you can only get a snapshot of your total sales performance on eBay. The reports go back a maximum of only six months—so print out your reports each month—and you can review reports only for as long as you were signed up for them.

> **NOTE** *eBay Sales Reports look at your history for the month; when reviewing fee data in these reports, the information will not match your eBay invoice exactly if your billing cycle ends on a day other than the last day of the month.*

How to Access Sales Reports and Sales Reports Plus

The first time you want to access sales reports, you must subscribe:

1. Go to www.ebay.com and click the My eBay button at the top of any eBay page. You will be asked to sign in.

2. On your My eBay page, in the left navigation list, click on Subscriptions underneath My Account.

3. A list of services you can subscribe to will appear. Under Sales Reports, click the Subscribe link next to the report you wish to subscribe to (Sales Reports or Sales Reports Plus).

Once you have subscribed to Sales Reports, you can access the reports anytime by logging in to My eBay and clicking on Sales Reports underneath My Subscriptions. Your latest monthly report is always shown by default. To access previous reports, click the Archived Reports link in the left part of the page.

eBay Sales Reports Plus

eBay Sales Reports Plus is free for eBay Store owners; otherwise, a monthly charge is levied for its use. In addition to the basic information offered in the free sales reports, the Sales Reports Plus tool provides the following:

- Both listings and item-level information in the Sales Summary
- Buyer counts—total, unique, and repeat
- Sales metrics by category
- Sales metrics by format (auction, Fixed Price, stores inventory)
- Sales metrics by ending day or time for auction listings
- Detailed eBay fees
- A summary of unpaid item requests
- Marketplace data

A navigation menu in the left column lists the sections: Sales Summary, Sales By Format, Sales By Category, Marketplace Data, and Archived Reports.

Sales Summary

The Sales Summary part of the eBay Sales Report Plus is identical to that of the Basic Sales Report and includes sales activity, fees, and unpaid item statistics.

Sales By Format

The Sales By Format section of the Sales Reports Plus window contains a Format Summary chart that shows you where your monthly sales are coming from: Auction, Fixed Price, or Stores Inventory. While sellers should have a general idea where they are listing items and where sales are coming from, Figure 3-5 shows how these at-a-glance summaries can be helpful in checking your assumptions and tracking the data over time.

$ALES STRATEGY   *You can use the Sales By Format section of eBay Sales Report Plus to help you choose whether to use auctions or Fixed Price format for your items. (I'll talk about Advanced Listing Strategy #2: Choose auction-style listings vs. Fixed-Price format in Chapter 9.) Make sure you download reports so you can track the performance of auctions versus Fixed Price format over time.*

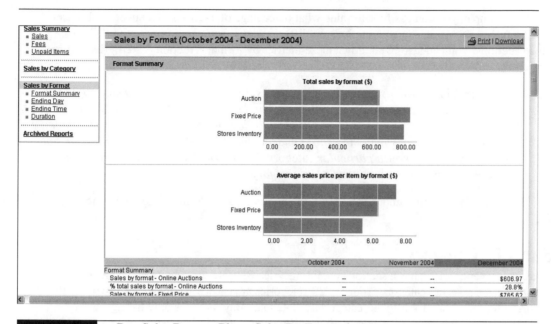

Format Summary	October 2004	November 2004	December 2004
Sales by format - Online Auctions	--	--	$606.97
% total sales by format - Online Auctions	--	--	28.8%
Sales by format - Fixed Price	--	--	$765.62

FIGURE 3-5   eBay Sales Reports Plus—Sales By Format lets you see at a glance the total sales by format and the Average Sales Price per item by format.

Under the Total Sales by Format chart is another chart called Average Sales Price Per Item By Format. Under those charts are detailed numbers (including the STR), which allows you to compare metrics by format. For example, you can compare the ASPs of your auctions to your Fixed Price items.

Another interesting piece of data eBay provides in these charts is the number of unique buyers (one person who makes five purchases is still one *unique* buyer, but will show up five times under the "Total Buyer" count). If your unique buyer count is lower than your total buyer count, that means customers are purchasing multiple items from you. Getting a customer to purchase several items instead of one is something sellers strive for; some sellers run promotions, such as offering free or combined shipping, if a customer purchases a certain number of items from their store. Having a customer buy multiple items not only makes you more money, it makes it easier for you as a seller—and *saves* you money—if you receive one payment and can ship all the items in one shipment.

Sales Reports Plus allows you to look at the following metrics by ending day, ending time, and auction duration:

■ STR

■ ASP

■ Average bids per item

For example, you can easily determine what percentage of auctions that ended on Fridays successfully sold; or, if you end auctions on different days, you can compare the STRs of those auctions. You can also break down these metrics by format (Auction, Fixed Price, Stores Inventory, and Total).

TIP   *Be careful how you use these broad statistics. Many factors can influence STRs. For example, if all your DVD auctions end on Friday, and all your clothing auctions end on Monday, the type of items offered may have more to do with your STR than the day of the week on which the listings ended. eBay Sales Reports Plus reports do not allow you to see how a particular* category *did in terms of ending day. However, you can break out your* monthly *sales by category.*

You can click Duration under Sales By Format to get the ASPs and STRs by listing duration (1, 3, 5, 7, and 10 days).

Sales By Category

eBay Sales Reports Plus has a section containing Sales By Category charts that break out your monthly sales by eBay category. Your top 20 categories are shown, and you can download the report to see sales data for all your categories. Note that eBay includes only listings in the first category that sellers choose for those listings; eBay does not include a listing in a category's results if it was chosen as a second category.

$ALES STRATEGY   *You can use the Sales By Category section of eBay Sales Reports Plus to help you choose categories. (I'll cover this in Basic Listing Strategy #4: Locate the best category in Chapter 8.) The Sales By Category section can also help with Advanced Listing Strategy # 1: Research what to sell (Chapter 9), by helping you identify strong and weak categories.*

In Figure 3-6, you can see that the two charts at the top show total sales by category and the number of successful items by category. These numbers include data on auctions, Fixed Price listings, and store items.

In addition to providing bar charts of sales by category, eBay breaks out statistics for each category. It includes the following metrics:

- Sales
- Month-to-month sales growth
- Ended items
- Successful items (#)
- Successful items (%)
- Average sales price per item
- Total buyers

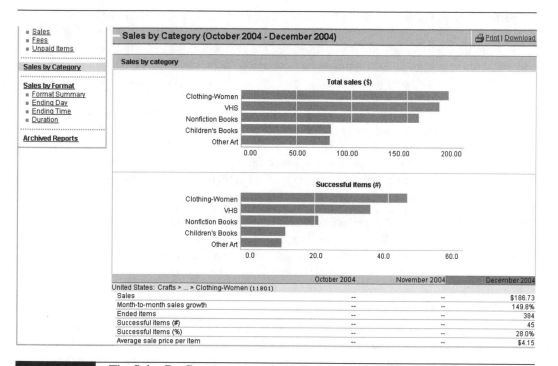

FIGURE 3-6   The Sales By Category report in eBay Sales Reports Plus is useful for seeing your category's performance for the most recent three months.

Successful items (%) is the STR. If you listed 66 auctions that ended in the month of February, and 11 auction items sold successfully, that would mean a 11/66, or a 17 percent STR on your auction items. On eBay Sales Reports, you'll notice these numbers don't seem to compute for the statistics listed by category if you have an eBay Store. This is because in this section of the report, Ended Items and Successful Items (#) include store items, but Successful Items (%) does not include store items. You'll have to take eBay's word on STR by category or check it against your own records.

In March 2005, eBay added the ability to break out category data by format as well, so you can see, for example, how your clothing items performed in store format versus auction format.

Using Sales By Format allows you to compare all listings by auction, Fixed Price, and store format. Using Sales By Category allows you to compare sales by category. Don't get too bogged down in trying to play with these numbers to see what they mean, however. The data revealed in these broad comparisons of monthly sales is only one part of the equation. You need to know what you did differently from month to month to understand the implications of the data.

A perfect example is the Month-To-Month Sales Growth metric (shown near the bottom of Figure 3-6). This is useful information if you listed the same number of like items in that category from month to month. But if you decreased the number of like items in a category, it would not be surprising to find that your sales decreased accordingly. On the other hand, if you start listing items in a category different from those you had listed in the past, these statistics will help you determine whether the new items are better sellers.

Seasonal factors can heavily influence sales metrics, too. Seasonal factors include the types of seasonal items you are selling (mittens and snow boots are seasonal items) as well as seasonal retail trends. eBay sales are typically slower in the summer months, and this will impact your sales. Sophisticated retailers compare year-to-year performance to try to account for seasonal differences. This means they compare the report for the month of January for the current year with the report for the month of January for the previous year.

NOTE *eBay Featured and Anchor Store subscribers also receive a Sales By Category—All Sellers report. This shows sales performance averaged across all sellers in the categories and formats in which they sold. Note that this data is provided only for categories that are at least four levels deep in eBay's category structure.*

eBay Marketplace Research

As this book was going to press, eBay introduced the eBay Marketplace Research subscription service. Formerly, this data was available only through licensees such as the market-data tools covered in Chapters 4 through 6. The eBay tool has some features unavailable from licensees, including the ability to research specific sellers, international data, and Top Searches. Figure 3-7 shows Top Searches for the Pottery And Glass (Ceramiques et Verres) category on eBay France.

Likewise, companies that license eBay data have some features unavailable through eBay Marketplace Research. I explain the basics of eBay's new service in Appendix B.

Archived Reports

When you log into My eBay and access your Sales Reports, you'll notice that the current month's statistics are provided. To access previous months' reports, you can click Archived Reports in the left column.

I recommend downloading all your reports to your computer and also backing them up onto a disk, memory stick, or whatever media you use to back up data. Don't rely on eBay to store your sales data for you. (I know of cases in which data has been lost.)

eBay provides its reports in a monthly format. If you download data and import it into a spreadsheet, you can compare data over time, and you can also combine report data to create quarterly or annual reports. If you aren't good with spreadsheets, consider taking a class, buying a book, asking for help in an online forum, or hiring someone to help you set up a system so you can review your sales performance on a regular basis. I suggest *Excel QuickSteps* by Guy Hart-Davis (McGraw-Hill, 2004).

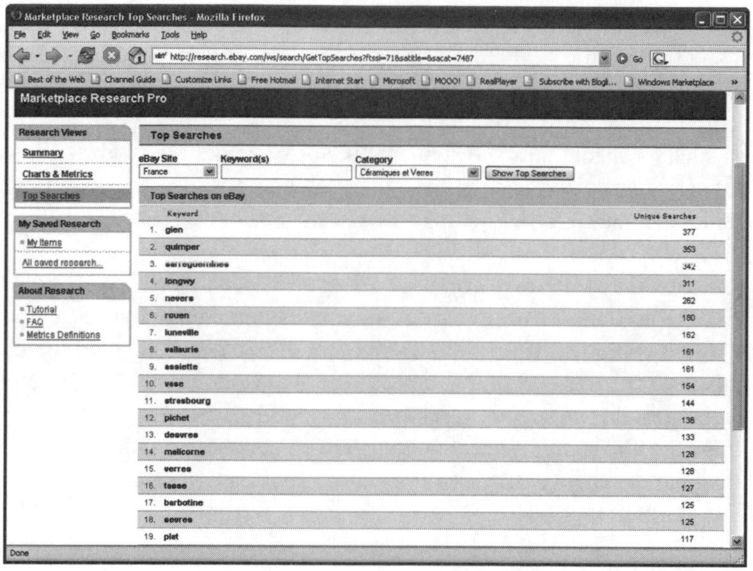

FIGURE 3-7 eBay Marketplace Research lets you see what the top searches are across all of its international websites, including eBay France, shown here.

Measuring Success with eBay Sales Reports

Allison Hartsoe, President and CEO of Internet Business Skills (www.internetbusinessskills .com), helps entrepreneurs increase revenue and reduce costs using Internet technology and has advised many small businesses on how to use eBay effectively. Allison uses eBay Sales Reports to determine how well her clients are performing on eBay.

Allison said two of the most useful and interesting metrics on eBay Sales Reports are the percentage of repeat buyers and the STR. (Repeat Buyers % is found on the Sales Summary page when you sign in to eBay Sales Reports. Sold Items % is found on the Sales Summary page and on the Sales By Format pages.)

"What's most interesting on the eBay Sales Reports that is not easily found on other reports is the repeat buyer percentage. We use this number to determine if a customer is a good candidate for eBay's e-mail newsletter capability. As that number edges up to 10 percent, it's time to launch the newsletter and start giving buyers reasons to tell their friends about the great deal they got and come back to buy."

(continued)

Allison also reviews the percentage sold metric (STR) and compares it to the category average, which she finds using tools like Terapeak, Andale, and DeepAnalysis. This comparison helps her determine whether clients can improve their current performance.

"Each category has a specific percentage success rate that varies over time but can be found with tools such as HammerTap's DeepAnalysis or sites like Medved," Allison said. "We consider the category percentage the 'baseline.' When our sellers are significantly above that percentage, it's a sign their listings are optimized. In other words, almost every time they list, they sell product.

"Recently, we took on a seller in a competitive space who was doing well from a gross sales point of view. However, when we reviewed the sales percentage figure (STR), we discovered he was not selling as often as his competitors. As a result, he paid more in fees and put less in his pocket at the end of the month. He was 11 percent under the category average for percentage sold and never even knew it."

Once she knew the client's STR was lower than average, she did more research to find out what he was doing differently than his competitors, and she was able to suggest ways to increase his STRs—and profits.

Whether you use eBay Sales Reports or another tool to look at your sales data, understanding spreadsheets can help you organize your data in meaningful ways so you can apply the information you glean going forward.

eBay Stores Traffic Reports

The benefits of having an eBay Store are the lower listing fees (a monthly subscription fee pays for itself quickly for high-volume sellers), along with the ability to offer a wide range of items in a storefront that buyers can peruse or search.

One of the biggest challenges eBay Storeowners face, however, is driving traffic to store listings. If you have been selling on eBay using auctions, you know buyers flock to the eBay site, enter search terms for items, and click through to your listings when a match occurs. But did you know that store items do not show up in basic eBay.com searches? (Searches *will* display 30 store listings, but only if fewer than 21 listings are found in auction or Fixed Price format.)

Storeowners spend a lot of time—and, in some cases, a lot of money—using techniques to drive traffic to their store items. It's important for them to get feedback on whether those efforts pay off in terms of traffic and sales. The goal is to spend marketing resources on the most effective drivers of traffic, and to pull back on techniques that aren't working.

eBay Storeowners can use Traffic Reports to help them determine which marketing techniques are driving traffic to listings.

How to Access eBay Store Traffic Reports

Here's how to access eBay Store Traffic Reports (you must have a store in order to access Store Traffic Reports):

1. Go to www.ebay.com and click the My eBay button at the top of any eBay page. You will be asked to sign in.

2. On your My eBay page, in the left navigation area under My Subscriptions, click the Manage My Store link.

3. Under Reports in the left navigation area, click the Traffic Reports link. You will have to sign in again to eBay.

4. Agree to the Omniture Authorization, since the reports are hosted on a third-party website (Omniture).

5. On the My Summary page, you can navigate to view your reports.

In Chapter 7, I discuss another traffic-tracking tool called Sellathon ViewTracker, and I recommend you test both services. Most sellers I've spoken with who have used ViewTracker get addicted to it, but they also find eBay Traffic Reports useful.

eBayTraffic Reports are free for eBay Storeowners and vary according to the type of eBay Store you own. All storeowners can access traffic reports that indicate which pages and listings were most often visited by their customers, and which websites and search keywords brought the most visitors to their stores and listings. Featured and Anchor storeowners also have access to advanced path, bidding, and buying reports.

Path reports indicate how and from where visitors entered your store and from which pages they exited your store. Bidding and Buying reports indicate which sites and search keywords led to the most bids and sales. This can be some of the most useful information available to any storeowner, since it can help you pinpoint which marketing techniques are working for you.

Three Kinds of eBay Stores

eBay has three types of stores (http://pages.ebay.com/help/sell/storefees.html):

- Basic
- Featured
- Anchor

Basic stores come with five customizable pages and the ability to send e-mail newsletters to 100 buyers per month. Featured and Anchor stores cost more than Basic stores, but they come with more features, including advanced reports, exposure on eBay Stores pages, promotional dollars to spend on the eBay Keyword Program, and a free subscription to Selling Manager Pro.

NOTE   *eBay sellers with Basic stores who don't have access to eBay's Path and Bidding and Buying reports may be especially interested in Sellathon's ViewTracker service, reviewed in Chapter 7, since it gives additional information beyond eBay Traffic Reports.*

eBay Traffic reports are powered by Omniture's SiteCatalyst, a web *analytics* tool used by some of the largest e-commerce sites on the Internet. Unfortunately, it is not possible to exclude your own IP address from being populated in the Traffic report, so you will have to factor this into your analysis. You need to have Internet Explorer 5.5 or later installed on your machine, and a Flash player may also need to be installed.

$ALES STRATEGY   *The Site Traffic reports of the eBay Store Traffic Reports can help you develop your listing strategies by showing you the popularity of your listings.*

Types of Store Traffic Reports

When you initially access the eBay Store Traffic Reports, you'll be taken to the My Summary page. On the left side of the page, you'll see a navigation system. Clicking My Summary will always bring you back to the main My Summary page (Figure 3-8). Under Traffic Reports are the three types of reports you can generate: Site Traffic reports, Finding Methods reports, and Custom Reports (you'll see more reports if you have a Featured or Anchor store, as in Figure 3-8).

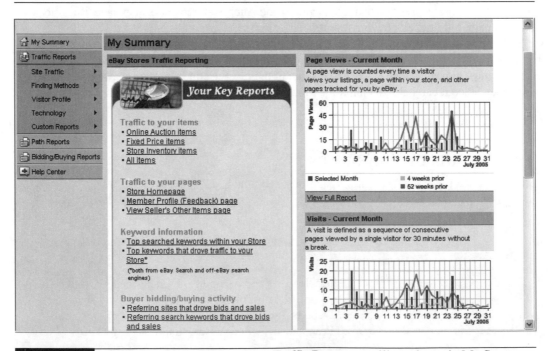

FIGURE 3-8   When you log in to eBay Store Traffic Reports, you'll see the main My Summary page.

> **NOTE** *A calendar feature at the top left side of most pages (not shown in Figure 3-8) lets you switch between day and monthly views. You can click the word* Range *(next to the word* Calendar*) to specify a date range.*

Site Traffic Reports

Site Traffic reports provide information about how many buyers are visiting your eBay pages. You can see how many unique visitors come to your eBay pages in a given day or month, how many times a particular user views your pages in a given time period, and how many visits your pages receive.

Sellers have more than just listing (View Item) pages, and when counting traffic, eBay Traffic Reports include visits to all of these pages:

- Listing pages
- Member Profile (Feedback) pages
- Seller's Other Items page
- About Me page
- Store Home page
- Any other page that eBay can identify with a single seller

Site Traffic reports can provide an indication of how popular your pages and listings are, and this information is useful for comparing these metrics over time. Ideally, you will be able to see relationships between your offerings and popularity and between your marketing efforts and popularity.

Site Traffic reports are useful for testing different approaches to listing techniques. For example, let's say you list two identical items using slightly different keywords in the title, but everything else is identical. If one listing is getting more traffic than the other, it may indicate the keywords you use in the popular listing are more effective and would guide your use of keywords in future listings.

Site Traffic reports are also useful in helping you determine the most popular days for visits to your pages, as well as tracking seasonal differences, assuming you capture the Site Traffic report data and track it over time. (Downloading reports to an Excel spreadsheet can help you with tracking.) You'll learn about more ways to use traffic data and apply it to your listing and marketing strategies in Chapters 8 through 10.

Finding Methods Reports

Finding Methods reports provide information about how buyers are finding your eBay pages. A buyer's ability to find your listings is the key to success in online sales. Finding Methods reports can help you figure out where your traffic is coming from. For example, the Referring Domains report shows you where your visitors were looking before they arrived at your store or listings. This kind of information can help guide your marketing strategies, which are covered in Chapter 10.

$ALES STRATEGY *Finding Method reports can help you with Marketing Strategy #3: Improve your advertising and publicity (Chapter 10), by showing you where traffic is coming from. The Search Keywords reports can help you with Basic Listing Strategy #5: Uncover the most effective keywords (Chapter 8).*

Unfortunately, Basic storeowners can't access the more detailed reports available to Featured and Anchor storeowners.

TIP *Your searches will be counted in the data you receive on these reports. eBay advises that when you search your own store, you identify your searches by entering search terms using a unique combination of uppercase and lowercase letters. For example, for the term* cookbook, *you could enter* COOKbook. *This will help you differentiate your searches from those of potential buyers.*

Custom Reports

Custom Reports include data about most popular pages, most popular listings, homepage page views, and search terms used within your store.

Individual Traffic Reports

The following reports are available from eBay's basic traffic reports. Improving your listing and marketing techniques will drive more traffic to your eBay Store, leading to more sales, so traffic is an important metric to monitor.

Unique Visitors Report

This Site Traffic report shows you how many *unique* visitors your pages receive for a particular day or month. If one person visits your listing multiple times in a day, he or she will be counted only once for that day, unless the person is accessing your listing from different computers (from work and from home, for example). Knowing how many different people saw your listing is more useful than knowing how many visits your store had in a day—in most cases, 100 different people viewing your store is better than one person clicking 100 times.

Page Views Report

This Site Traffic report shows you the number of times visitors have viewed all of your pages. You can click the link next to Selected Page (at the top right of the page) to isolate data to a particular page (the default is the entire site). A page view is counted every time someone views any of your pages currently being tracked.

Figure 3-9 shows a Page Views Report from March 2005. You can see a nice overview of traffic to all of your eBay pages by date, and you can see the entire month on one graph. See "Most Popular Pages Report" later to see a count of visits by page and see which pages are most popular.

3

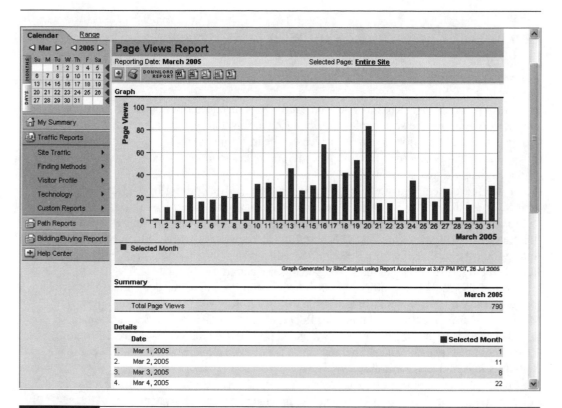

FIGURE 3-9	The Page Views Report shows you how much traffic is visiting your eBay pages on each day of the month.

Visits Report

This Site Traffic report shows you the number of visits made to your pages, allowing you to see how the total number of visits has changed during a given time period. This is different from the Unique Visitors Report in that one person may visit your pages multiple times in a day, and this single visitor will be counted for each visit he or she makes. eBay defines a *visit* as a "sequence of consecutive page views without a 30-minute break. A visit always contains one or more page views. A unique visitor always performs at least one, but possibly more visits."

Referring Domains Report

This Finding Methods report shows you the domains your visitors visited before visiting your store or listings. A *domain* is a high-level Internet address such as ebay.com or paypal.com. (The Referring Domains Report does not show you the actual page the visitor is coming from—only the domain.) Visitors moving between pages on eBay are not considered in these reports.

Consultant Plays Traffic Cop with eBay Reports

Allison Hartsoe, who we met earlier in the chapter, helps entrepreneurs use eBay effectively. Allison explained how she uses eBay Traffic Reports to increase the number of visitors to her clients' eBay Stores.

One of Allison's first steps is to use eBay Traffic Reports to determine whether a customer's store is *optimized* for the search engines (*optimized* means that search engines display your listings when someone does a search), which can be instrumental in driving visitors to an eBay Store. Allison uses the Search Engines Report under Finding Methods to see which search engines visitors are using.

"If we see a client with 85 percent or more of their traffic coming from eBay search, then we know their eBay Store is not being picked up well by Yahoo!, MSN, AIM, Google, or Froogle," Allison said. "We then go back to their eBay Store, turn on their external feed function, enter solid keywords in the Search Engine keywords section of their eBay Store settings, and we update the store description." Allison said she monitors the Search Engine Report weekly to see how the search-engine mix is changing.

Allison also uses eBay Traffic Reports to find the top five keywords that are most effective for her client. She gets this information from the Search Keywords Report under Finding Methods, and from the Store Search Terms Report under Custom Reports. She supplements these two reports with category keywords found in eBay Pulse reports (www.ebay.com/pulse). "By matching the two and adding these words to the title or store categories, we make sure we capture as many buyers as possible."

Finally, Allison monitors the Page Views Report under Site Traffic Reports as a predictor of future sales. "We look for a steady increase in page views month over month," Allison said. "Since some products are seasonal, and eBay itself can be seasonal, we will sometimes recommend running ad campaigns through eBay Keywords [eBay's optional marketing program] to boost traffic during a slow down."

eBay uses the term *Typed/Bookmarked* as a referrer type. A *referrer* is simply the place a visitor was before visiting your pages. Typed/Bookmarked is a catch-all category for visitors who came to your listings or store without a referring URL; this can indicate that the visitor typed your store's URL directly into the browser address bar, or he or she may have clicked a bookmark (favorite) or a link from an e-mail application such as Outlook or Eudora.

NOTE   *In Chapter 7, I'll talk about the pitfalls of analyzing traffic data. In many cases, it's difficult to identify where all traffic is coming from, so make sure you understand the limitations before you make broad assumptions about your traffic data.*

Despite the fact that you won't know the domain from which *every* visitor arrives, you will know the domains from which many of your visitors come, and this can prove to be helpful information. For instance, if you sell movie posters and see that some traffic is coming from a website about movie posters, you might consider advertising on that site or you might look for similar websites about movie posters on which to advertise.

Search Engines Report

This Finding Methods report helps you identify which search engines people are using to find your eBay Store and listings. For example, the Search Engines Report will provide a count of the number of people who found your store or listing on Google (or Froogle), along with the percentage. Figure 3-10 shows that, in the month of July 2005, 40 percent of traffic generated from search engines came from Yahoo!, 40 percent came from Google, and 20 percent came from eBay Search (the eBay.com Search box). (The report does not track traffic arriving from other sources; it tracks only search engine searches, including eBay's own search engine.)

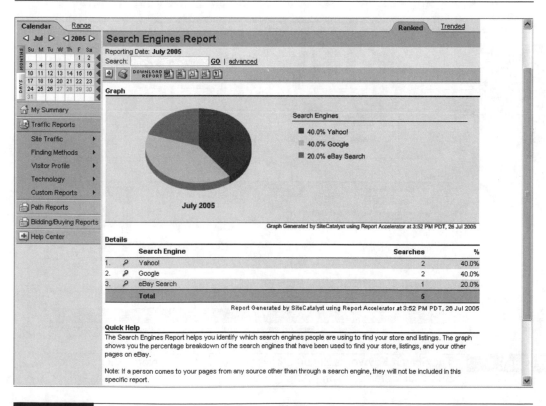

FIGURE 3-10   Search Engines Report shows which search engines are driving traffic to your eBay Store.

Search engine traffic is an important measurement that can help you make sure your store is *optimized* for search engines, and it can be used to measure the success of your paid search marketing efforts. (Marketing strategies are covered in Chapter 10.)

Search Keywords Report

This Finding Methods report, shown in Figure 3-11, displays a breakdown of each search keyword that has been used to find your store and listings (including eBay Search and search engines such as Google). Identifying which keywords are most effective in finding your store and listings can help you determine which keywords to use in your listing titles and descriptions.

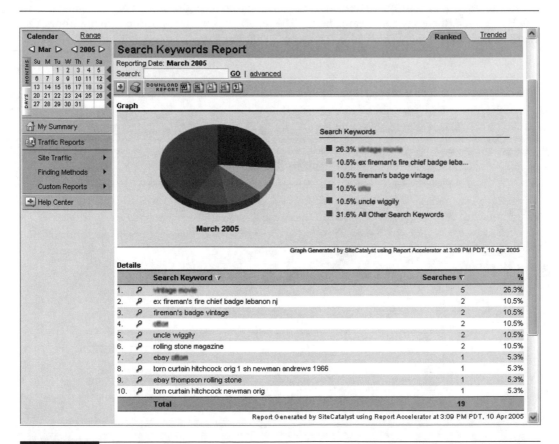

FIGURE 3-11 The Search Keywords Report allows you to see the keywords shoppers used to find your store and listings.

TIP
Click the magnifying glass next to each keyword to see which search engine was used for that search term.

Most Popular Pages Report

This Custom report displays your most popular pages along with the number of times these pages have been viewed. If some pages are not being viewed, you can try to determine why that is so.

TIP
You can use the search box at the top of the page to filter the report for specific pages (that is, use Item Online Auction to filter only for listings pages for your auctions).

Most Popular Listings Report

This Custom report displays the number of times your listings (as opposed to all pages) have been viewed, helping you to identify popular items.

TIP
You can use the search box at the top of the page to filter the report. For example, you can enter the name of the format (Online Auction, Fixed-Price, Store Inventory, and so on) to filter only for those types of listings.

Store Home Page Views Report

This Custom report displays the number of times your eBay Store homepage has been viewed, which is helpful if you want to assess the effectiveness of your marketing strategies and promotions in driving traffic to your store homepage.

Store Search Keywords Report

This Custom report displays a count of how many times a keyword was searched within your store. This report includes keywords used for title searches as well as title and description searches. You can use this report to identify which keywords are most frequently searched within your store, helping you determine the best words to use in your listing titles and descriptions.

TIP
If people are searching your store for items you don't stock, the Store Search Keywords Report may help you identify new products to consider selling. (We'll see a case in Chapter 9 where a PowerSeller found a new brand of sunglasses by studying search terms, and the item turned into a big seller.)

Selecting a Date Range

You can change a report's date ranges from the default, which is the current month. You can use the calendar on the left side of the report page to change the month you are viewing. Above the calendar are two tabs, Calendar and Range. You can click Range and then specify the date range for the data you wish to view, as shown in Figure 3-12.

FIGURE 3-12   eBay Traffic Reports allow you to select the days, months, or date ranges you want to view.

Downloading eBay Store Traffic Reports

Each report type offers several download options. Directly under the report title, date, and search box is a row of icons. Download options include Word, Excel, PDF, HTML, and comma-separated formats. Simply click an icon and a dialog box appears. You can choose to download the report immediately, or you can send it to a recipient via e-mail. You can also choose to compress the data by checking the box next to Compress: Send As A Zipped File (if you choose to compress the file, you will need a program like WinZip to unzip the file). You are required to enter an e-mail address even if downloading immediately, since eBay will e-mail you the report if it takes too long to generate.

Featured and Anchor Store Traffic Reports

Sellers who have a Featured or Anchor eBay Store have access to additional traffic reports from eBay called Path Reports and Bidding/Buying Reports.

Path Reports

Under Path Reports on the navigation pane on the left side of the reports window, choose Complete Paths and then Full Paths to see how visitors navigated through your store listings, which can help you measure the success of your cross-promotion techniques. Figure 3-13 shows the two sections of the Full Paths Report—the Graph section, which indicates the percentage of visitors who took a particular path, and the Details section, which shows the actual path the visitor took in visiting your listings.

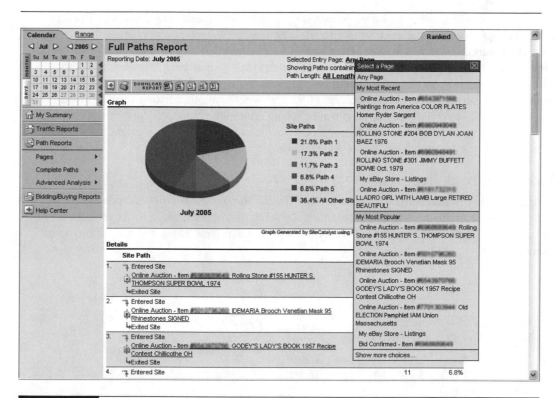

FIGURE 3-13   This Full Paths Report shows you exactly how people are navigating your listings, helping you measure the success of your cross-promotional activities.

In Figure 3-13, in addition to other information, you can see in the Graph section that 21 percent of your visitors took Path 1 to arrive at your listing. In the Details section, you can see that 34 people entered the listing for an auction for a *Rolling Stone* magazine featuring a Hunter S. Thompson article, and then exited the site. If you add a link to another listing in your store, this report would indicate whether people were clicking the link by identifying where each person visited after they left this particular listing. I'll cover cross-promotional strategies and how to measure them in Chapter 10.

Under Path Reports, choose Complete Paths and then Path Lengths to see the number of people who visited and how many of your listings were visited before they left your store (for example, 2000 people may have viewed only one listing before leaving your store, while 50 people may have viewed three listings before leaving). Choose Complete Paths and then Time Spent Per Visit to see how long visitors spent viewing your listings.

Advanced Analysis shows where people are coming from (via the Previous Page Report) and which pages people are clicking to after viewing a particular page on your store (Next Page Report). Figure 3-14 shows the Next Page Report for a particular eBay listing; it shows that after viewing this listing, 82.2 percent of visitors (37 visitors) left your store, 8.9 percent (4 visitors) placed a bid, 4.4 percent (2 visitors) went to your eBay Store page, 2.2 percent (1 visitor) went to the bid confirmed page, and 2.2 percent (1 visitor) went to another listing located in your store inventory. Knowing whether people are clicking around in your store can help you figure out better cross-promotional techniques and help you determine which items might make good complementary sales (shoes and socks, for example).

Bidding/Buying Reports

Bidding/Buying Reports are different from basic Traffic Reports in that they include counts from actual bidders and buyers only, not *all* visitors. Knowing data about a bidder or buyer is much more valuable than knowing data about a visitor who came to your listing and did not bid on or buy anything.

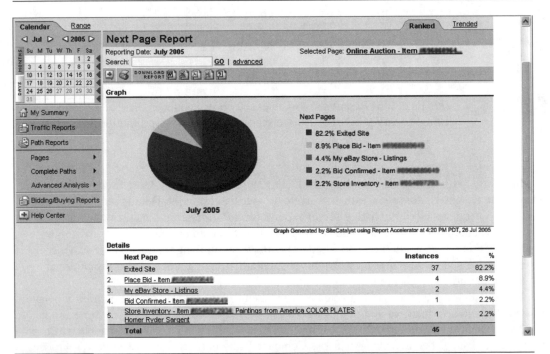

FIGURE 3-14   The Next Page Report can help you see where people are going after leaving one of your store pages. This report can help you devise better cross-promotional strategies.

Suppose, for example, that you spend most of your marketing budget on Google marketing, and that's where much of your traffic comes from. But you determine that the majority of *bidders* and *buyers* come from Yahoo! This could cause you to rethink your marketing budget allocations.

A Bids Report displays the total number of bid confirmation page views that occurred with your auction listings on a given day, while the Buy It Now Report does the same for Buy It Now, Fixed Price, and store inventory listings. The Bids Report in Figure 3-15 shows the number of bids this seller received each day of the month.

eBay makes available the following Bidding/Buying Reports:

- Listings
- Referring Domains
- Original Referral Domains
- Search Engines
- Search Keywords
- Entry Pages
- Original Entry Pages

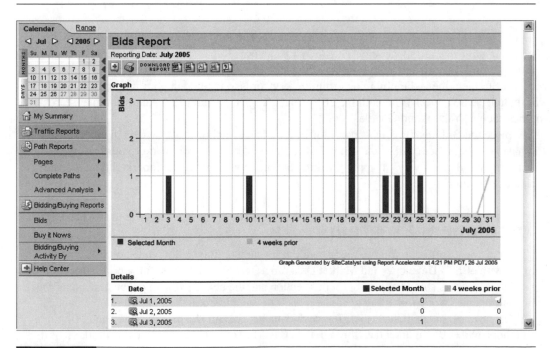

FIGURE 3-15   This Bids Report shows bidding activity for each day of the month.

Bookmark It!

The eBay Help file outlines the types of reports available and defines the terms used in the reports:

- eBay Help File for Sales Reports Plus   http://pages.ebay.com/help/sell/sales-reports-plus.html

eBay has also set up a discussion board where sellers can talk to each other and share advice about using the Sales Reports. You can also sign up for the eBay Sales Reports News Group to receive announcements from eBay relating to Sales Reports. Other eBay groups may be of interest to you as well, and you can find them on the eBay Groups sellers' page.

- eBay Sales Reports Discussion Board   http://forums.ebay.com/db1/forum .jsp?forum=4024
- eBay Sales Reports News Group   http://groups.ebay.com/forum.jspa?forumID= 100016610
- eBay Groups for Sellers   http://groups.ebay.com/index.jspa?categoryID=35

Referring Domains Report tells you where bidders and buyers are coming from—helpful in fine-tuning your marketing strategy. The Search Keywords Report breaks out bid confirmation or Buy It Now confirmation page views by the particular keywords users were searching on from various search engines—helpful in determining keywords to include in your listing titles. This will include search terms from both the eBay search engine and all of the major Internet search engines such as Yahoo! and Google.

Explore the Bidding/Buying Reports for Featured and Anchor Store owners in more detail if you have access to them. All of the eBay Traffic Reports can help you market your listings more effectively. We'll cover ways to apply this kind of data to your listing and marketing strategies in Chapters 8 through 10.

eBay Developers Program

If you are a crack software programmer as well as top-notch eBay seller, you should become familiar with eBay's Developer and Market Data programs. Even if you're not a programmer or top seller, all readers should at least skim this section and the next section to get an understanding of how companies work with eBay to create tools for eBay buyers and sellers. In future chapters, you'll learn about Andale (Chapter 4), Terapeak (Chapter 5), and DeepAnalysis (Chapter 6), three tools that provide eBay market data through the eBay Market Data Program. You will likely find that such tools can serve your needs more efficiently than designing your own tool. (Be sure and read the introductory sections of Chapter 4, even if you don't wish to use Andale, since it gives background on all three market-data tools covered in this book.)

eBay allows developers to use its API to enable their own tools and software to communicate with eBay. You can use eBay's API to perform searches, retrieve information about listings, and do much more.

eBay requires companies to join its Developers Program before they can access the eBay API. Several tiers exist in eBay's Developers Program—some for individuals, some for professionals, some for enterprises, and even one for affiliate marketers. Different pricing structures (and restrictions) apply to each tier, and you must sign up for the program and be approved by eBay. You can find out more about tiers at http://developer.ebay.com. Individuals can join the program at no cost and receive 10,000 free API calls per month. All others (Basic, Professional, and Enterprise members) pay an annual fee plus fees for API calls and technical support.

NOTE   *eBay eliminated Developer fees as this book was going to press.*

Prior to the creation of the Developers Program, third-party vendors would "scrape" eBay's site, accessing data without eBay's permission. (Some services still scrape eBay.) While services such as auction-management and listing tools help sellers by automating their activities, scraping eBay data utilizes eBay resources. Every time an auction is launched to the eBay site, eBay resources are being used. Listing, bidding, searching, sniping, even checking to see how auctions are doing all make demands on eBay's servers.

eBay developed the API for developers to reduce the burden on its systems and to make it easier for software vendors to keep up with frequent code changes. With the eBay API, developers communicate directly with the eBay database.

Using the API, developers can create programs that do the following:

- Submit items for listing on eBay
- Get the current list of eBay categories
- View information about items listed on eBay
- Get high bidder information for items
- Retrieve lists of items a particular user is currently listing through eBay
- Retrieve lists of items a particular user has bid on
- Display eBay listings on other sites
- Leave feedback about other users at the conclusion of a commerce transaction

Bookmark It!

More information on eBay's Developers Program can be found online, where you can learn how to access to documentation, live help, discussion forums, and more:

- eBay Developers Program   http://developer.ebay.com/DevProgram
- eBay Market Data Program   http://developer.ebay.com/marketdata

eBay lists commercial applications developed through the Developers Program in its Solutions Directory at http://solutions.ebay.com. eBay organizes the directory into three main sections:

- **Selling Solutions** Includes listing management tools, photo hosting and management tools, e-mail management tools, and checkout processing tools.

- **Buying Solutions** Includes search tools, auction monitoring tools, and payment tools.

- **Other Solutions** Includes data analysis tools, developer tools, marketplace research tools, and wireless tools.

eBay also offers developers a certification program, for which an annual fee is charged to participate. eBay describes the program at http://developer.ebay.com/certifiedprovider. The Certified Providers Catalog, found at http://developer.ebay.com/certifiedprovider/catalog.aspx, lists the Certified Providers and in some cases has links to videos where companies describe their services.

In the next section, we take a look at the program eBay set up to allow access to its historic data, which is specifically targeted to those interested in developing data-analysis tools and services.

eBay Market Data Program

eBay created its Market Data Program, formerly called the Data Licensing Program, to allow third parties to access eBay's historical transaction data without having to access the website directly through the API. Instead, vendors can access data directly from eBay's data warehouse.

The eBay Market Data Program provides access to closed listing information and includes prices, item descriptions, selling price, feature usage, number of bids, and other transaction details. Personal information, such as user IDs and feedback and reserve price information, are not included as part of the data. The program includes data from eBay.com (the U.S. site) and other sites including Germany and the UK (with a separate licensing fee for each country site).

According to eBay, its Market Data Program lends itself to a variety of products, such as the following:

- **Analytics** To explore pricing or product decisions
- **Price guides** To understand fair-market value of goods
- **Merchandise indicators** To discover where supply constraints exist
- **Efficacy** To decide which merchandising features work
- **Consulting and training** To help eBay sellers understand marketplace dynamics

eBay offers two data licensing options. The "For eBay" license is designed for those creating applications specifically for users of eBay to help them better understand what's happening in the marketplace. The "Off eBay" license is designed for those who want to tap into the consumer activities on eBay but aren't selling services to eBay buyers or sellers, such as consumer or market research firms, retailers, manufacturers, government agencies, and statistic syndication services.

eBay has strict limits on who can use the data and how it may be used. eBay charges a combination of fixed fees and revenue sharing for participating in the program. Annual licensing fees offer different levels of pricing based on the volume of data required and are higher for commercial users. eBay also takes a revenue share from licensees. (Fees are likely to change over time.)

Licensing Options

eBay makes its data available in two plans. The Value Guide package includes listings that have sold successfully. The Efficacy package has more detailed information and includes successful and unsuccessful listings. Developers choose which categories they wish to license and select from two pricing tiers:

- **Standard pricing**   Offers 50 percent of listings and is made available on a weekly basis, with a 21-day delay.
- **Premium pricing**   Offers 100 percent of listings and is made available on a daily basis, with a 2-day delay.

Check the site for the most up-to-date pricing and fees. Most readers will find the fees prohibitive for purchasing eBay data for their own use; most firms license eBay data to develop commercial services, and we'll review three of those services in Chapters 4 through 6.

Services That Dish Up eBay Data

The Professional Golf Association's Value Guide (http://valueguide.pga.com) offers free trade-in and resale values for nearly all brands and models of golf clubs. eBay data powers the pricing guide, and the service was one of the first to license eBay market data.

SmartCollector (www.smartcollector.com) provides pricing data and other services to collectors on its website. See the "SmartCollector Publishes eBay Pricing Data" sidebar.

PriceMiner is an online pricing guide that includes listing results from eBay as well as from GoAntiques.com and TIAS.com, two online antiques malls. PriceMiner charges for a monthly subscription and offers a wireless plan, where you can access data from your cell phone or other Internet-enabled portable device.

Expect to see more pricing guides and services as companies realize the potential of eBay market data.

SmartCollector Publishes eBay Pricing Data

SmartCollector (www.smartcollector.com) is an example of a company that uses eBay's Developers Program and Market Data Program to provide a unique service for a niche market.

SmartCollector founder Jeff Sloan is a collector in addition to being a successful businessman and venture capitalist. He saw the need for a service for collectors like himself to organize information about their collections. Jeff founded SmartCollector with Chris Cameron to provide a service that blends two critical needs of collectors: a tool to manage their collection portfolio and a service that analyzes item value and market trends.

SmartCollector licenses eBay data through the eBay Market Data Program, creating current and historic market statistics to fuel its data analysis services. SmartCollector is also a member of eBay's Developers Program. While it has plans to add additional services, SmartCollector offers three main services: Manage It, Value It, and Trend It.

Manage It is a tool for collectors to add information about their collection that shows everything you own and have bought and sold. As of this writing, the service is free. Value It searches eBay closed listing data, but there are some key differences between conducting price research at SmartCollector and searching closed listings at eBay, according to the service.

- On eBay, you can search 15 days of completed items. SmartCollector offers 120 days of historical sales using Value It.

- eBay Completed Items searches include successful and unsuccessful auctions. SmartCollector concentrates only on successful transactions, as those are the clearest indicators of current value.

- SmartCollector organizes the data for easy navigation and search refinement, and Value It can chart sales and bid patterns for any items that you research.

Trend It analyzes trends by eBay categories and delivers statistics including listing volume, bid volume, total sales, average bids per listing, average price per listing, and Buy It Now totals. You can also compare trends across categories. For example, you can find out how sales of die-cast toys compare to action figures over the past year in sales and average prices, or see which antiques categories are showing the greatest sales growth.

You can search 15 days of eBay sales history for free after registering with the site. Membership to access Value It and Trend It Research Tools is free.

SmartCollector licenses data from the following eBay categories:

- Collectibles
- Antiques
- Entertainment—Memorabilia
- Books—Antiquarian & Collectible
- Sports—Sports Memorabilia

- Jewelry & Watches—Vintage Antique
- Pottery & Glass—Pottery & China
- Pottery & Glass—Glass—Art Glass
- Dolls & Bears—Dolls
- Toys & Hobbies—Classic Toys
- Toys & Hobbies—Diecast
- Toys & Hobbies—Vintage Antique Toys
- Toys & Hobbies—Action Figures
- Toys & Hobbies—Model RR, Trains
- Toys & Hobbies—TV, Movie, Character Toys
- Toys & Hobbies—Games—Board, Traditional Games

Wrapping Up

With the introduction of eBay Sales Reports Plus and eBay Traffic Reports, sellers can learn how to take advantage of sales data to become more profitable. Hopefully, eBay will continue to add features and capabilities to these reports to make them even better and more widely available to all eBay sellers.

With the introduction of its Market Data Program, eBay paved the way for companies to mine eBay data in more sophisticated ways, both for in-house use and for commercial applications. We'll look at three services in Chapters 4 through 6 that use eBay market data to provide sellers with metrics such as ASP by category and by keyword searches.

Chapter 4

Evaluating Research Tools, and All About Andale

eBay data tools can make you an expert in the eBay marketplace. They can be used to help you find out which items are hot sellers on eBay. You can search an item by keyword and view metrics such as the average price, number of bids, success rates of listings, and more. You can find out what features the best-selling listings used (by comparing metrics by features used) so you can make decisions about your own listing and marketing strategies. You can even search an entire eBay category and look for trends to jump on new opportunities or quickly exit a declining market.

This information is available to anyone who wants it—whether you sell on eBay or not. But because these tools are relatively new and a monthly subscription charge is necessary to use them, the percentage of sellers doing active research is still very low. Yet this is the very data to which eBay sellers long to have access!

If you are looking to grow your eBay business and want to sell smarter on eBay, you should take a look at market-data tools and the information they can provide. PowerSellers who use these tools have an edge over their competitors.

In this chapter and in Chapters 5 and 6, you'll read about tools from companies that are members of eBay's Developers Program or Market Data Program, as described in Chapter 3. It's a good idea to skim these chapters to learn about the information you can glean from market-data tools. This will help you decide which tools you want to take for a test drive.

Subsequent chapters describe how to apply the information to your listing and marketing strategies. Return to Chapters 4 through 6 when it's time to test the tools; these chapters walk you through features and help you get acquainted with exactly how the tools work.

What You Should Know About the Data eBay Releases

eBay limits the amount and type of data it makes available through its Market Data Program. Personal information, such as user IDs, feedback, and reserve price information, are not included. Chapter 3 covers other restrictions.

eBay delivers information to vendors with at least a three-day delay, or *lag time*. eBay does not include active listings in the market data, and it sets limits on the date ranges provided through the Market Data Program.

Vendors can change the amount of data they include in their tools. When reviewing results of data-analysis tools, always make sure you understand from which time period the data is coming to take into account such factors as seasonal variations in sales results. As of this writing, Andale and DeepAnalysis each offer the most recent four weeks of eBay market data. Terapeak offers the most recent three months of data, and it provides two years' worth of data through its Browse Category feature.

Evaluating eBay Market-Data Tools

Each of the three vendors that licenses eBay market data has taken a different approach to working with that data. Each tool accesses unique data when making reports, and each offers unique command, menus, and reports.

Table 4-1 summarizes the features of each market-data tool to help you make the best decision about which ones to use. Remember that vendors are constantly making changes and improvements to their tools (and eBay makes lots of changes, too). If some features are particularly important to you, it's a good idea to check out the current product information to determine whether the services have made changes.

How the Tools Work: Hosted vs. Desktop Systems

Andale and Terapeak are *hosted* systems, so the number crunching is done on *their* servers. This means you can sign in from any computer, a plus if you are off-site or traveling. DeepAnalysis is a *desktop* system, so you have to wait for the data to come back to *your* machine. As a result, DeepAnalysis has ways you can limit the data to subsets to make the process quicker—but keep in mind that less data can be a disadvantage when calculating averages. Using DeepAnalysis also requires more disk space on your computer.

Feature	Andale	Terapeak	DeepAnalysis
Hosted or desktop	hosted	hosted	desktop software
eBay categories (excluding eBay Motors and Real Estate)	all	all	all
Currency (how often it's updated)	weekly	daily	daily
Lag time	7 days	3–4 days	3–4 days
Coverage (how much historical data is available)	4 weeks	3–4 months, plus 2 years of category research	1 year (as of 2006)
Ability to export reports	no (print reports only)	yes	yes
Special features	n/a	Refine search by item specifics, category, UPC, or ISBN; automatic weekly update e-mails; hot lists updated daily	Unique seller codes help track top sellers; ability to filter search results

TABLE 4-1   Key Features of Market-Data Tools

Relevance: Excluding Auctions from Results Lists

DeepAnalysis offers a feature that makes it particularly powerful: it gives you the ability to remove irrelevant listings from your results so you can recalculate sell-through rates (STRs) and average selling price (ASP) information for only those listings that match your needs.

Comprehensive Coverage: Categories Included

Initially, Terapeak included only half of eBay's categories (those that made most of the revenue on eBay). But now all three products include all eBay categories—excluding eBay Motors and Real Estate, categories that eBay does not include in the Market Data Program.

Special Features

Terapeak allows you to refine your category research by item specifics, and DeepAnalysis has plans to offer this feature.

Terapeak does not include a daily analysis section in its Report Tool that would allow you to see a summary of successful ending days, but it does give you an *hourly* analysis so you know what time of day listings ended versus the number of those listings that sold successfully. You can use the Terapeak Trends Tool to help you determine the most successful days of the week for a search, but it's not as easy to read and takes extra steps. (See Chapter 5 for details.)

DeepAnalysis identifies each seller with a unique number that makes it possible to track a seller over time; though you won't be able to identify the seller by eBay User ID, this can still provide useful competitive information, which I'll cover more in Chapter 6.

Currency and Lag Time

eBay imposes a three-day lag on data. This means companies don't get today's listing data for another three days. Beyond that, Terapeak and DeepAnalysis update data daily, giving them a three- to four-day lag time. Andale has a one-week lag time.

Dates of Coverage

Terapeak has archived data going back two years for category research, and closed listings go back three to four months, depending on the category. Andale and DeepAnalysis offer four weeks' worth of recent data. DeepAnalysis makes one year's worth of data available (as of 2006).

Saving and Exporting Reports

Terapeak and DeepAnalysis allow you to save and export reports so you can use them in spreadsheets such as Excel. Andale lets you save the search, but not the data. Andale does have a print-friendly format so you can print reports.

Andale Research Tools

Andale (www.andale.com) is an auction-management service provider founded in April 1999. It offers a wide range of auction-management tools, including eBay listing tools, on an a la carte subscription basis, meaning you pay monthly fees only for the tools you want. Andale Counters (developed by a company called Honesty) were for many years the only tool eBay sellers could use to measure traffic to their listings. Andale now offers a suite of data-analysis tools under the umbrella of Research Tools, as shown in Figure 4-1.

Research Tools include Andale Research, What's Hot, Sales Analyzer, Suppliers, and Counters. Users subscribe to any of the Research Tools they want on a monthly subscription basis. You can subscribe to all of them under the Research Pack plan.

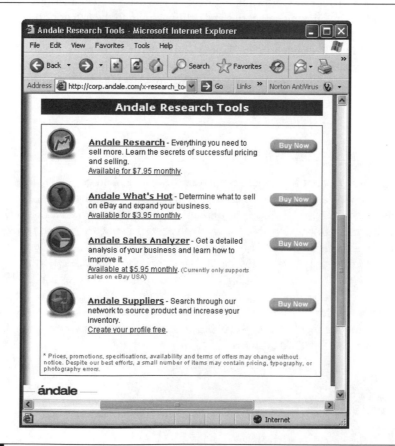

FIGURE 4-1   Andale offers Research Tools available on a monthly subscription basis.

TIP   *I recommend using the more full-featured but more expensive Terapeak or DeepAnalysis, since the information you gain should pay for itself in increased profits for all but the lowest volume sellers. The investment in time and money in learning these tools and using them regularly will certainly pay off for you in increased sales.*

Some of the Andale Research Tools mine eBay Data (What's Hot and Andale Research). Andale's Counters and Sales Analyzer measure your own eBay sales. Andale's Suppliers is a searchable directory of suppliers of merchandise to help eBay sellers find sources of inventory.

What's Hot

You can browse and search for hot sellers on eBay using Andale's What's Hot tool. Log in to the Andale site (www.andale.com) and go to the Research Tools area, then click What's Hot. When you click the Find Out What's Hot button, you'll see a list of eBay's main categories with a count of hot items in each category, as shown in Figure 4-2. The list is updated weekly. You can browse categories on the left by clicking categories and drilling down to the category that interests you.

You can also conduct a search for a particular item. Enter a search term in the Find Out How Well Your Items Will Sell search box. In Figure 4-3, results are shown for the search terms *south beach diet*. You can glance down the columns to see the following information for each item listed: Quantity Listed, Quantity Sold, Percent Of Sold Items, Average Sale Price, and Price Range.

Meet a Vendor: Andale

Janet George and Prashant Nedungadi are part of the team at Andale responsible for Andale Research Tools (www.andale.com). Janet, vice-president of product management, and Prashant, chief technology officer, said because eBay is a price-competitive market, it's critical for sellers to have and manage information about how effective their listings are on eBay, including the effectiveness of advertising on sell-through rates and margins.

Janet and Prashant say data analysis is all about the seller's business performance and their customers. "It is the single most important thing to measure success and to be able to grow the business. It does not matter if the seller is doing business on eBay for the first time or is a PowerSeller. The ability to measure sellers' success and know the dynamics of the changing, growing marketplace, where business is conducted, gives sellers a definite competitive edge to grow their business."

Andale, Inc.
300 Ferguson Drive
Mountain View, CA 94043
Telephone: 650.230.3000
Customer Support: 877-4ANDALE

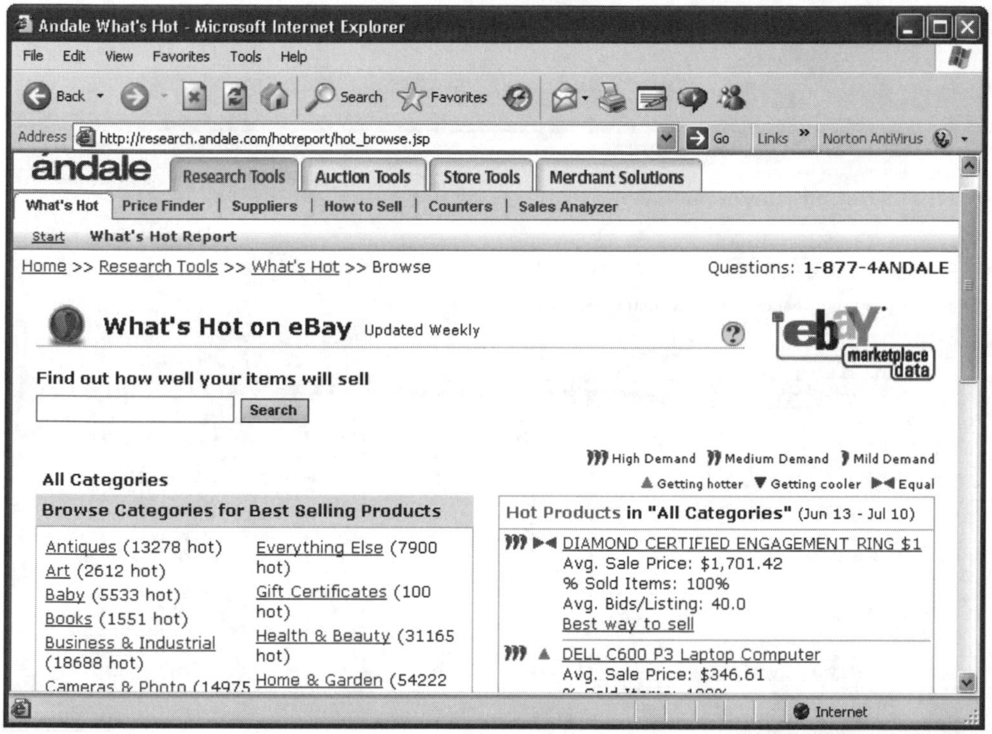

FIGURE 4-2   Andale's What's Hot On eBay list lets you find out what's hot in a particular eBay category.

> **NOTE**   *Remember that different sellers may use different keywords in their titles. Spend some time thinking about the words sellers might have used in their titles, and conduct multiple searches. And as a seller, you need to think about what terms buyers will enter to find your items. In Chapter 8, I reveal how to use market-data tools to uncover the most effective keywords.*

Andale uses a chili pepper ranking system to indicate how hot a category or item is: three chili peppers indicate high demand, two chili peppers indicate medium demand, and one chili pepper indicates mild demand. You can run an unlimited number of What's Hot reports for a flat monthly fee.

> **$ALES STRATEGY**   *Andale's What's Hot report can give you ideas on what to sell. See Chapter 9 for more information on Advanced Listing Strategy #1: Research what to sell.*

Once you find something that interests you using Andale's What's Hot tool, you can use the Andale Research tool for more information.

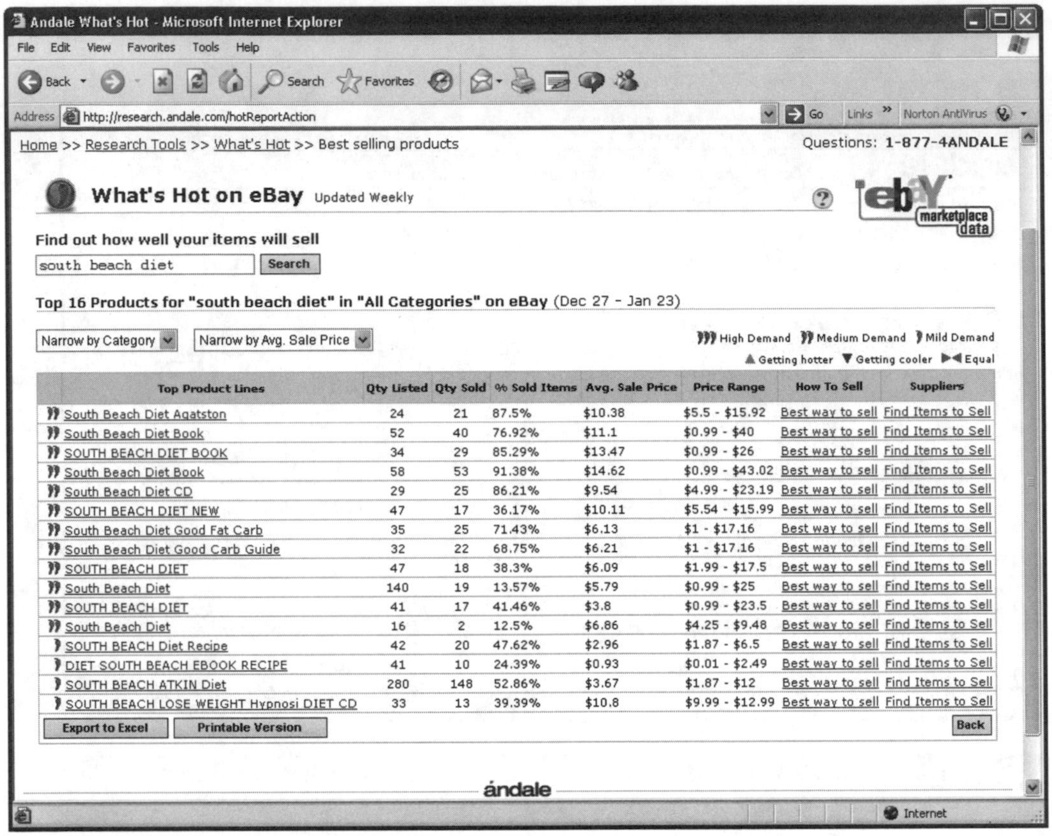

FIGURE 4-3   Andale's What's Hot report shows top products for your search term and uses a chili pepper rating system to indicate the degree of hotness.

Andale Research

Andale Research analyzes more than 80 million closed eBay listings to determine the average sale prices (ASPs), volume (number of items), and STRs of products sold on eBay.

Log in to the Andale site and go to the Research Tools area; then click Andale Research, which has two main features: Price Summary and How To Sell. Enter your search term in the Research Item search box and click the Research button. The search results page appears.

TIP   *If you click the Advanced link to the right of the Research Item box, you are taken to a form where you can narrow your search further by selecting a category, choosing words to exclude, or specifying a price range.*

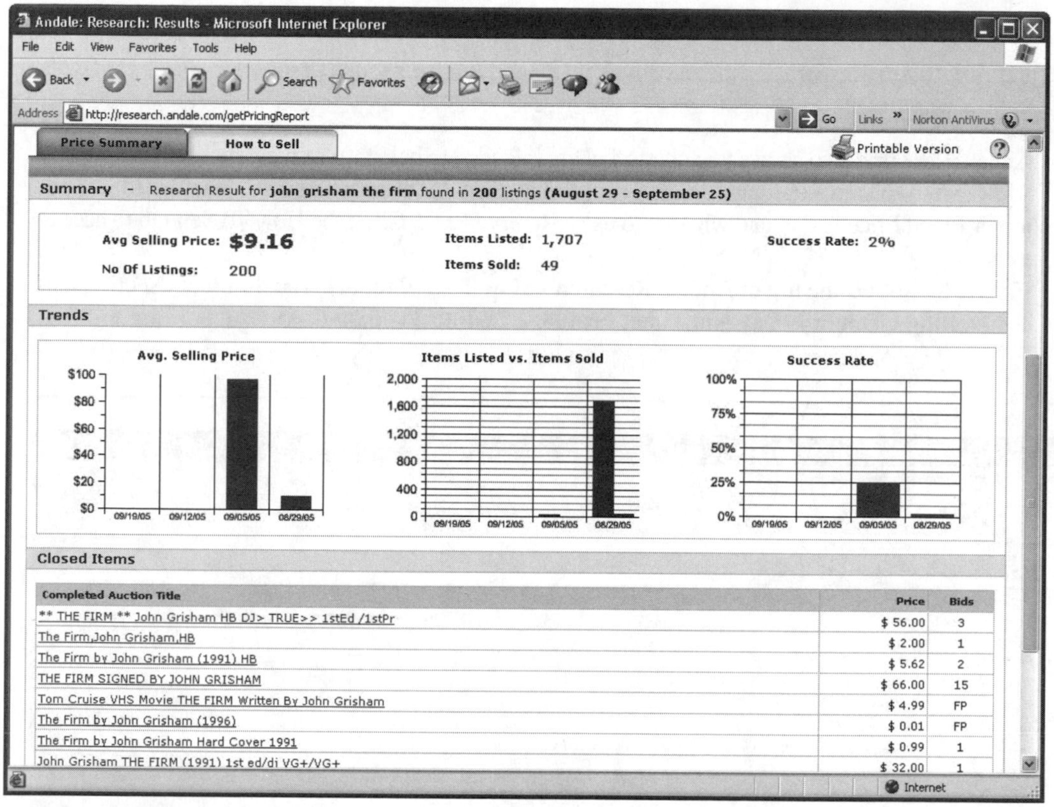

FIGURE 4-4   Andale Research shows you ASP for a search for *John Grisham The Firm*, along with the number of listings and the STR.

Under the Refine Search Results section is the Price Summary information, shown in Figure 4-4, which includes a Summary section listing the ASP, quantity listed, quantity sold, and the STR (% Successful).

Under the Summary section is the Trends section containing three graphs: ASP; Items Listed vs. Items Sold; and Success Rate. In the Trends section, you'll find the Closed Items section, which includes ten listings and a link to view all closed listings. Reviewing these listings will help you determine whether you need to refine your search.

Here is an example of why you might need to look at the raw data behind the analysis. (The lesson in this example applies to all market-data tools.) In Figure 4-4, Andale Research determined that the ASP for a search *John Grisham The Firm* was $9.16. But a look at the listings used to compute the ASP shows the results include different kinds of items—including hard cover, first editions, first editions/first printing, audio books, and VHS movies. You can refine the search by limiting it to a particular category, which will help you get a more accurate average for the particular item in which you are interested.

NOTE   *In Andale Research, you can change your search results to maximize price instead of STR, if you prefer.*

Andale Research also shows you charts that are intended to help you refine your listing strategies, including when to start your auction, which optional eBay features to use, and whether to run an auction or Fixed Price listing and whether to use a Reserve Price. Click the How To Sell tab to access these charts.

Figure 4-5 shows the top of Andale Research's How To Sell report. The Summary section lists the best-selling Category; Day and Time; Features; Listing Type; and Price, according to STR.

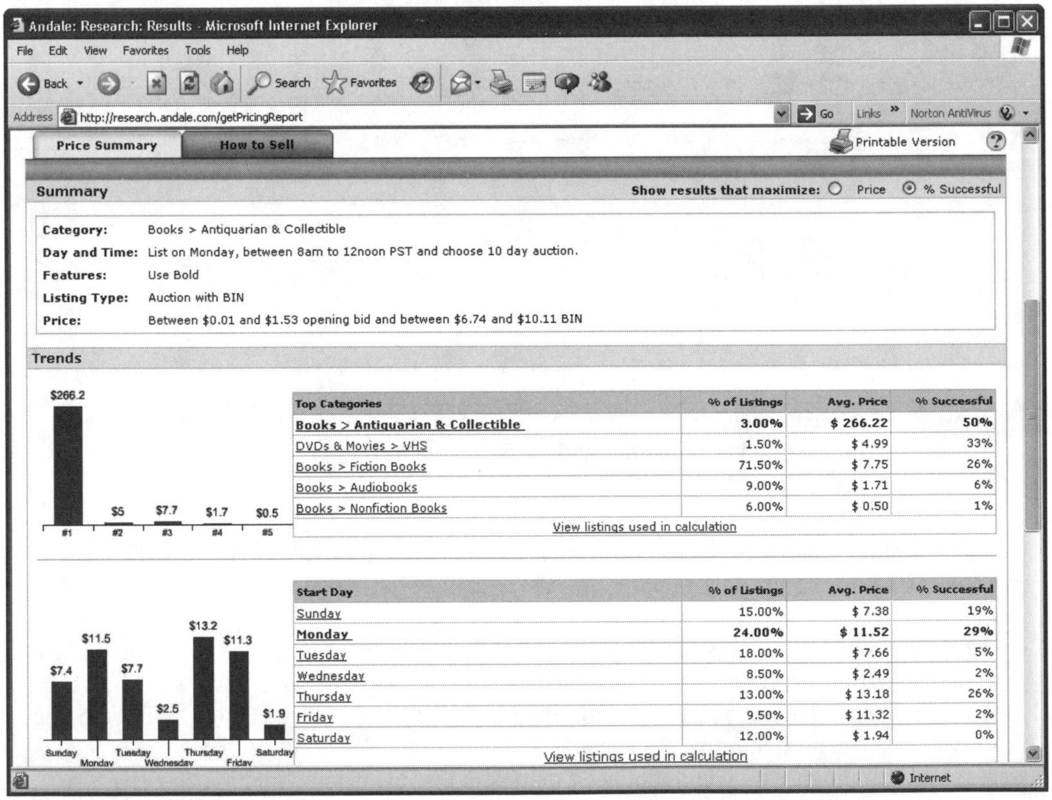

| FIGURE 4-5 | The Top Categories chart shows the Antiquarian & Collectible Books category achieved the highest STR (and ASP) for the search term *John Grisham The Firm*. The Start Day chart shows Monday was a good starting day for these listings. |

You can change this criterion to ASP by selecting the Price radio button next to Show Results That Maximize: on the top right-side of the page.

The Trends section includes four charts: Top Categories, Start Day, eBay Marketing Features, and Listing Type (see Figure 4-5 and Figure 4-6). Andale applies bold type to the best listing strategy as determined by its analysis.

The Andale Research tool can help you develop many of your listing strategies. Review the charts that contain data on when to start your auction, whether to use optional features, and which optional features to use.

Andale Smart Analysis

Andale uses the "Smart Andale analysis method," which is based on its "smart research intelligence engine" that tries to remove irrelevant eBay items when calculating averages and How To Sell recommendations on researched items. For example, Andale says that if you are searching for *Sony digital camera*, its smart research intelligence engine will try to weed out accessories such as stands and cases from the result. The problem with this, however, is that it takes away your ability to control the analysis. Using this feature *assumes* the engine really is smart. However, you are better off clicking the All Items Data Search located to the right of the Research Item button, so the tool uses

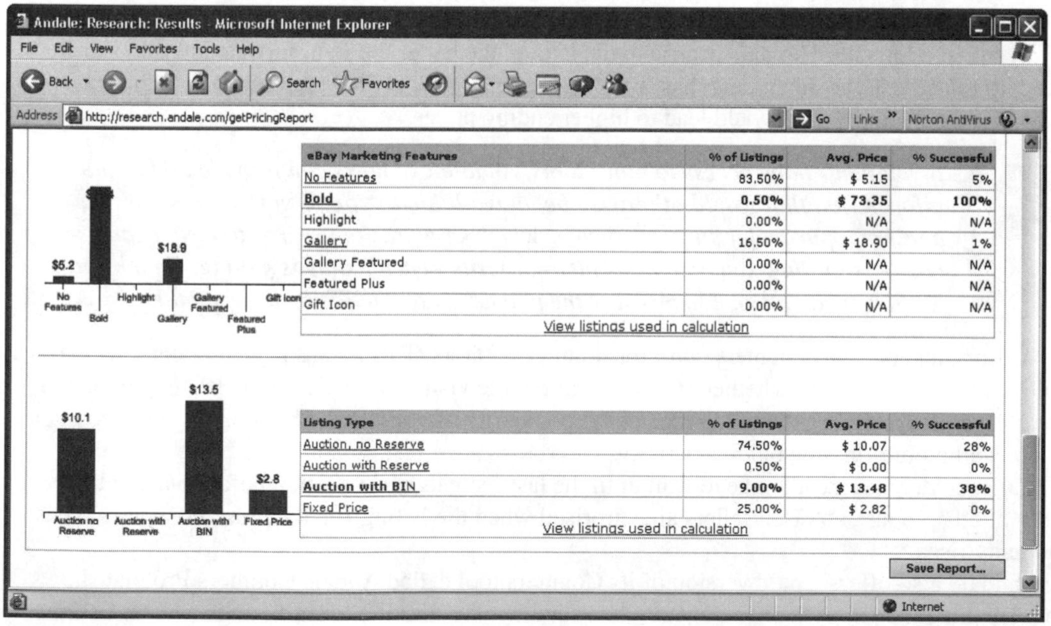

eBay Marketing Features	% of Listings	Avg. Price	% Successful
No Features	83.50%	$ 5.15	5%
Bold	**0.50%**	**$ 73.35**	**100%**
Highlight	0.00%	N/A	N/A
Gallery	16.50%	$ 18.90	1%
Gallery Featured	0.00%	N/A	N/A
Featured Plus	0.00%	N/A	N/A
Gift Icon	0.00%	N/A	N/A
View listings used in calculation			

Listing Type	% of Listings	Avg. Price	% Successful
Auction, no Reserve	74.50%	$ 10.07	28%
Auction with Reserve	0.50%	$ 0.00	0%
Auction with BIN	**9.00%**	**$ 13.48**	**38%**
Fixed Price	25.00%	$ 2.82	0%
View listings used in calculation			

FIGURE 4-6   Other charts in the How To Sell report show usage and results for listings with optional eBay features, including the use of Reserve Price and Buy It Now.

all eBay items returned in the search results when calculating recommendations. Try to select the best keywords and category to match your needs so you won't get irrelevant listings in your results.

When using Andale Research, I recommend the following:

- When you do a keyword search, limit results to the category that best matches your needs.

- Review the listings that make up the results to make sure they are relevant to your search and contain enough listings over a long enough period of time to make valid recommendations.

- Always click All Items Data Search instead of relying on the Smart Andale analysis method, which is the default setting.

- Consider the fees and other factors that may impact your profitability.

- Review Chapter 2 thoroughly to learn about potential pitfalls of data analysis and always keep them in mind.

Counters

Most eBay users are familiar with Andale Counters since eBay offers them free to all sellers. You can use Counters to track the number of times your listings have been viewed by visitors, an indicator of interest in your items. You can display the counter so visitors know how many others have visited the listing (good if you expect lots of traffic to your listing), or you can keep the counts hidden so only you know this number (good if you expect low traffic to your listing). Potential bidders looking at the counter are likely to make assumptions about the quality of the item you have for sale. The more traffic to the listing, the better the item for sale, the shopper is likely to think. (On the other hand, bargain shoppers may look for low-trafficked listings so there is less bidding activity that would lead to higher ending prices.)

$ALES STRATEGY *If you don't have access to other tools, Andale Counters can provide additional information that would otherwise be unavailable to you. If you are conducting a test of a particular strategy, such as which keywords to use in a title, you can use counters to show you how many hits—or visits—each listing is getting. On a basic level, you can attempt to measure the popularity of one listing over another.*

Unfortunately, basic counters don't track unique visitors. This means if your counter displays 100 hits, you don't know whether 100 different people visited your listing or 10 people visited 10 times each. You can get a rough idea of the popularity of your listing by looking at the counter results and monitoring the bidding activity.

Of course, many people like to wait until the last seconds of an auction before placing their bid (called sniping), so often sellers are surprised when the listing finally ends and the price has suddenly risen.

Andale also offers a paid version of its Counters tool called Andale Counters Pro that shows counter hits for listings broken down by hour and by day for all current listings and for listings that closed within the past ten days. You can see at a glance which days were most popular for an item.

$ALES STRATEGY *Andale Counters Pro lets you see traffic by hour and by day, which can help you with Basic Listing Strategy #1: Find the best time to end an auction, explained in Chapter 8.*

Sellers can also compare the hits on up to three of their items or run current price, hits, and bids comparisons on other items in their categories, as shown in Figure 4-7. Andale Counters Pro data can be exported or printed.

Sales Analyzer and Sales Analyzer Pro

Andale Sales Analyzer Pro is designed to provide information about your own sales history. You enter your eBay user ID and that of other marketplaces, and it will come back with data summarizing your past sales across eBay, Amazon, Yahoo!, and other marketplaces, as shown in Figure 4-8. Sales Analyzer Pro also shows you the number of sales by type (auction versus Buy It Now versus Fixed Price) as well as the number of sales by new customers and by repeat customers.

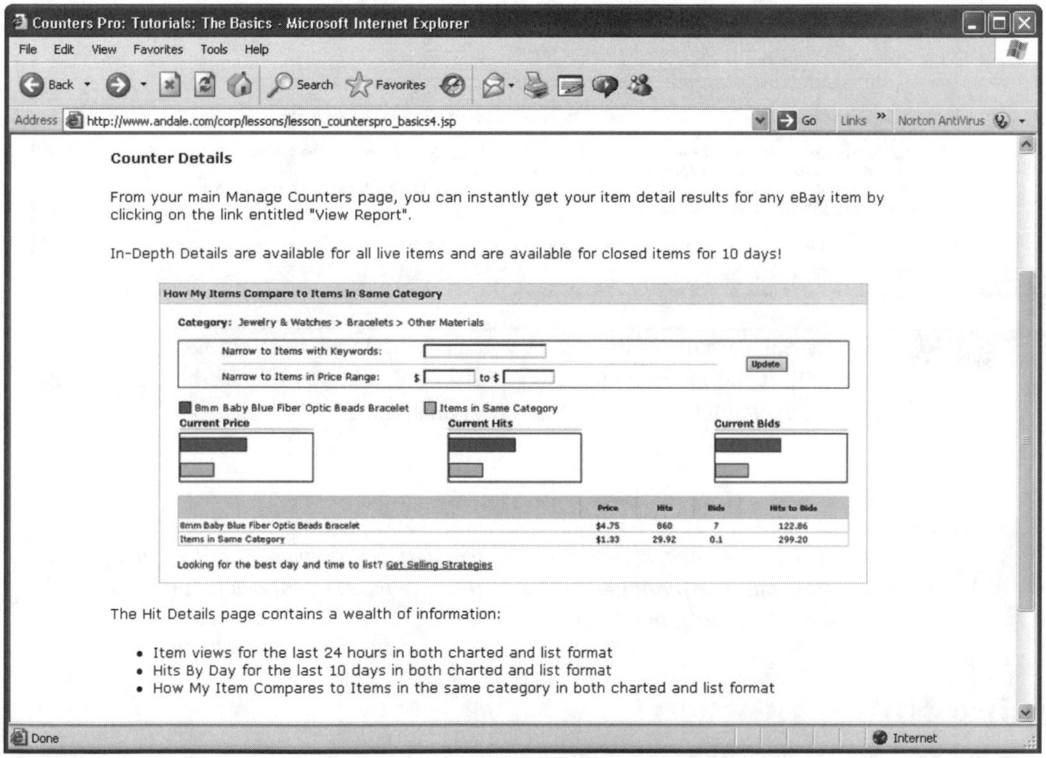

FIGURE 4-7   Andale Counters Pro allows you to see the number of hits and bids for your item so you can compare it with other items in the same category.

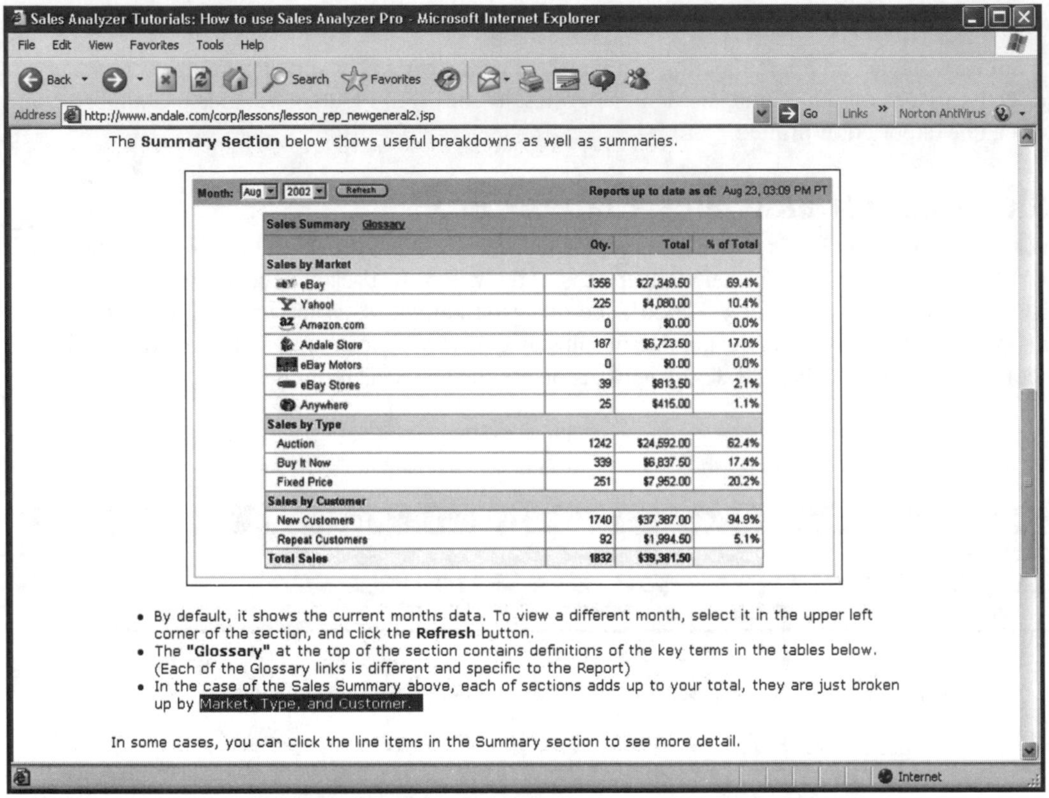
Sales Analyzer Tutorials: How to use Sales Analyzer Pro - Microsoft Internet Explorer
File Edit View Favorites Tools Help
Back Search Favorites
Address http://www.andale.com/corp/lessons/lesson_rep_newgeneral2.jsp
Go Links Norton AntiVirus
The Summary Section below shows useful breakdowns as well as summaries.
Month: Aug 2002 Refresh
Reports up to date as of: Aug 23, 03:09 PM PT
Sales Summary Glossary
Qty. Total % of Total
Sales by Market
eBay 1356 $27,349.50 69.4%
Yahoo! 225 $4,080.00 10.4%
Amazon.com 0 $0.00 0.0%
Andale Store 187 $6,723.50 17.0%
eBay Motors 0 $0.00 0.0%
eBay Stores 39 $813.50 2.1%
Anywhere 25 $415.00 1.1%
Sales by Type
Auction 1242 $24,592.00 62.4%
Buy It Now 339 $6,837.50 17.4%
Fixed Price 251 $7,952.00 20.2%
Sales by Customer
New Customers 1740 $37,387.00 94.9%
Repeat Customers 92 $1,994.50 5.1%
Total Sales 1832 $39,381.50
• By default, it shows the current months data. To view a different month, select it in the upper left corner of the section, and click the Refresh button.
• The "Glossary" at the top of the section contains definitions of the key terms in the tables below. (Each of the Glossary links is different and specific to the Report)
• In the case of the Sales Summary above, each of sections adds up to your total, they are just broken up by Market, Type, and Customer.
In some cases, you can click the line items in the Summary section to see more detail.
Internet

FIGURE 4-8 Andale Sales Analyzer Pro shows you unit and dollar sales across all the places you sell, including eBay, Amazon and Yahoo!, and you can see how many new customers you have compared to repeat customers.

$ALES STRATEGY *Use Andale Sales Analyzer to compare your sales across channels (Marketing Strategy #5: Expand your presence, reviewed in Chapter 10). But if you are selling on multiple marketplaces, auction-management services have more advanced features with full integration into your accounting programs.*

Wrapping Up

The beginning of this chapter talked about the kinds of information market-data tools provide eBay sellers. Although all market-data tools provide basic metrics like ASP and STR for eBay listings, each vendor takes a different approach to working with the data. It's important to understand the features provided by each tool so you can make an informed decision about which tool is right for you.

Andale is a basic tool, and it is priced accordingly. It's best used to get a general sense of an item's ASP and STR if you are on a low budget. But if you want to dig deep into the world of eBay market data, keep reading. Terapeak, covered in Chapter 5, and DeepAnalysis, covered in Chapter 6, allow you more flexibility in item and category research. Understanding trends at a category level can help you be a smarter and more competitive seller on eBay.

4

Chapter 5

Taking the Guesswork out of eBay Selling with Terapeak

Using Terapeak, you can find out the average selling price (ASP) and sell-through rate (STR) for any item or category on eBay. Terapeak, like other eBay market-data tools, can help make you an expert in the eBay marketplace, with many kinds of reports at your fingertips.

Chapter 4 provided an overview of the three market-data tools covered in this book: Andale Research, Terapeak, and DeepAnalysis and reviewed the key features of Andale Research Tools. This chapter reviews the features of Terapeak and explains how to use the service.

You can use the overview in Chapter 4 and the contents of this chapter to help you figure out whether you want to use Terapeak. You can also use this chapter to help you navigate Terapeak if you decide to subscribe to the service—keep this chapter open as you explore Terapeak reports and features.

Terapeak (www.terapeak.com) is a service from Advanced Economics Research Systems (AERS) Inc. Founders (and brothers) Anthony and Andrew Sukow say they got the idea for Terapeak when they wanted to know more about how their own eBay software listings were affected by variations in the way they ran their auctions.

Terapeak licenses data from eBay; all data is based on successful listings unless otherwise specified. As of this writing, Terapeak provides only eBay market data, but it may offer tools for sellers to analyze their own eBay sales performance in the future.

Terapeak also offers custom reports and consulting services to organizations wishing to use eBay market data to assess current market value and after-market demand for goods and to identify lifecycle stages and trends in consumer behavior.

Meet a Vendor: AERS (Terapeak)

Terapeak cofounders Andrew and Anthony Sukow work with eBay statistics every day, so it's a good thing they like numbers. As AERS chief technical officer and chief executive officer, respectively, they help clients figure out how to make sense of eBay data.

Andrew and Anthony say most of their customers use Terapeak to research items they are thinking of selling and to research hot categories, but they say some people are doing some innovative things with the product as well.

"eBay affiliates are buying reports on keywords to find word combinations that other people have not thought of in various categories," Andrew said. "We have stock analysts who are experimenting with sales reports on certain companies' products in order to predict quarterly earnings. Some big sellers are sending us lists of their items to analyze so they can figure out what ones need price adjustments and how to maximize revenue on every transaction."

The most important metrics, according to the Sukow brothers, are ASP ("knowing what it's worth will tell you where to start your price") and STR.

Why is researching eBay important? Says Andrew, "I have seen sellers improve their listing effectiveness by as much as 60 percent. This is what happens when you start to sell smarter. Researching is just like studying for an exam. If you don't study, you'll probably flunk it."

Anthony adds, "Those who choose to not research are flying blind. They have no idea of the impending boom or doom. They can only say, after the fact, 'I wish I would have known.'"

AERS Inc.
PO Box 3075 STN CSC
Building R McKenzie Avenue
Victoria, B.C. V8W 3W2 Canada
Telephone: 250-472-4371
Customer Support: support@terapeak.com

Understanding Terapeak Navigation

At the top of every Terapeak page is a navigation bar with the following choices: Home, Browse Categories, Search Listings, Hot List, and Help, as you can see in Figure 5-1. You can select the category you want to research by clicking Browse Categories, and you can search listings by clicking Search Listings. Terapeak also provides a list of popular categories that you can access by clicking Hot List.

Terapeak Main Tools

Terapeak has five main tools:

- **Report**   Provides at-a-glance views of key metrics
- **Listings**   Shows details about closed listings

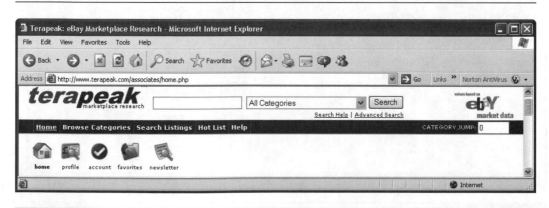

FIGURE 5-1   Terapeak's navigation bar allows you to switch to a different function by clicking a button.

- **Sellers** Lists top sellers and is sortable by criteria
- **Trends** Provides an overview of a category and how it has changed over time
- **Features** Indicates how many listings used optional eBay features and the accompanying success rates

You can access these tools by clicking Browse Categories or by clicking Search Listings. You'll see the icons for these tools directly under the navigation bar at the upper-left side of the page, as shown in Figure 5-2. In the Search Listings section, you'll see all the same icons except for the Features tool.

eBay restricts licensees from revealing counts by category, but it lets vendors report numbers when searching by keywords. This means if you are using the Browse Categories page to look at Terapeak data, you'll see relative numbers and ratios (such as 40 percent of listings), not absolute

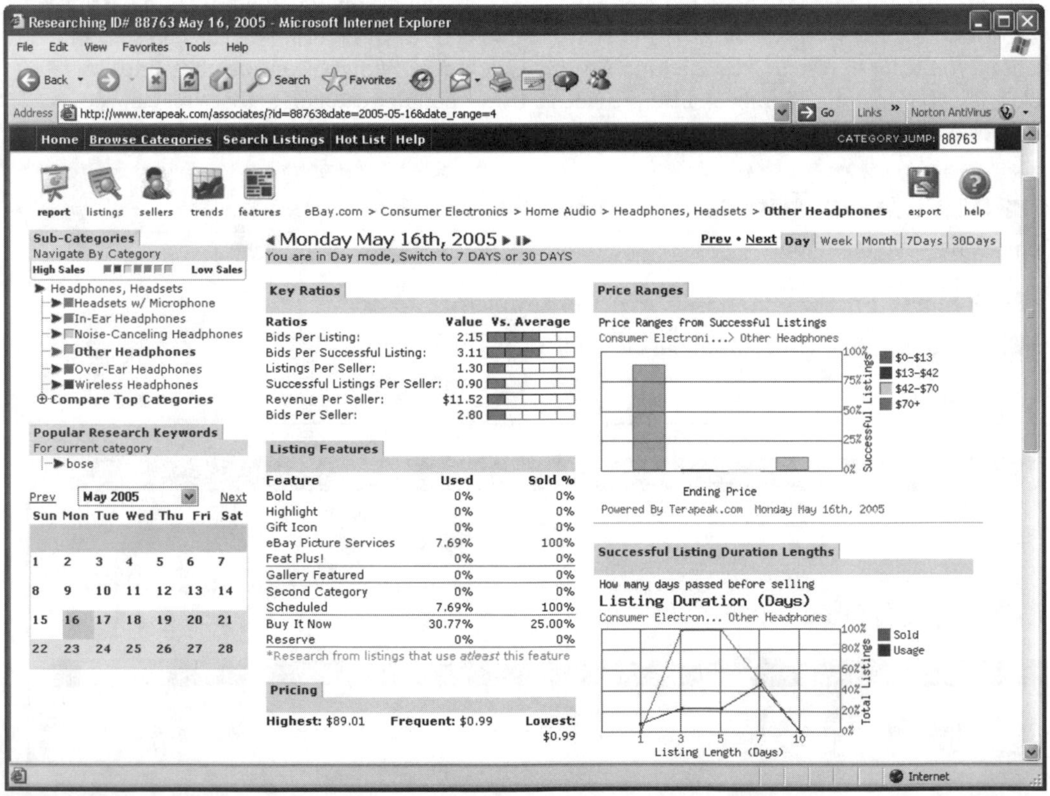

FIGURE 5-2   When browsing a category in Terapeak, you can navigate to closed listings, top sellers, category trends, and selling features, or go to the main Report page shown here.

numbers (such as 2200 listings). But if you are using the Search Listings view to look at Terapeak's data, you will see both relative numbers and absolute numbers, so you know exactly how many listings make up the results.

Let's say, for example, that 1000 music CD listings were active in a given time period, of which 50 percent closed successfully with a sale. The Browse Categories report would show you percentage values—50 percent of listings in this category ended successfully—but it would not reveal that 1000 listings were considered. eBay intentionally restricts this information so people cannot gauge the size of each of its categories, which is precious competitive information. It also doesn't want people adding up the revenue of all its categories, revealing eBay.com's gross revenue.

However, Terapeak's Search Listings reports do offer exact details in addition to percentage values. In our example, they would reveal that of 1000 listings, 500 (or 50 percent) ended successfully. It can be helpful to supplement your Browse Categories reports with Search Listings reports to try and get as much useful information as possible.

Whenever you are searching by keywords instead of browsing listings by category, you should make sure that you look at the listings that make up the search results (by clicking the Listings tool icon) to help determine whether you should narrow or broaden your search. In other words, for example, if you are searching for plates using the search term *Sheffield plates*, you can click the Listings tool icon to see if irrelevant items are included in the results, such as books about Sheffield plates. If you can formulate an accurate search strategy, you can get some very detailed information about the product for which you are researching.

Category "Trails"

When you are drilling down in categories, you'll see links across the top of the page, under the navigation bar, that display a trail of data that lets you know how far down you've drilled into a category, as shown in Figure 5-3. You can broaden the category view by clicking up one or more levels. (Software programmers call these navigation aids *breadcrumb trails*.)

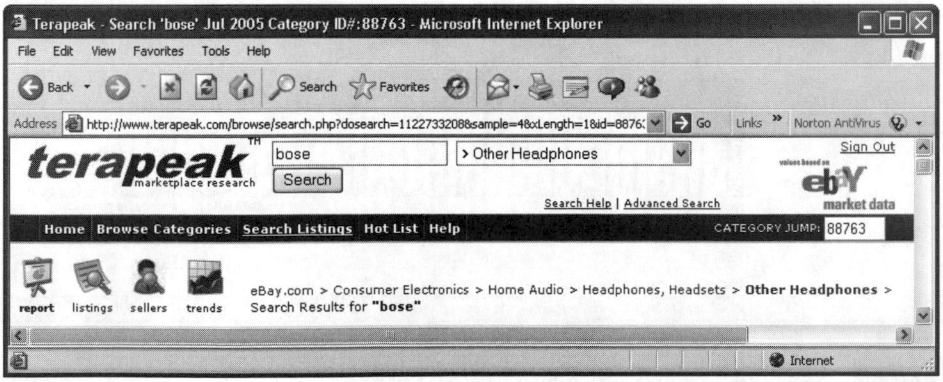

FIGURE 5-3   This category trail shows you have drilled down into the Consumer Electronics category all the way down to Other Headphones subcategory.

Viewing and Comparing Subcategories

You can also navigate categories in another way: on the left side of the results pages for a Bose headphones search, for example, you will see a list of Sub-Categories displaying all the subcategories under Headphones, Headsets (see Figure 5-4). This is a handy feature because it lets you see all subcategories at a glance, making it easier to navigate among categories in which you may be selling. In addition, many sellers like to compare similar categories to help them identify opportunities. They might spot a faster growing category with higher ASPs in an area in which they already have some expertise, for instance. Terapeak also provides a way for you to compare categories graphically, as shown in Figure 5-4.

Jumping Categories

To the right of the top menu bar, as shown in Figure 5-3, a CATEGORY JUMP field displays the category number for the results you are viewing, updating automatically as you change categories.

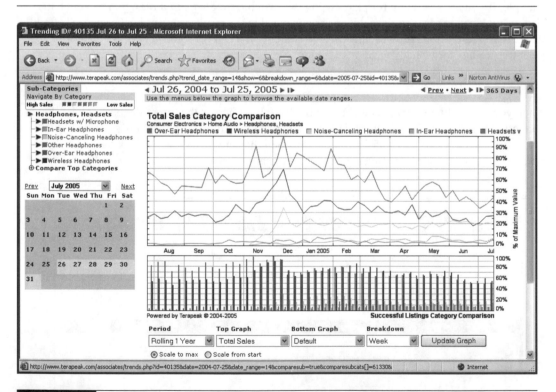

FIGURE 5-4   Clicking Compare Top Categories on the Sub-Category list shows you a graph that plots those categories on a chart, making it easier to compare them.

Knowing the category number can help when you sell your item on eBay. Or, if you want to change categories in a hurry and know the category number, you can enter it into the field.

Viewing by Date or Range

You can view data by day, week, or month using the date navigation tools directly under the category trail (see Figure 5-2). Directly to the left of the date navigation tools, you can see which mode you are in (Day, Week, or Month) and the specific date or date range. A Calendar feature appears on the left side of most pages, also shown in Figure 5-2.

It's important to note the difference between looking at a report after selecting Week versus selecting 7 Days. Selecting Week shows you data from the calendar week, Sunday through Saturday. So, for example, if the current date is Tuesday, September 27, 2005, and you select Week, you'll see only data from Sunday, September 25 to Tuesday September 27. Basically, selecting Week shows data from the current calendar week, starting on Sunday, up to the current day. If you select 7 Days, however, you will see data for the most recent *seven days* for which Terapeak has data (a rolling seven-day view). So, for example, if the current date is Tuesday, September 27, 2005, and you select 7 Days, you'll see data from Tuesday, September 20, through today's date—a full seven days' worth of data. The same methodology applies to choosing Month versus 30 Days.

Date and date range are important to understand, because if you are looking at data using the Week view, for example, you may *think* you are looking at a full week's worth of data, but that might not be the case. And remember that when you assess the performance of eBay listings from one period to another, it's always important to have comparable data so you are comparing apples to apples.

Hot List

You can use Terapeak to see eBay's top-growing categories by clicking the Hot List button on the navigation bar to see which categories are categorized as Super Hot, Very Hot, and Hot. The categories must meet minimum levels of performance and show growth in the number of bids they receive from month to month. According to Terapeak's criteria,

- Every Hot category must have more than $25,000 in revenue for the past 30 days.
- Each Hot category must have at least 700 bids in the past 30 days.

A category's degree of "hotness" is found by adding up the bids for the past 30 days and comparing to the prior 30-day period and computing the bidding growth rate. Then Terapeak does the same for total listings to compute the listing growth rate:

- If the bid growth exceeds the listing growth by 35 percent, the category is Super Hot.
- If bid growth exceeds listing growth by between 15 to 35 percent, the category is Very Hot.
- If bid growth exceeds listing growth by less than 15 percent, the category is Hot.

Terapeak factors in the bidding growth because this indicates that demand for the category is growing. If bidding were stable, that would be fine for existing sellers if the number of listings remained the same (and no new sellers entered the category, for example). But categories for which demand is growing can support additional listings, making it more attractive for sellers assessing whether to begin selling in that category.

To access the Category Hot List feature, sign in to the Terapeak site at www.terapeak.com and click Hot List on the navigation bar. You will see a list of categories that match Terapeak's hot criteria (see Figure 5-5). The list is displayed in columns: Sales Rank (measure of total dollar sales), Category Name, Status, and Success (out of all listings, how many ended in a sale).

Clicking any of the column names will sort the results by that criterion. For example, when results are displayed in order of Success rate, you can click the Status header and results will be organized by the hotness level, with Super Hot listings at the top, then Very Hot, and finally Hot. The Sales Rank metric helps you, since some Super Hot categories may have a low average selling price.

$ALES STRATEGY *Terapeak's Category Hot List can help you get ideas for products to sell; this is covered in more detail in Chapter 9.*

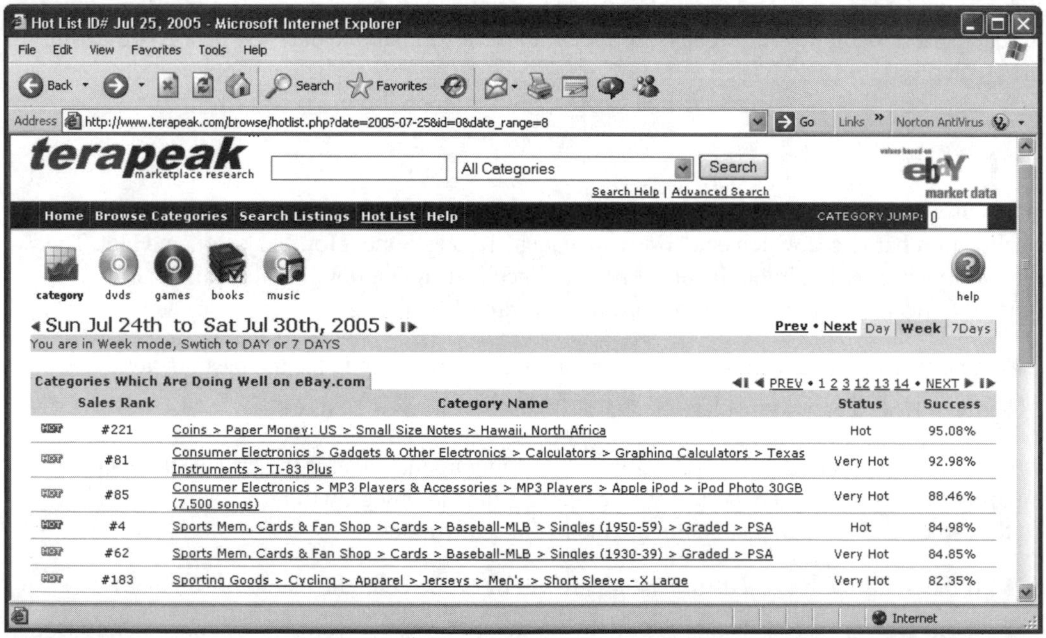

FIGURE 5-5 Terapeak's Hot List displays fast-growing categories on eBay, helping you identify possible areas in which to sell.

Item Specifics Provides More Research Options

To get to the heart of Terapeak data, you can click either Browse Categories or Search Listings on the main navigation bar. But before we get into the details of what kinds of reports and data are available, you should understand a few things about Item Specifics.

Terapeak can fine-tune your search using Item Specifics. I talked about eBay's Item Specifics feature in Chapter 2; this feature allows sellers to describe product attributes in special searchable fields, making it easier for buyers on eBay to find just the items they are looking for.

As discussed in Chapter 2, eBay breaks out market data only for Level 3 and lower categories. Because some categories encompass only to Level 2, such as the Books category, data tools cannot do analysis on those categories. Figure 5-6 shows what happens when you Browse Categories and choose Books > Children's Books: you see the message "Categories At Level 2 Are Not Enabled For Research."

On the left side of the page you'll see an Item Specific Research area (shown in Figure 5-7). You can use the pull-down menu under Category and select Nursery Rhymes, for example, to get data for those items in which the seller selected Nursery Rhymes using Item Specifics, as you can see in Figure 5-7. This lets you get around the category-level limitation by using Item Specifics.

You can also search by condition (new or used) and other Item Specifics in this area (provided the category has such an attribute field, as the books category does). Keep your eye out for Item Specifics fields to help you fine-tune your research.

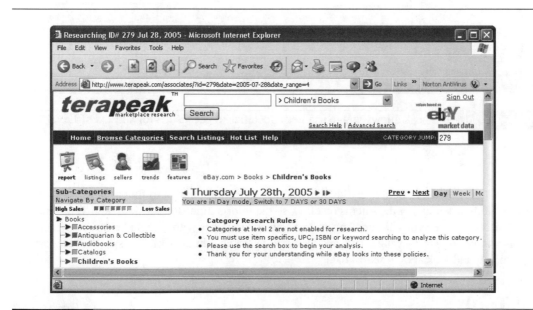

FIGURE 5-6   Level 1 and Level 2 categories cannot be analyzed with market-data tools, as you will see if you browse the Books > Children's Books category.

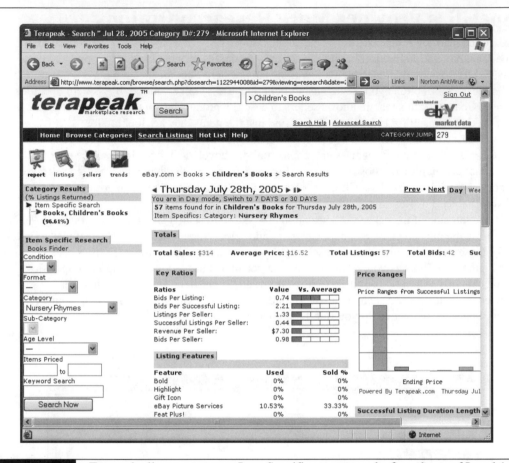

FIGURE 5-7   Terapeak allows you to use Item Specifics to get results for subsets of Level 1 and Level 2 categories—for example, Nursery Rhymes in the Children's Books category.

The only drawback to Item Specifics is that some sellers don't bother to fill out Item Specific attribute fields when listing their items on eBay, so the information is not available in Terapeak data. To deal with this, you can supplement Item Specific searches with straight keyword searches (such as *nursery rhymes*—using a Title and Description search—in the Children's Books category, for example), and look at both sets of data.

Report Tool

Now that we've covered how to navigate the Terapeak service and reviewed the Hot List feature, we can turn our attention to the service's five main tools, which are accessed by clicking Browse Categories or Search Listings. These five main tools are Report, Listings, Sellers, Trends, and

Features. (Note that Terapeak calls the page that appears after you click the Report tool icon, the Research Report. I will refer to it as Report tool for simplicity's sake.)

The Terapeak Report tool gives you at-a-glance views of key metrics, including key ratios, bids per listing, revenue per seller, feature usage statistics, pricing statistics, and listings duration. You can access the Report tool by clicking the Report icon from the Browse Categories or Search Listings page.

Key Ratios

Key ratios tell you the number of bids per listing, bids per successful listing, listings per seller, successful listings per seller, revenue per seller, and bids per seller, as shown in Figure 5-8.

If you are tracking the same category over time, it could be useful to keep an eye on key ratios to see if any sudden significant changes occur that indicate you should take a closer look at the listings and sellers making up a category.

Another tool lets you see how these metrics compare with metrics in the category as a whole. Hold your cursor over the five-box graph next to each metric, and you'll see whether the metric in this subcategory is poor versus the average, average, or very good versus the average in the broader category as a whole. In the example shown in Figure 5-8, Bids Per Listing is Average (as indicated by three shaded boxes), but the Revenue Per Seller is Very Poor vs. the Average (indicated by one shaded box).

If the item or subcategory you are researching is not doing as well as the category as a whole, you may want to dig further to see if you can find a better item to sell in this category.

Listing Features

Listing Features tells you the percentage of listings that used optional features (Bold, Highlight, Gift Icon, eBay Picture Services, Featured Plus, Gallery Featured, Second Category, Scheduled, Buy It Now, Reserve), and of those, what percentage successfully sold, as shown in Figure 5-9.

The Browse Categories view will show you relative numbers (percentages only, not the actual number of auctions), so use this in conjunction with the Features tool (covered later in the chapter), which gives you the actual number of auctions that used the features.

Key Ratios		
Ratios	**Value**	**Vs. Average**
Bids Per Listing:	2.15	
Bids Per Successful Listing:	3.11	
Listings Per Seller:	1.30	
Successful Listings Per Seller:	0.90	
Revenue Per Seller:	$11.52	
Bids Per Seller:	2.80	

FIGURE 5-8   The headphone listings comprising this report get an average 2.15 bids per listing and generate an average of $11.52 in revenue per seller.

Listing Features		
Feature	**Used**	**Sold %**
Bold	0%	0%
Highlight	0%	0%
Gift Icon	0%	0%
eBay Picture Services	7.69%	100%
Feat Plus!	0%	0%
Gallery Featured	0%	0%
Second Category	0%	0%
Scheduled	7.69%	100%
Buy It Now	30.77%	25.00%
Reserve	0%	0%

*Research from listings that use *atleast* this feature

FIGURE 5-9   No headphone listings included in this report used the Bold feature, but of the 7.69 percent that used eBay Picture Services, 100 percent sold.

$ALES STRATEGY   *Use the Listing Features report to help you figure out what features to use in your listings, and whether to use Reserve Price. In Chapter 9, I'll discuss this report regarding Advanced Listing Strategy #4: Evaluate optional features and upgrades, and Advanced Listing Strategy #3: Analyze effectiveness of reserve price.*

Pricing

Pricing tells you the highest selling item, the lowest selling item, and the most frequent price. This very general snapshot can be helpful, but you should always get more details by clicking the Listings tab to see a list of all item listings, where you can sort by ending price.

An example using denim jackets demonstrates why looking at listings can help you interpret the general numbers you encounter in all data-analysis tools. Figure 5-10 shows a Terapeak Report view for a search on *denim jacket* in the Clothing, Shoes & Accessories category, where we have zoomed in on the Pricing snapshot. You can see that the highest selling item went for $6500.01, the lowest item went for a penny, and the most frequent selling price for denim jackets in this category was $9.99. These numbers beg for a closer look.

You can click the Listings tool icon to see the actual auctions on which the report is based. Clicking Listings brings up a page of all 10,409 listings for denim jackets, shown in Figure 5-11.

Clicking the End Price column sorts the data so highest priced items show up at the top of the results, as shown in Figure 5-12. This is an "ah-ha" moment, when you see that the highest priced items are for *vintage* denim jackets, earning hundreds or even thousands of dollars for each jacket. Not all denim jackets are created equal, but if you have your hands on some denim jackets you want to sell on eBay, this report and the listings behind it indicate you might do very well in terms of selling price.

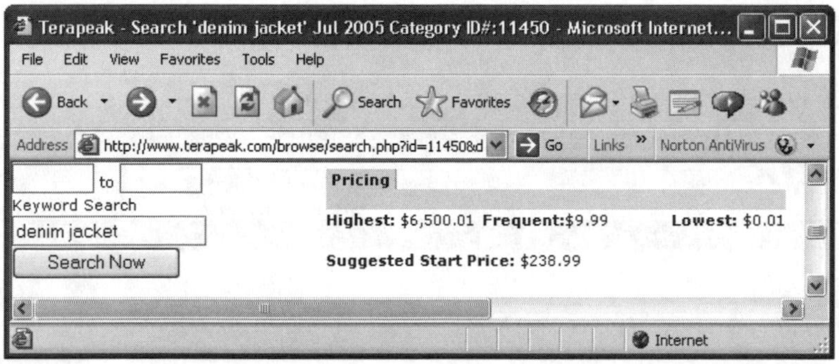

FIGURE 5-10   The pricing data in this report shows denim jackets in the Clothing, Shoes & Accessories category ranged from $9.99 to $6500—an incredibly broad range.

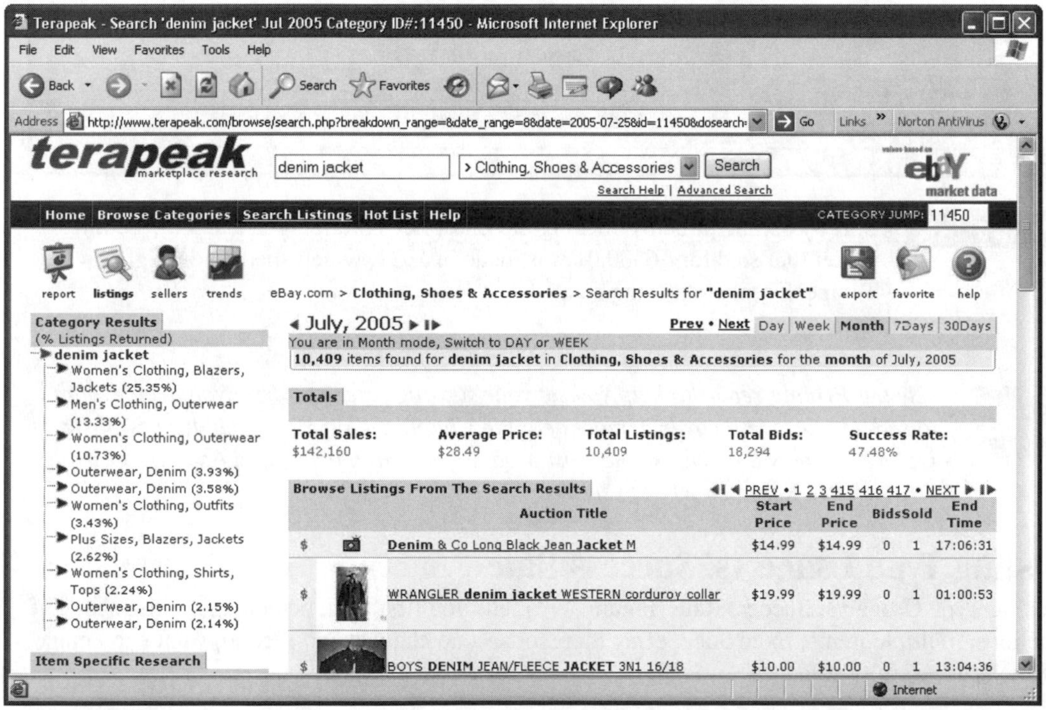

FIGURE 5-11   Click Listings when you are looking at search results, and you'll see a list of the actual eBay listings upon which the report is based—in this case, closed listings for denim jackets.

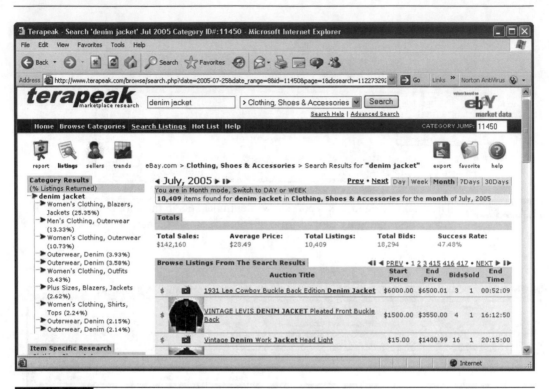

| FIGURE 5-12 | Sort by selling price by clicking the End Price column to see that the denim jacket that sold for $6500.01 was made in 1931, which sheds more light on the Terapeak report's pricing data. |

$ALES STRATEGY   *Use the Pricing report to help you set your starting price and help you decide what to sell—topics we'll cover in more detail in Chapters 8 and 9, which discuss Basic Listing Strategy #3: Choose the most profitable starting price, and Advanced Listing Strategy #1: Research what to sell.*

Listing Type Usage vs. Success Rate

Listing Type Usage vs. Success Rate (Figure 5-13) tells you first what percentage of listings were auctions, multiple items, fixed price, eBay Store, or second chance; and second, what percentage of each successfully sold.

$ALES STRATEGY   *Use the Listing Type Usage vs. Success Rate report to help you figure out whether to use auctions or Fixed Price listings, which I'll cover in Chapter 9, dealing with Advanced Listing Strategy #2: Choose auction-style listings vs. Fixed-Price format. Remember to take into account the role auction listings play in driving traffic to eBay Store inventory.*

Listing Type Usage VS Success Rate					
TYPE	**Bid Auctions:**	**Multiple Item:**	**Fixed Price:**	**eBay Store:**	**Second Chance:**
USAGE	59.09%	0.00%	9.09%	31.82%	0.00%
SOLD	34.62%	0.00%	25.00%	21.43%	0.00%

FIGURE 5-13   This report shows 59.09 percent of listings were in auction format, of which 34.62 percent sold; 9.09 percent were Fixed Price format, of which 25 percent sold; and 31.82 percent were eBay Store listings, of which 21.43 percent sold.

Hourly Analysis (PST)

Hourly Analysis tells you the total number of listings ending versus the listings that sold successfully, plotted for each hour of the day, as shown in Figure 5-14. This information tells you when the busiest hour of the day is and the hour of the day with the greatest percentage of items successfully sold. (Terapeak recommends looking at hourly analysis from a week or month view to remove random variations found in a specific day's analysis.)

In general, I like my auctions to end at a time when many people are online searching for items to purchase. With this tool, I can test my assumptions about the best times to end an auction, and I can even try to determine whether optimal ending time varies by item or category.

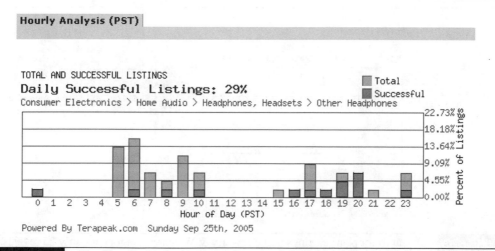

FIGURE 5-14   The Hourly Analysis report shows activity by hour for the item or category you are researching.

Second Chance Offers

Sellers can send Second Chance Offers to any non-winning bidders if the winning bidder does not pay the seller, if a seller has duplicate items, or if the reserve price is not met in a Reserve Price auction. Second Chance Offers can be created immediately after a listing ends and for up to 60 days. (Sellers should be sure that everything has been done to resolve any issues with the original buyer before sending a Second Chance Offer.) Second Chance Offers contain a Buy It Now price equal to the non-winning bidder's bid amount.

$ALES STRATEGY *Use the Hourly Analysis report to help you with Basic Listing Strategy #1: Find the best time to end an auction (Chapter 8). (It helps you find the best time of day, but not the best day of the week.)*

Price Ranges

The Price Ranges feature breaks selling prices into groups and shows you the percentage of successfully sold listings in each group (see Figure 5-15). This visual look at pricing conveys pricing information quite clearly. The data is available only in a single-day view, so it's best to generate reports for at least a week (one day at a time) to get a truer picture of selling prices.

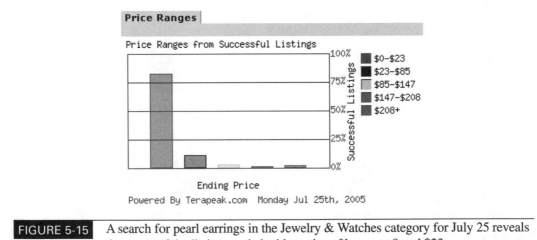

FIGURE 5-15   A search for pearl earrings in the Jewelry & Watches category for July 25 reveals that most of the listings ended with a price of between 0 and $23.

$ALES STRATEGY *Use the Price Ranges report to help you with Basic Listing Strategy #3: Choose the most profitable starting price (Chapter 8), and Advanced Listing Strategy #1: Research what to sell (Chapter 9).*

Successful Listing Duration Lengths

Listing Duration tells you the percentage of successfully sold items by listing duration (1-, 3-, 5-, 7-, or 10-day auctions).

In Figure 5-16, you can see the Successful Listing Duration Lengths report. It shows about 20 percent of the auctions used a 3-day duration and had 100 percent STR (all of them sold). More than 40 percent of the listings were 7-day listings, and they had about a 45 percent STR.

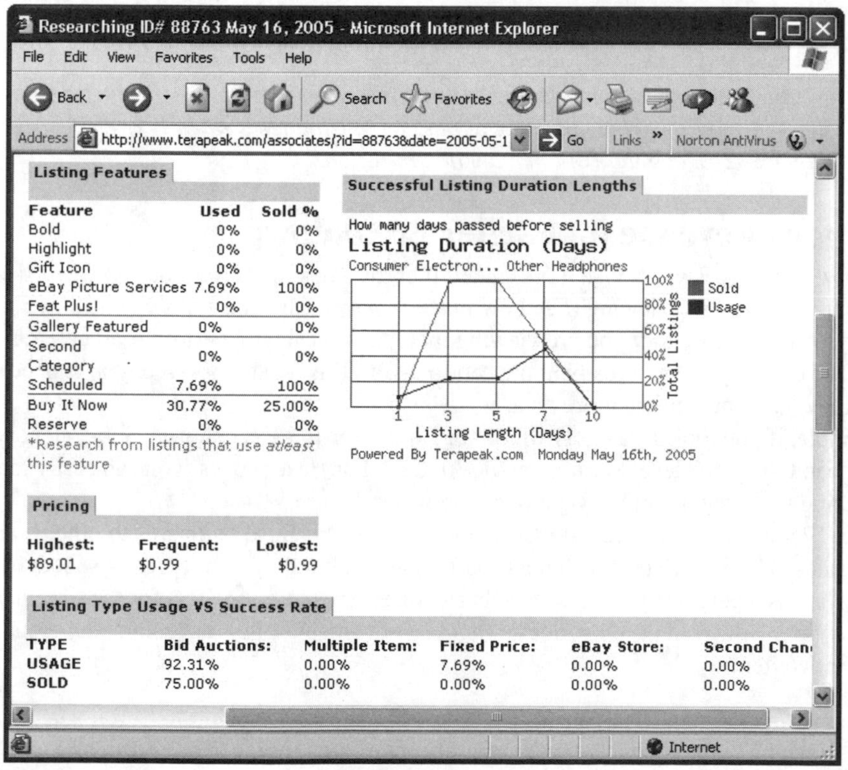

5

FIGURE 5-16 Successful Listing Duration Lengths on Terapeak's Report page reveals usage and success rate of auctions by duration.

No items were listed with a 10-day duration, so it has a zero STR. eBay charges extra for 10-day listings, which may be why in this particular category and timeframe no seller used that duration. We'll talk in later chapters about the tradeoff between a longer duration, which gives your item more exposure, versus a shorter duration, which allows potential buyers to purchase an item more quickly.

Remember from Chapter 2 that eBay treats Buy It Now (BIN) auctions differently than you might expect. Let's say you run a 7-day BIN auction, and someone purchases the item the first day with a BIN bid. Rather than being counted as a 7-day auction, eBay counts it as a 1-day auction! So factor this in when you are looking at the "usage" part of the chart and know that the lower-duration listings are being "overcounted" somewhat as a result. (This is true for all eBay data, not just data coming from Terapeak.)

Knowing how long an item was listed before being purchased is useful, but it means you lose a valuable piece of information: the true STRs for auctions by duration. You don't really know how many items that were sold in three days were actually 3-day auctions versus 5-day, 7-day, or 10-day auctions. This is another case where reviewing listings can be helpful in giving you a reality check—you can see in the actual listing the duration and when it was sold.

$ALES STRATEGY   *Use the Successful Listing Duration Lengths report to help you decide how long your auctions should be. I'll talk more about this in Chapter 8 when I cover Basic Listing Strategy #2: Determine optimal auction duration.*

Subcategory Revenue and Seller Breakdown

Sub-Category Sales gives you a visual presentation of the sales in each of the subcategories within the category you are viewing (See how much money each subcategory contributes). This appears only when the category you are viewing includes subcategories (as not all categories are subcategorized). So if you are already at the "bottom" of eBay's category tree, you'll need to "back up" a level so you can see more data.

For example, if you look at category 61332 for Bose Over-Ear Headphones, Sub-Category Sales does not appear. Go up one level to category 61330, Over-Ear Headphones (you can easily move up a category using the category trail navigation aid shown in Figure 5-3).

Figure 5-17 shows you the breakdown so you can see how Bose compares to other brands in terms of sales. The Sub-Category Sellers chart underneath tells you how many sellers each subcategory has as a percentage (see what subcategories have more sellers) for the time period you are reviewing. However, the chart doesn't tell you how many sellers are selling large quantities versus one or two items.

$ALES STRATEGY   *Use the Sub-Category Revenue & Seller Breakdown report to help you with Basic Listing Strategy #3: Choose the most profitable starting price (Chapter 8), and Advanced Listing Strategy #1: Research what to sell (Chapter 9). You can also use this report in doing competitive research (Chapter 11).*

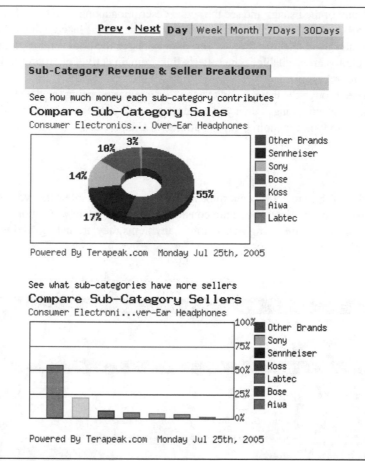

FIGURE 5-17   This section of the Terapeak Report shows the percentage of each brand (subcategory) in terms of total dollar sales.

Listings Tool

Terapeak's Listings tool shows you a list of actual eBay listings that make up your search results for the time period you specify. Column headers are Auction Title, Start Price, End Price, Bids, Sold, and End Time, which you can see by referring back to Figure 5-11. The column headers are hyperlinked, allowing you to sort the list by starting price, ending price, number of bids, whether it sold, and ending time. Listings that sold are highlighted in green with a dollar sign icon to the left of the listing.

TIP   *Use Terapeak's Listings Tool to help you confirm that the results accurately represent your search when generating reports in Terapeak.*

You can click any of the listings and see the actual description along with the seller and winning buyer's user IDs. eBay does not archive photos with the data. Photos listed using eBay's Picture Services are generally available for 60 days (Terapeak accesses the photos through eBay's API program). Other photos are available if the seller's links remain active, but many sellers remove photos once their listings end.

You can browse through the listings and change the time period using the date tabs. It's always important to look at closed listings when you conduct a search to make sure the results contain relevant listings and to look for anomalies, as outlined in Chapter 2.

Sellers Tool

Terapeak's Sellers tool (Figure 5-18) is enormously useful and is available when you search listings (not when you browse categories). If you are considering selling in a new category, you should know how many top sellers are listing items, how many items they are listing, and what kinds of STRs they are achieving.

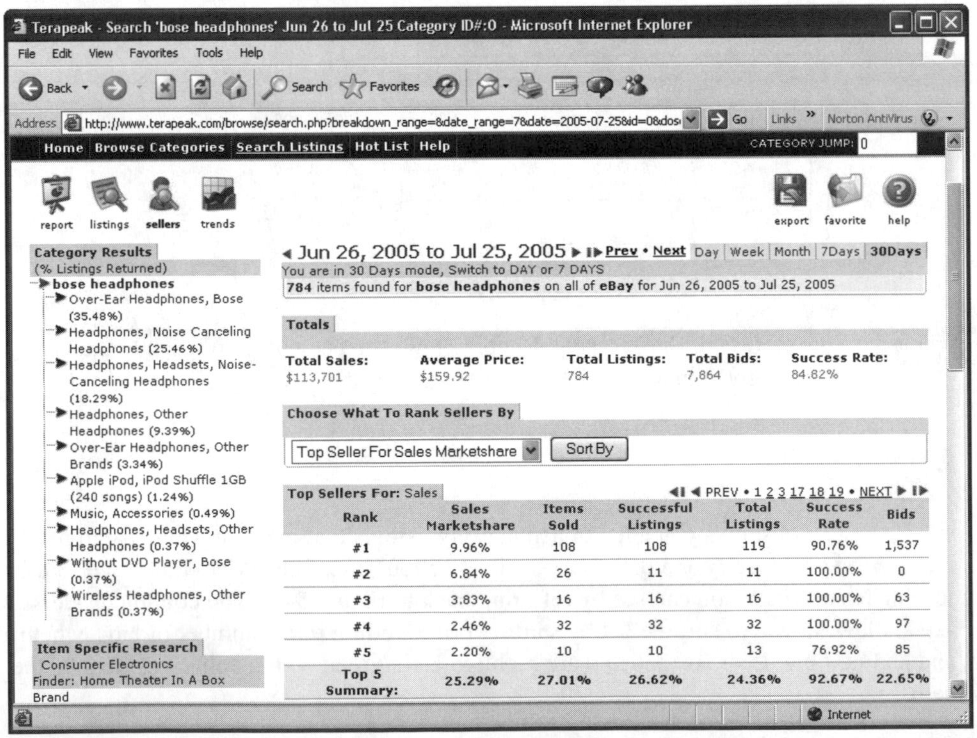

FIGURE 5-18   Terapeak's Sellers tool lists top sellers and is sortable by criteria such as market share and number of items sold.

At the top of the Sellers tool page, you'll find a summary of sales information for *all* sales:

- Total Sales
- Average Price
- Total Listings
- Total Bids
- Success Rate

Under that summary is a list of sellers in order of sales, with the number one seller listed first. You can sort sellers by the following criteria:

- Top Seller For Sales Marketshare
- Top Seller For Items Sold
- Top Seller For Successful Listings
- Top Seller For Total Listings
- Top Seller For Bids

Because eBay places restrictions on how its data can be used due to privacy concerns, Terapeak cannot reveal the user IDs for sellers, but the information provided in the results can still give you lots of good competitive information. It can also be frustrating, however. For example, if you sort by Top Seller By Bids, it would be nice if you could click the seller's listings to see what that seller is doing to attract so many bids.

The only way around this shortcoming is to go to eBay directly and familiarize yourself with top category sellers by doing searches of eBay.com listings and eBay Store listings. The more you study listings and store inventory in a category, the better idea you will have of who are the top sellers, and the better educated guesses you will make in how those top sellers are represented on Terapeak Seller reports.

For example, if you determine from the Seller report in Figure 5-18 that the number one seller of Bose headphones listed 119 items last month, and the next seller in terms of number of listings sold 32 items, you just might be able to identify that top seller by searching eBay.com and eBay .com Stores. (It's always a good idea to supplement data-analysis reports with your own research on the eBay site anyway.)

After showing the list of individual data for the top five sellers, the Sellers tool inserts a line that summarizes the data for the top five sellers for the product or category you are looking at, as shown in Figure 5-18. (It's interesting to note that the top five sellers made up one-quarter of the dollar sales [Sales Marketshare] for this item.) The report then continues with its list of sellers ranked by order.

Terapeak's Sellers tool give you the Rank and percentage (depending on how you've sorted the results), Items Sold, Successful Listings, Total Listings, Success Rate, and Number Of Bids. You'll see for some sellers that the number in the Items Sold column are higher than the Total Listings. This can be accounted for by Dutch auctions, in which sellers list multiple items in one listing.

Sorting by different criteria will bring back different seller rankings. You can look in the Items Sold column to try to track a particular seller. For example, if the number one seller by Listings sold 43 items, you can see where the seller who sold 43 items falls in the rankings by Sales Marketshare. (This is a bit awkward, however, and is due to the fact that the tool is not allowed to reveal sellers' user IDs.)

You can change the date range for the Sellers tool report. Looking at Top Sellers for a month may be more useful than viewing data for any one particular day, in case that day is an anomaly. A month's worth of data will smooth out some of these daily anomalies. You can also click the Listings tool to review the actual listings that make up the search results.

On the left side of the page, Category Results are listed so you can narrow down your search results to a particular category. Looking at Figure 5-18, you could click Over-Ear Headphones, Bose to see listings for that subcategory.

Under the list of Category Results is a tool that allows you to narrow your search by price, called Price Specific Research.

$ALES STRATEGY *Use the Sellers tool to conduct competitive research and see where your sales rank compared to other sellers. Looking at Figure 5-18, you might see you are the number 3 seller in terms of dollar marketshare (if you sold 16 items and had 100 percent sell-through).*

Trends Tool—Browsing Categories

The Trends page gives you an overview of a particular category and how it has changed over time. You can view the following charts by clicking on the pull-down box labeled Top Graph (the page displays only one at a time in the top graph):

- Total Sales (dollars)
- Total Listings
- Successful Listings
- Listing Success
- Total Bids
- Average Price
- Listing Types (excludes regular auction format)
- Listings Per Seller
- Bid Per Listing

The Trends tool page gives you a "big-picture" view of the category you are researching by showing you data over time (Figure 5-19). You can change the date range (period) and timeframe (breakdown) using the pull-down menus under the charts; click the Update Graph button whenever you make a change.

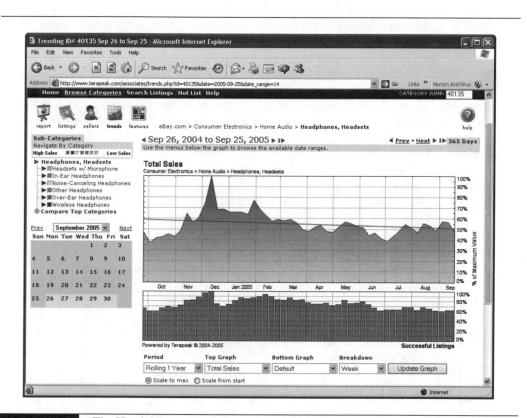

FIGURE 5-19   The Headphones, Headsets category did well in terms of sales during the holiday season (November and December).

All charts are in percentages and do not provide actual numerical data because of restrictions in eBay's data licensing agreement. While you cannot tell how many actual listings make up the category, knowing how a category is changing (if average prices are falling, for example), is certainly helpful. And, of course, you can use the Trends feature when searching keywords (as opposed to browsing categories), which tells you absolute numbers; this is covered in the next section, "Trends Tool—Searching Listings."

You can use the three pull-down boxes directly under the graphs to select date ranges and type of graph: Period, Graph, and Breakdown. Use these to plot any of the available graphs by whatever timeframe you wish. Use the Bottom Graph pull-down box to specify what data should appear in the bottom graph.

$ALES STRATEGY   *Use Terapeak's Trends tool to help you view the current state of a particular category and track it over time. This helps in benchmarking your own activities and with Advanced Listing Strategy #1: Research what to sell (Chapter 9).*

Terapeak has a great tool that lets you compare categories. Under the pull-down boxes are two boxes with arrows pointing to each other: This Category's Children and Compared Categories. Highlight the category you want to compare and click the right arrow. Figure 5-20 shows a graph comparing consumer electronics headsets for two categories, Headsets w/ Microphone and Noise-Canceling Headphones. This graph compares the total (dollar) sales.

After you have chosen the categories you'd like to compare in the box on the right, click the Update Graph button under the graph and above these boxes. You can use the pull-down menus to the left of that button to compare various metrics (discussed at the beginning of this section).

This information allows you to compare the subcategories of the category you are researching, helping you decide whether one category is more attractive for selling than another (assuming you have taken into account other factors, such as inventory costs, whether you have a supplier, and so on).

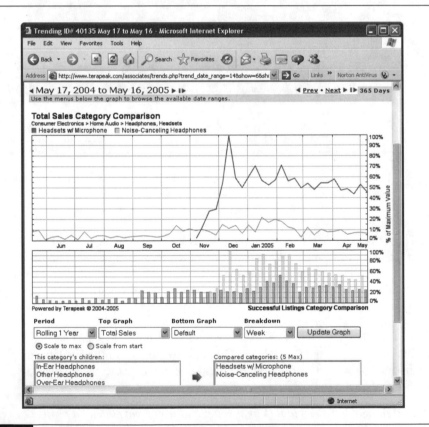

FIGURE 5-20   In this Terapeak Category Comparison report, you can see that noise-canceling headphones had more dollar sales than headsets with microphones.

Beware eBay Category Changes

eBay makes frequent changes to its category structure. This will have an effect on trended data in categories over time. If a category has a sudden increase or decrease in listings, it may be due to a subcategory being added or moved to another (or brand-new) category.

eBay announces category changes on its General Announcements Board (in the Community section at www2.ebay.com/aw/marketing.shtml) and details the changes on Seller Central (under Services) on this page: http://pages.ebay.com/categorychanges.

It's always wise to compare more than one metric, so run reports for all of the graphs available to you. For example, noise-canceling headphones cost more, so it's no surprise that the aggregate sales figures would be higher. But if you're considering selling home audio equipment, you might be interested to know whether headsets with microphones had fewer listings, more bids, and a higher STR than its sister categories.

In some cases, an item you are selling might legitimately fall under more than one category, so knowing which category performs better might be another reason to compare category metrics.

You can see whether a particular category is increasing or decreasing by various metrics. In Chapter 1, we looked at how comparing an item's Average Selling Price to the Category Average Selling Price can help you make strategic decisions about your business. Likewise, you can compare other metrics in a category to particular items, as well as comparing category performance to your own sales history in that category.

We'll talk more about this in Chapter 9 when looking at data to help make decisions about what to sell. Just remember that seasonal factors can heavily influence sales in any given category, and like many retail sites, eBay has its own seasonal rhythms, historically experiencing higher sales in winter months for the site as a whole. Review Chapter 2 for other factors that can influence sales.

Trends Tool—Searching Listings

While the Trends Tool gives you data in percentages when Browsing Categories, the Trends Tool—Searching Listings works the same way but gives data in dollars and units.

The Trends tool under Search Listings contains the following graphs, accessible through the Graph pull-down box labeled Top Graph (see Figure 5-21):

- Total Sales
- Total Listings
- Successful Listings
- Listing Success
- Success Rate
- Total Bids

- Average Price
- Items Sold
- Bids Per Listing
- Listings Per Seller

The Trends tool allows you to compare ASP and STR by day of the week. Remember that in the Report tool, you can see various charts, including an "hourly analysis" that tells you the total number of listings ending versus the listings that sold successfully. Unfortunately, Terapeak does not include a "daily analysis" section in the Report tool, so use the Trends tool to help you determine the most successful day of the week for a category. Figure 5-21 shows an example of a Trends tool report for plasma screen TV.

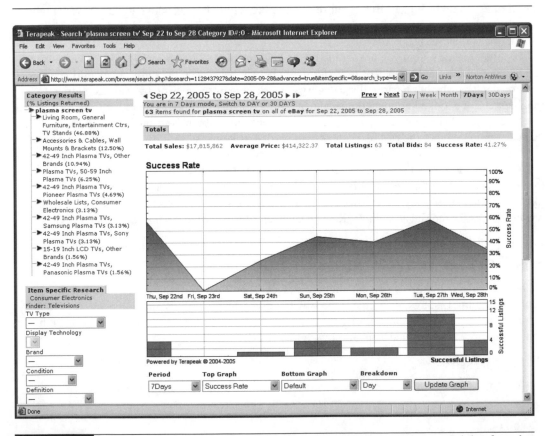

FIGURE 5-21   The Trends tool under Search Listings shows Friday was not a good day for sales of plasma screen TVs for this particular week.

Here's how the Trends tool could be used to get the data for plasma screen TV listings:

1. Click Search Listings, enter the search term **Plasma Screen TV** in the Search box, and click the Search Listings button.

2. Click the Trends icon.

3. Underneath the graph, use the pull-down menus to select 7 Days under Period, Success Rate under Top Graph, and Day under Breakdown.

4. Click the Update Graph button.

Now you will see a graph that plots out a week of listings containing the term *Plasma Screen TV*, as shown in Figure 5-21. You can see which days were best in terms of STRs. One week's worth of data is not enough to tell you which days are best for ending a plasma screen TV auction listing, but if you track the data over time, you should see patterns emerge.

$ALES STRATEGY   *Use Terapeak's Trends tool to help you with basic and advanced listing strategies; Trends reports give you absolute data, as opposed to the relative data of the Browse Categories tool. Check closed listings to make sure the information represents what you are researching.*

Features Tool

The Features tool tells you how many listings used optional eBay features and the accompanying success rates. This tool allows you to dig up more information than the Listing Features section of the Report tool alone. I recommend that you use both when trying to determine which optional eBay features you should pay for in your listings.

The more data points (listings) in a category, the more interesting the Features Tool becomes. While you are looking at a particular category, click the Features icon under the Navigation Bar. Click the Bold box and then click the Display Feature Information button. You'll see a count of how many listings used eBay's optional Bold feature only—with no other optional features—and the accompanying success rate. This will help you determine whether using the Bold feature will increase the STR (success rate) of your listings, important since you pay a fee to use those optional features.

Next, check the boxes for Bold, Gallery, and Highlight, and click Display Feature Information. You'll see results showing how many listings used all three features and how many listings used some combination of those three features, as shown in Figure 5-22. You can also click all the boxes and get results for listings that used all of those features or some combination.

NOTE   *Keep in mind that experienced sellers tend to use optional features on items they perceive as having a higher value. The listings that used optional features in these reports might have had a better chance of selling anyway because of their condition, rarity, or demand. If you have doubts, you can go to the Listings tool and review the listings yourself.*

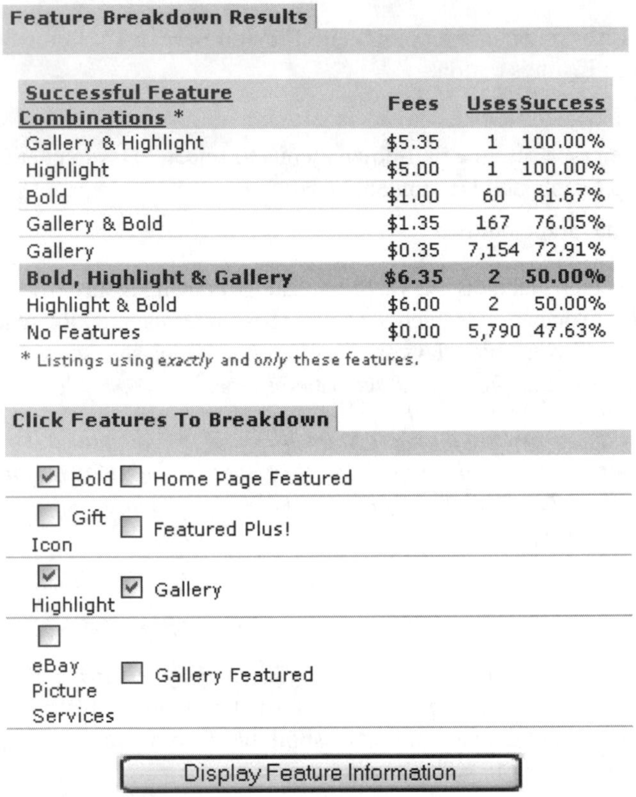

Feature Breakdown Results

Successful Feature Combinations *	Fees	Uses	Success
Gallery & Highlight	$5.35	1	100.00%
Highlight	$5.00	1	100.00%
Bold	$1.00	60	81.67%
Gallery & Bold	$1.35	167	76.05%
Gallery	$0.35	7,154	72.91%
Bold, Highlight & Gallery	**$6.35**	**2**	**50.00%**
Highlight & Bold	$6.00	2	50.00%
No Features	$0.00	5,790	47.63%

* Listings using *exactly* and *only* these features.

Click Features To Breakdown

- ☑ Bold   ☐ Home Page Featured
- ☐ Gift Icon   ☐ Featured Plus!
- ☑ Highlight   ☑ Gallery
- ☐ eBay Picture Services   ☐ Gallery Featured

[Display Feature Information]

FIGURE 5-22   The Features tool lets you see how many listings used optional features and the average STR for those listings. You can see that Gallery was a popular feature in this category.

$ALES STRATEGY   *Use the Features tool to help you decide which optional features you might want to use to draw traffic to your listings. We'll cover this in Chapter 9 on Advanced Listing Strategy #3: Analyze effectiveness of reserve price and Advanced Listing Strategy #4: Evaluate optional features and upgrades.*

Save Report

While using Terapeak, you'll notice on some pages an icon in the shape of a computer disk with the words *Save Report* next to it. If you click this icon, you will be automatically prompted to save an Excel file containing the report information. This allows you to track data over time and arrange and compile the data any way you like.

If you want to track STRs for a group of categories, you can download the data to your spreadsheet each month and create a graph in your spreadsheet to see the changes over time.

Wrapping Up

Terapeak's team is immersed in eBay data—they live and breathe numbers and devote their business to figuring out the best way to dig through market data and make meaning of it to help eBay sellers improve their performance. From the time it introduced the tool, Terapeak has made major improvements and fine-tuned its approach.

Terapeak offers sellers a goldmine of information. Like any research tool, you must use it correctly and be careful of drawing general assumptions from the data. But with practice using Terapeak along with your experience as an eBay seller, you will be able to use Terapeak to help you make wise business decisions about what to sell, when to sell, and how to sell.

Terapeak offers tutorials, workshops, and a support forum. If you decide to use the tool, learn to use it most effectively to make you more money in your eBay business.

Chapter 6

Digging Into Data with DeepAnalysis

DeepAnalysis (www.hammertap.com) was the only tool of its kind for several years and was wildly popular with eBay sellers because it allowed them to print out detailed reports about any eBay seller, providing valuable information about competitors. Bright Builders (a division of HammerTap) acquired DeepAnalysis in 2004. The company has since entered into eBay's Market Data program, and as a result of eBay's requirements, the company changed some of the functionality offered to users.

DeepAnalysis is a client-based program, as opposed to Terapeak's hosted service. This means you must install DeepAnalysis software on your computer. When using DeepAnalysis, your search request is transmitted to the DeepAnalysis website, where the search is conducted, and the results are downloaded to your computer. You can purchase and download DeepAnalysis from the HammerTap website, where you'll see the welcome screen shown in Figure 6-1.

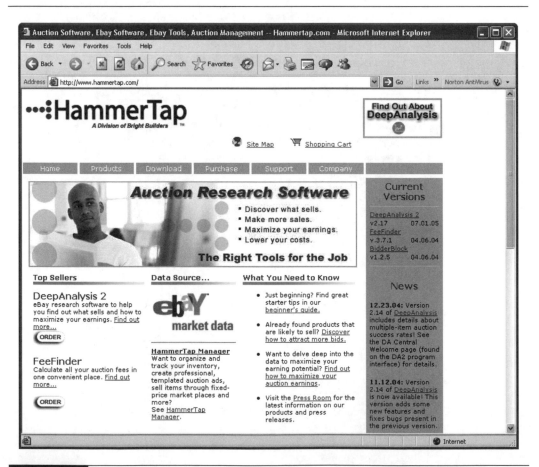

FIGURE 6-1   Bright Builder's HammerTap website lets you purchase and download the DeepAnalysis software program to your computer.

DeepAnalysis Version 1 vs. Version 2

Many people are familiar with version 1 of DeepAnalysis (DA1). After Bright Builders acquired HammerTap DeepAnalysis, it developed version 2 (DA2) and began licensing data through eBay's Market Data program. With DA1, users could conduct research on competitors' sales. But because eBay prohibits research on an eBay seller without the eBay seller ID and password, this is no longer possible. With DA2, users may do statistical research on their own accounts (or the accounts they manage) but not on others' accounts. While this restriction may seem unfortunate if you want to analyze your competitors, remember that it also protects *your* data from your competitors' eyes. All tools powered by the eBay Market Data program include this restriction.

6

In testing the service for this book, we conducted searches on a fast computer with a cable modem, and search results for two weeks' and four weeks' worth of data came back quite quickly. If you have a slow connection or slow computer, it will take longer to get results. As the company expands the amount of archived data from which to draw, you may have to develop strategies for overcoming slow searches if you have older equipment and slower connection speeds—the best way to do that is to narrow your search as much as possible by narrowing the date range and number of search results.

Meet a Vendor: Bright Builders (DeepAnalysis)

Jen Cano is Director of Public Relations for Bright Builders, the makers of DeepAnalysis. Jen said every eBay research effort should answer one or more of these three questions:

- ■ What sells?
- ■ How can I increase my sales rate?
- ■ How can I maximize my profits?

Jen said beginners use DeepAnalysis to find out what will sell and how much they can make, and experienced sellers use it to find out how to boost their sales rates and increase their profit margins by finding successful starting prices, keywords for listing titles, and presentation styles.

She recommends DeepAnalysis customers do research for specific categories and products. "For example, the most successful day of the week to end an auction will be different for Home Décor than for Video Games because the buyer demographic is different."

(continued)

Jen summed up her philosophy as, "Don't mimic the competition, exceed it."

Bright Builders

1510 N Technology Way

Orem, UT 84097

Telephone: 800-342-1990

Customer Support: support@hammertap.com

www.hammertap.com

www.brightbuilders.com

We reviewed version 2.16.1111, which has the ability to return 500, 1000, 2000, 5000, 10,000, 20,000, 50,000, and 100,000 results for the last four weeks. So if you have a very slow connection, start by selecting a week's worth of data for 500 search results, and work your way up. If searching a category, add keywords to narrow the results.

DeepAnalysis looks at the latest four weeks' worth of data, updating data daily, and the company plans to add one year's worth of data over time. DeepAnalysis does not yet support Item Specifics searches but will add support for it in a future release.

DeepAnalysis is available only for the Windows operating system. The system requirements for DeepAnalysis are as follows:

- Internet access
- Windows 98 Second Edition, 2000, or XP
- At least 15MB disk space

DeepAnalysis Navigation

Research tools—eBay Auction, eBay Seller, and eBay Category—are located in the upper-left corner of the DeepAnalysis page, as shown in Figure 6-2.

To the right of research tools, you'll see a research form with various fields and commands. The research form changes depending on whether you are searching eBay auctions, eBay sellers, or eBay categories. This form may look a bit confusing, but once you understand how it works, it's simple to use. DeepAnalysis displays the form at the top of every page for all searches.

You conduct a search on DeepAnalysis, and the software provides a summary under the Findings tab, as shown in Figure 6-3.

When you examine reports using this tool, keep in mind that you may be looking at a subset of the actual number of eBay closed listings that fit your search criteria, depending on the maximum

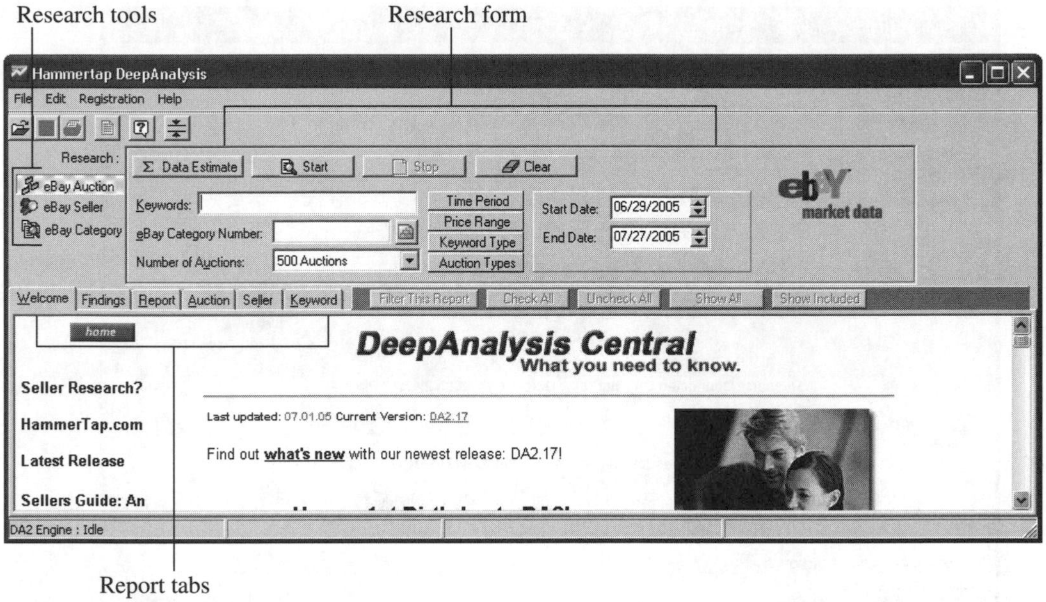

Research tools   Research form

Report tabs

FIGURE 6-2   Research tools are shown in the upper-left corner of the page, to the left of the research form.

number of results you tell DeepAnalysis to bring back to your computer based on your connection speed. So if DeepAnalysis finds 70,000 listings that match your criteria, but you've set a maximum of 500 results, DeepAnalysis will show you only 500 of the listings that matched your search, not the complete 70,000.

You can increase the amount in the Number Of Auctions field to get as many results as you can, and I recommend you do that. The more data points in an analysis, the better the analysis will be.

Use the report tabs just under the research form to navigate to the following reports:

- **Findings**   Provides listing summary information, shows what's hot, and displays success factors

- **Report**   Shows summaries of total sales, successful auctions, average sales price (ASP), and seller success rates (or sell-through rates, STRs)

- **Auction**   Shows a list of the actual eBay listings that make up your search results along with statistics about each listing

- **Seller**   Provides a spreadsheet of data organized by seller that allows you to identify top sellers by various metrics

- **Keyword**   Provides a list of words in auction titles and accompanying metrics such as ASP and STR to help you identify effective keywords to use in your titles

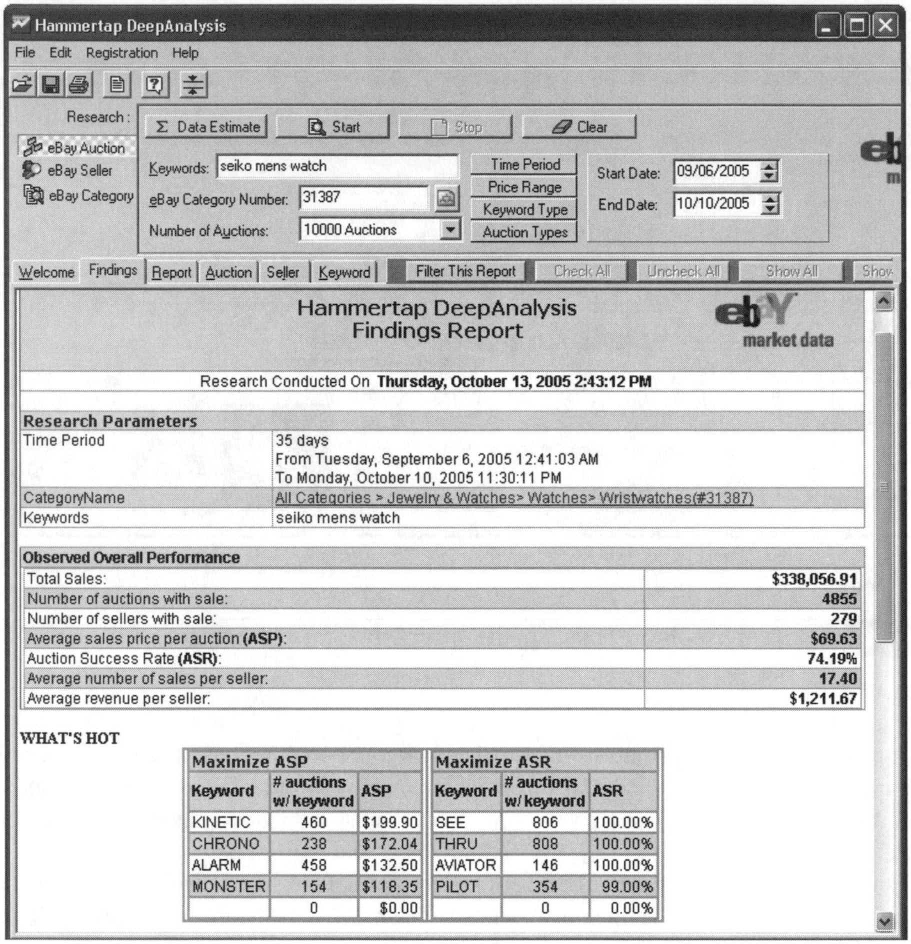

FIGURE 6-3   The Findings Report on the Findings tab displays the results of DeepAnalysis's research.

These report tabs stay the same whether you are doing research using an eBay Auction, eBay Seller, or eBay Category search.

Clicking the Welcome tab always takes you to the DeepAnalysis Central page (the same page displayed each time you open the program, as shown in Figure 6-2). Here you can see product news, read tips on using the software, and learn how to update to new releases.

After you enter information into the research form and click the Start button, a status bar at the bottom of the screen shows you the tool is working. Figure 6-4 shows the status bar in action: after you click Start, it displays Contacting Server, then Retrieving Data, then Analyzing Data so you can follow along as DeepAnalysis does its research.

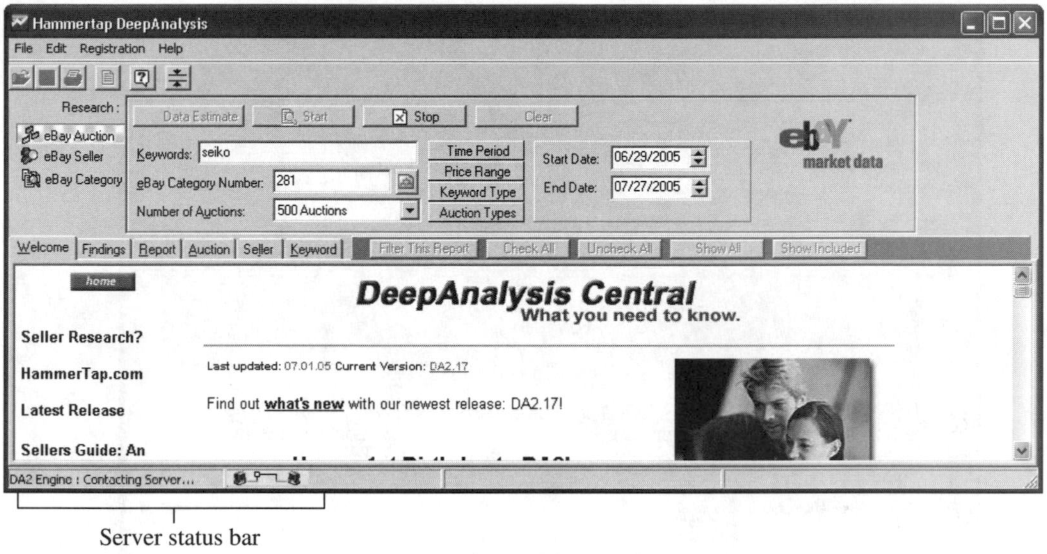

FIGURE 6-4   The status bar at the bottom of the screen lets you know when the tool is conducting research.

Findings Tab

After you've used the research form to do a search, you can see a summary page on the Findings tab. Figure 6-3 shows part of the Findings report for a search for *seiko mens watch* in the Wristwatches category (found under Watches in the main eBay Jewelry & Watches category). The Findings report displays the following information:

- **Summary information**   Counts and statistics on the research results
- **What's Hot**   Suggestions on keywords to increase selling price and STRs
- **Success factors**   Statistics on type of listings and features used to help you see which are the most successful

TIP

Adjust the Number Of Auctions field in the research form to a higher number if you aren't seeing enough results that match your search criteria.

Report Tab

Every page under the Report tab includes Research Parameters at the top of the page. This section includes the time period, category name, and keywords, and an Executive Summary, which is shown in Figure 6-5. The Executive Summary includes the following information:

- How many listings in total meet the research parameters
- Total sales in dollars

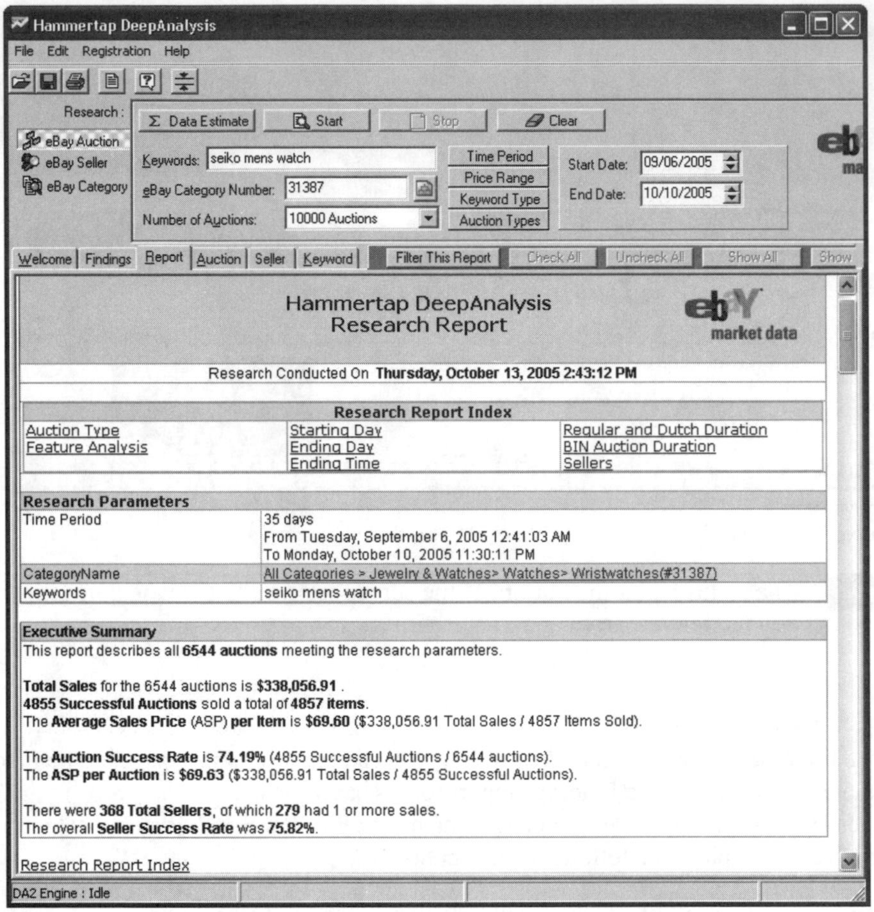

FIGURE 6-5   The Report tab shows an Executive Summary along with other key data.

- Number of successful auctions (how many listings sold successfully)
- Average sales price (ASP) per *item* (this accounts for multiple items found in Dutch Auction listings)
- Auction success rate (STR)
- Average sales price per *auction*

Auction Type

The Auction Type section (Figure 6-6) and graph (Figure 6-7) of the Report Tab page show statistical information by type of listing. Using the Auction Type report, you can see how many

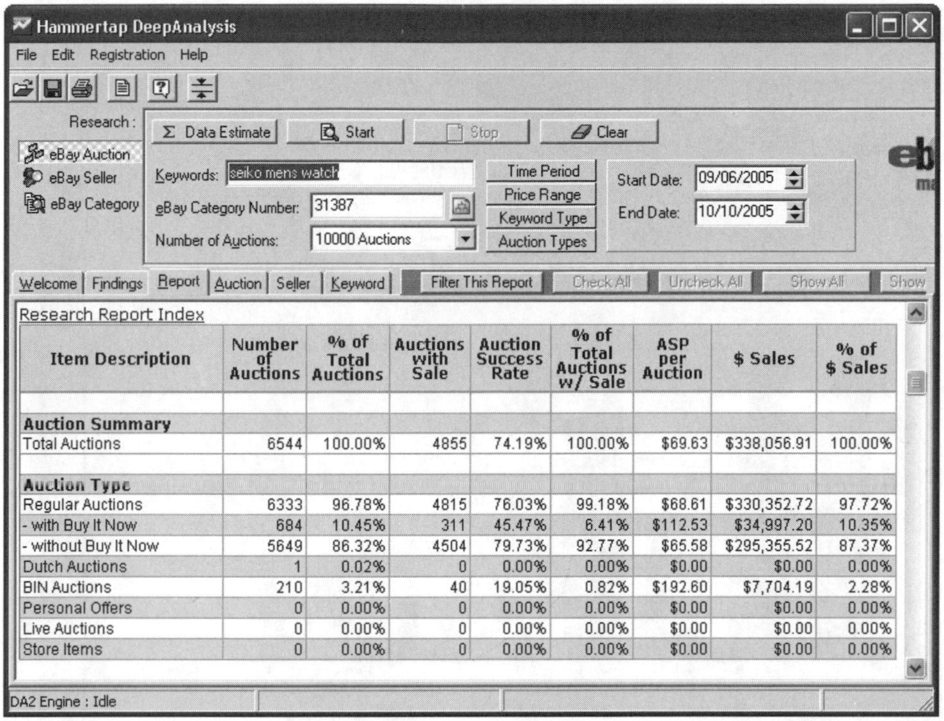

Item Description	Number of Auctions	% of Total Auctions	Auctions with Sale	Auction Success Rate	% of Total Auctions w/ Sale	ASP per Auction	$ Sales	% of $ Sales
Auction Summary								
Total Auctions	6544	100.00%	4855	74.19%	100.00%	$69.63	$338,056.91	100.00%
Auction Type								
Regular Auctions	6333	96.78%	4815	76.03%	99.18%	$68.61	$330,352.72	97.72%
- with Buy It Now	684	10.45%	311	45.47%	6.41%	$112.53	$34,997.20	10.35%
- without Buy It Now	5649	86.32%	4504	79.73%	92.77%	$65.58	$295,355.52	87.37%
Dutch Auctions	1	0.02%	0	0.00%	0.00%	$0.00	$0.00	0.00%
BIN Auctions	210	3.21%	40	19.05%	0.82%	$192.60	$7,704.19	2.28%
Personal Offers	0	0.00%	0	0.00%	0.00%	$0.00	$0.00	0.00%
Live Auctions	0	0.00%	0	0.00%	0.00%	$0.00	$0.00	0.00%
Store Items	0	0.00%	0	0.00%	0.00%	$0.00	$0.00	0.00%

FIGURE 6-6 The Auction Type section allows you to compare listing results by type, such as comparing the ASP of regular auctions versus BIN auctions.

sellers are conducting Dutch auctions (multiple-quantity listings), how many are using the Buy It Now feature, and how many are selling through eBay Stores, for example. You can then compare Auction Success Rate (STR) and ASP information.

You might look at the results in the Auction Type section and find that auctions using the Buy It Now (BIN) feature averaged higher selling prices and better STRs than auctions without Buy It Now, or you may discover the opposite. In *the seiko mens watch* example used in Figure 6-6, you can see that 10.45 percent of listings were regular Buy It Now auctions. Of those, 45.47 percent sold successfully, compared to 79.73 percent of regular auctions that did not use the feature. The Average Selling Price for regular Buy It Now auctions was $112.53 compared to $65.58 for those without the Buy It Now feature.

$ALES STRATEGY *Use the Auction Type section in the research reports to help you decide which type of format to use; this is covered in Chapter 9 with Advanced Listing Strategy #2: Choose auction-style listing versus Fixed-Price format. You can compare STRs and ASPs for different kinds of listings.*

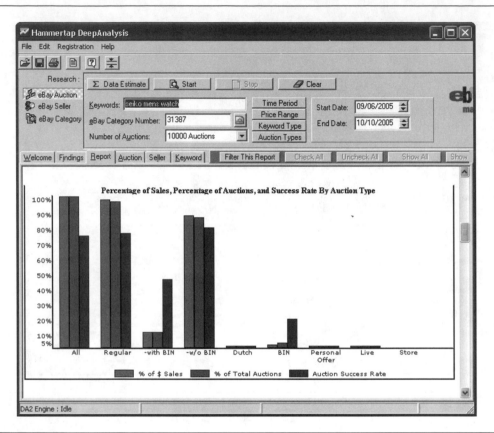

FIGURE 6-7   The Auction Type graph shows you a visual picture of usage and STR by type of listing.

Feature Analysis Section

The Feature Analysis section (Figure 6-8) shows how many listings used optional eBay features and upgrades. The Feature Analysis section tracks the following features:

- Reserve price
- Featured
- Gallery featured
- Gallery picture
- Bold
- Highlight
- Gift

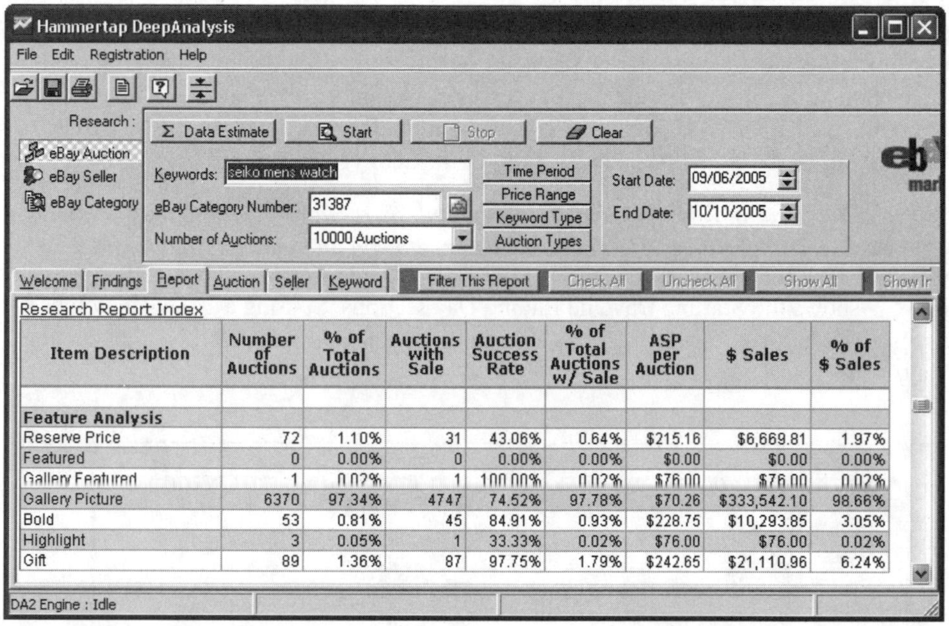

Item Description	Number of Auctions	% of Total Auctions	Auctions with Sale	Auction Success Rate	% of Total Auctions w/ Sale	ASP per Auction	$ Sales	% of $ Sales
Feature Analysis								
Reserve Price	72	1.10%	31	43.06%	0.64%	$215.16	$6,669.81	1.97%
Featured	0	0.00%	0	0.00%	0.00%	$0.00	$0.00	0.00%
Gallery Featured	1	0.02%	1	100.00%	0.02%	$76.00	$76.00	0.02%
Gallery Picture	6370	97.34%	4747	74.52%	97.78%	$70.26	$333,542.10	98.66%
Bold	53	0.81%	45	84.91%	0.93%	$228.75	$10,293.85	3.05%
Highlight	3	0.05%	1	33.33%	0.02%	$76.00	$76.00	0.02%
Gift	89	1.36%	87	97.75%	1.79%	$242.65	$21,110.96	6.24%

FIGURE 6-8 DeepAnalysis' Feature Analysis section measures the success of optional features such as Gallery and Bold.

It also shows the STR (Auction Success Rate), the ASP, and the dollar sales for those listings. Figure 6-8 shows that for this search, almost 98 percent of the auctions that used eBay's Gift feature sold successfully. Look at the % Of Total Auctions column to see that fewer than 2 percent of listings used this feature, however.

Keep in mind that some sellers are inclined to use features that cost extra money only on items they consider to be of higher value—meaning the listings with optional features may be better quality items worth more money. (This is especially true for the Reserve Price feature.) But it is useful to see how many listings used various features, and whether the ASP indicates it was worth it. Also, if many listings in a category use a feature—like Bold—you might want to consider whether *not* using Bold would put your listing at a disadvantage. Using the data in these charts provides only part of the information—review actual listings for more insight using the Auction tab, which I explain in the next section.

$ALES STRATEGY

Use the Feature Analysis section in research reports to help you decide whether to use Reserve Price and optional features and upgrades, discussed in Advanced Listing Strategy #3: Analyze effectiveness of reserve price, and Advanced Listing Strategy #4: Evaluate optional features and upgrades, in Chapter 9. You can compare STRs and ASPs for different kinds of features.

Starting Day and Ending Day Sections

Starting Day and Ending Day sections reveal information about usage, STRs, and ASPs based on the day of the week an auction started or ended. Many eBay sellers believe it's important to end an auction at the time when the most buyers are visiting the eBay site. (We'll talk much more about this in Chapter 8.) Using DeepAnalysis' Ending Day section, you can test your assumptions about the best day to end an auction for the item you're selling.

$ALES STRATEGY *Use the Ending Day section of the DeepAnalysis research report to help you with Basic Listing Strategy #1: Find the best time to end an auction (Chapter 8).*

Figure 6-9 shows the Starting Day and Ending Day sections. Starting a 1-day auction on a Monday is different than starting a 10-day auction on a Monday, so I prefer to study auction ending days.

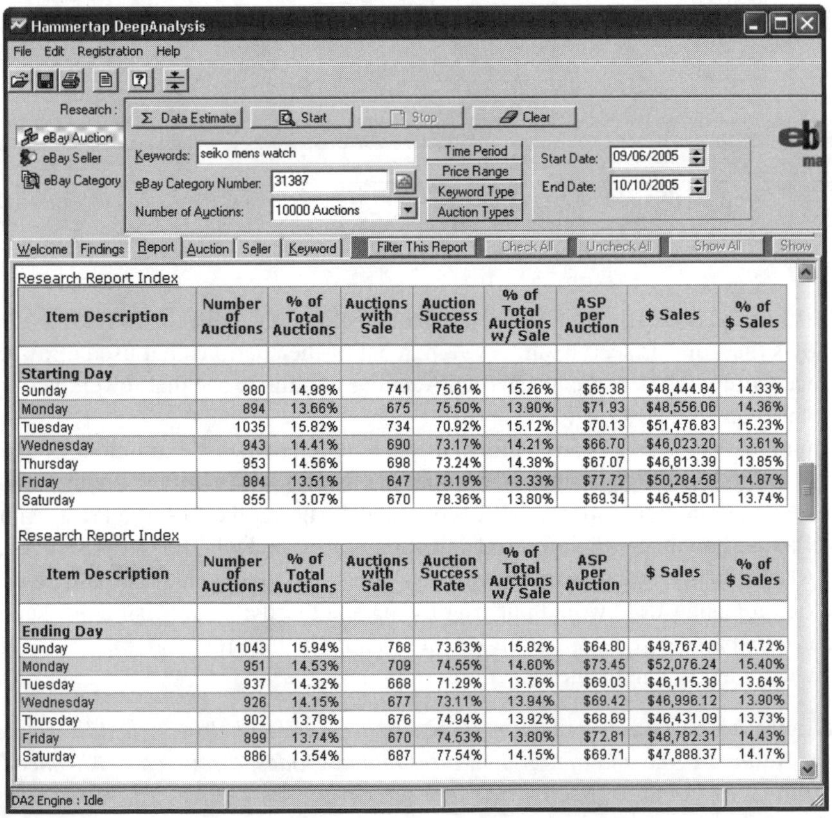

Item Description	Number of Auctions	% of Total Auctions	Auctions with Sale	Auction Success Rate	% of Total Auctions w/ Sale	ASP per Auction	$ Sales	% of $ Sales
Starting Day								
Sunday	980	14.98%	741	75.61%	15.26%	$65.38	$48,444.84	14.33%
Monday	894	13.66%	675	75.50%	13.90%	$71.93	$48,556.06	14.36%
Tuesday	1035	15.82%	734	70.92%	15.12%	$70.13	$51,476.83	15.23%
Wednesday	943	14.41%	690	73.17%	14.21%	$66.70	$46,023.20	13.61%
Thursday	953	14.56%	698	73.24%	14.38%	$67.07	$46,813.39	13.85%
Friday	884	13.51%	647	73.19%	13.33%	$77.72	$50,284.58	14.87%
Saturday	855	13.07%	670	78.36%	13.80%	$69.34	$46,458.01	13.74%

Item Description	Number of Auctions	% of Total Auctions	Auctions with Sale	Auction Success Rate	% of Total Auctions w/ Sale	ASP per Auction	$ Sales	% of $ Sales
Ending Day								
Sunday	1043	15.94%	768	73.63%	15.82%	$64.80	$49,767.40	14.72%
Monday	951	14.53%	709	74.55%	14.60%	$73.45	$52,076.24	15.40%
Tuesday	937	14.32%	668	71.29%	13.76%	$69.03	$46,115.38	13.64%
Wednesday	926	14.15%	677	73.11%	13.94%	$69.42	$46,996.12	13.90%
Thursday	902	13.78%	676	74.94%	13.92%	$68.69	$46,431.09	13.73%
Friday	899	13.74%	670	74.53%	13.80%	$72.81	$48,782.31	14.43%
Saturday	886	13.54%	687	77.54%	14.15%	$69.71	$47,888.37	14.17%

FIGURE 6-9 The Ending Day section reveals the most popular day to end an auction was Sunday, but not by much—and auctions ending on a Monday earned the highest dollar sales ($52,076.24).

Regular & Dutch Auction Duration and BIN Auction Duration Sections

The Regular & Dutch Auction Duration section reveals information about usage, STRs, and ASPs based on the duration of a listing. The BIN Auction Duration section does the same for listings using the Buy It Now feature. Figure 6-10 shows these two sections.

eBay allows sellers to run 1-day, 3-day, 5-day, 7-day, or 10-day listings. You can use the data in these sections to try to determine the most effective listing duration for your items. In Chapter 8, we'll talk in depth about the pros and cons of different auction durations.

$ALES STRATEGY *Use the Regular & Dutch Auction Duration section of the research report to help you with Basic Listing Strategy #2: Determine optimal auction duration (Chapter 8). Use the BIN Auction Duration section to find the optimal duration for Buy It Now listings.*

6

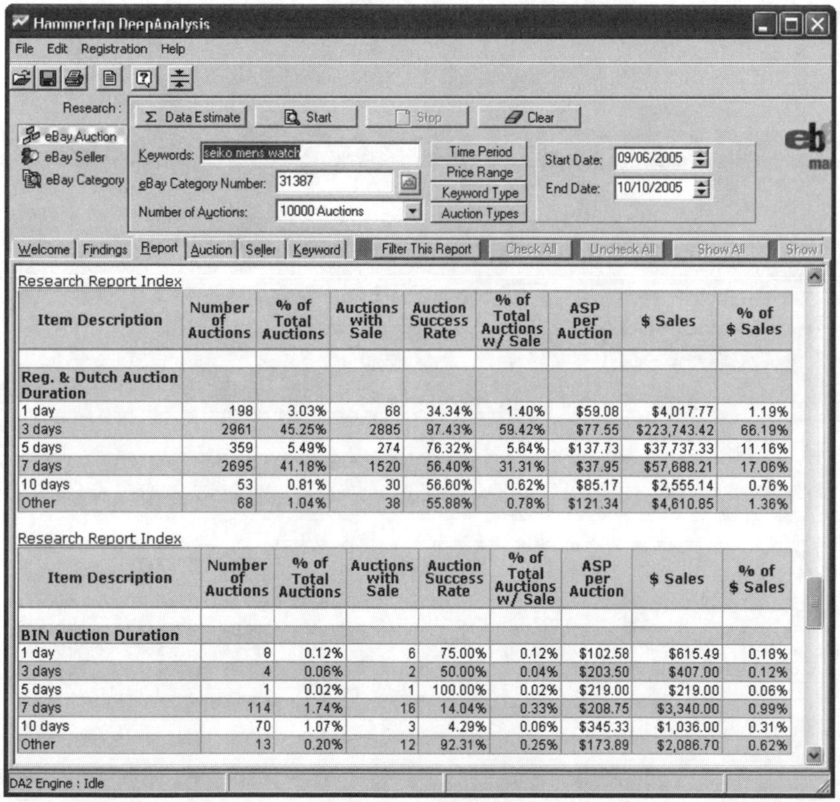

Item Description	Number of Auctions	% of Total Auctions	Auctions with Sale	Auction Success Rate	% of Total Auctions w/ Sale	ASP per Auction	$ Sales	% of $ Sales
Reg. & Dutch Auction Duration								
1 day	198	3.03%	68	34.34%	1.40%	$59.08	$4,017.77	1.19%
3 days	2961	45.25%	2885	97.43%	59.42%	$77.55	$223,743.42	66.19%
5 days	359	5.49%	274	76.32%	5.64%	$137.73	$37,737.33	11.16%
7 days	2695	41.18%	1520	56.40%	31.31%	$37.95	$57,688.21	17.06%
10 days	53	0.81%	30	56.60%	0.62%	$85.17	$2,555.14	0.76%
Other	68	1.04%	38	55.88%	0.78%	$121.34	$4,610.85	1.36%

Research Report Index

Item Description	Number of Auctions	% of Total Auctions	Auctions with Sale	Auction Success Rate	% of Total Auctions w/ Sale	ASP per Auction	$ Sales	% of $ Sales
BIN Auction Duration								
1 day	8	0.12%	6	75.00%	0.12%	$102.58	$615.49	0.18%
3 days	4	0.06%	2	50.00%	0.04%	$203.50	$407.00	0.12%
5 days	1	0.02%	1	100.00%	0.02%	$219.00	$219.00	0.06%
7 days	114	1.74%	16	14.04%	0.33%	$208.75	$3,340.00	0.99%
10 days	70	1.07%	3	4.29%	0.06%	$345.33	$1,036.00	0.31%
Other	13	0.20%	12	92.31%	0.25%	$173.89	$2,086.70	0.62%

FIGURE 6-10 The Regular and Dutch Auction Duration and BIN Auction Duration sections help you determine the optimal duration for your listings.

Sellers Summary and Top Sellers Sections

The Sellers Summary section of the research report shows how many sellers listed items, how many had a successful sales, and the ASP for the items in your search.

NOTE *At the time of this writing, the ASP Per Auction column appears to be showing the ASP per auction listed, not per auction sold. This isn't a helpful number, however, so perhaps Bright Builders will change how this number is calculated. You can get the ASP per auction sold in the Auction Summary section that appears below the Executive Summary section.*

Figure 6-11 shows the Sellers Summary and Top Sellers sections, which also break down data by the *top* ten sellers and by the *bottom* ten sellers. This is intriguing information. The Bottom 10 By No. Of Auctions row is not very interesting, but it's interesting to look at dollar sales (the $ Sales column) for the Bottom 10 By $ Sales row. Then compare it with dollar sales for the top ten sellers. Figure 6-11 shows for our example that the bottom ten sellers earned a total of $63.24, compared to the top sellers' $300,022.48.

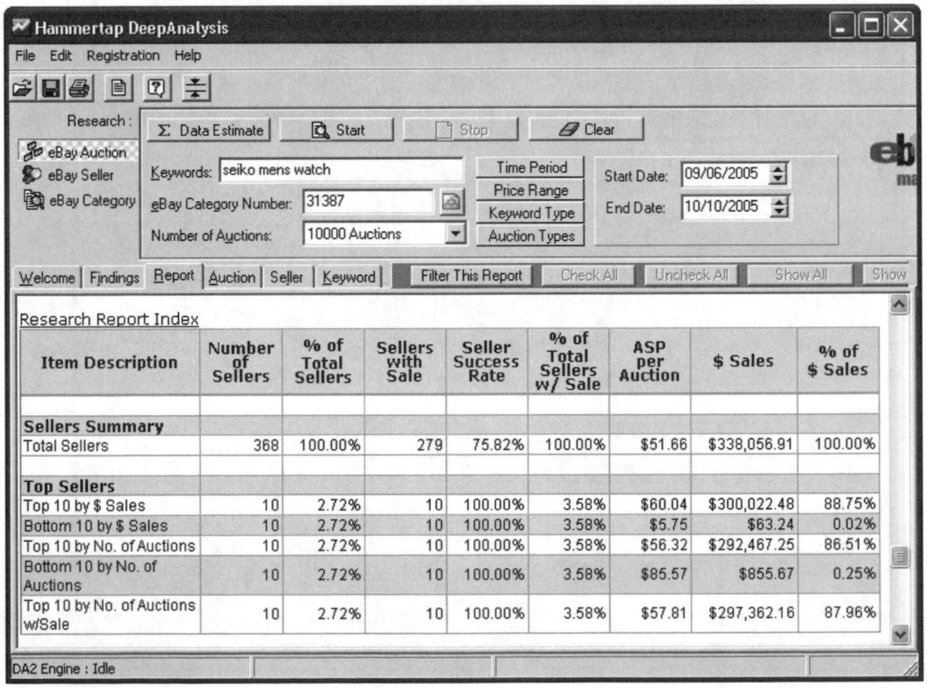

Hammertap DeepAnalysis

Research Report Index

Item Description	Number of Sellers	% of Total Sellers	Sellers with Sale	Seller Success Rate	% of Total Sellers w/ Sale	ASP per Auction	$ Sales	% of $ Sales
Sellers Summary								
Total Sellers	368	100.00%	279	75.82%	100.00%	$51.66	$338,056.91	100.00%
Top Sellers								
Top 10 by $ Sales	10	2.72%	10	100.00%	3.58%	$60.04	$300,022.48	88.75%
Bottom 10 by $ Sales	10	2.72%	10	100.00%	3.58%	$5.75	$63.24	0.02%
Top 10 by No. of Auctions	10	2.72%	10	100.00%	3.58%	$56.32	$292,467.25	86.51%
Bottom 10 by No. of Auctions	10	2.72%	10	100.00%	3.58%	$85.57	$855.67	0.25%
Top 10 by No. of Auctions w/Sale	10	2.72%	10	100.00%	3.58%	$57.81	$297,362.16	87.96%

DA2 Engine : Idle

FIGURE 6-11 The Sellers Summary and Top Sellers sections provide useful summary information for your search results.

It's also interesting to look at the percentage of dollar sales (% Of $ Sales) for the top ten sellers; you may find that the top ten sellers are making up 50 to 80 percent of the total dollar sales for your item. In this example, 2.72 percent of sellers made up 88.75 percent of dollar sales.

It's also interesting to compare the Top 10 By $ Sales row with Top 10 By No. Of Auctions w/Sale (STR) row in terms of ASP. In this case, there isn't much difference—top sellers by dollar sales earned $60.04 ASP per auction compared to $57.81 ASP per auction earned by the top ten sellers by number of auctions with a sale. But if the ASP for the top ten sellers by STR is much lower than that for the top ten sellers by dollar sales, that may indicate that some sellers are flooding the marketplace with a certain type of low-value item; it's certainly worth looking at, and you can go to the Seller tab to do more research.

$ALES STRATEGY   *You can use the Sellers sections to get a competitive picture for the product or category you are reviewing. Top-dollar sellers and top-volume sellers are not mutually exclusive, and it would seem logical that top-volume sellers are top-dollar sellers. Look at the intersection of the Top 10 By $ Sales row and the Percentage Of $ Sales column. You can see the market share for the top ten sellers in terms of dollar sales. If this market share is significantly higher than the market share for top volume sellers (Top 10 By No. Of Auctions w/Sale), it means some of those top-dollar sellers are working smarter and getting more money on fewer sales than the top-volume sellers.*

Auction Tab

The Auction tab shows you a list of the actual eBay listings that make up your search results. Figure 6-12 shows the Seiko watch example. Column headers are hyperlinked, allowing you to sort the list according to the following:

Item (eBay item number)	Title	Total Sales
High Bid	Start Price	Number Of Bids
Quantity Available	Quantity Sold	Reserve Met
Auction Type	Insertion Fee	Upgrade Fee
Final Value Fee	End Date	Duration
End Day	Category 1	Category 2
Top 10 By Sales	Top 10 By Start Price	Top 10 By Number Auctions
Top 10 By Auctions With Sale		

You can click a title and see the actual listing on eBay. eBay does not archive photos with the data, but photos listed using eBay's Picture Services are generally available for 60 days. Reviewing the listings can provide a good reality check to make sure you have developed an effective search strategy. It's always important to look at closed listings when you conduct a search to make sure the results contain relevant listings and to look for anomalies, as discussed in Chapter 2.

	Include	Item	Title	Total Sa ▽	High Bid	Start Price	# of Bids	Quantity Ava	Quantity Sold	Reserve Met	Auction Type	Insertion Fe
1	☑	5039751344	NEW Seiko Sportura Kinetic Chronograph Slvr Mens	$2,660.00	$2,660.00	$100.99	27	1	1	Y	Regular	$2.
2	☑	5034025925	VINTAGE SEIKO LaSALLE MENS 18K SOLID GOLD	$678.00	$678.00	$9.99	25	1	1	Y	Regular	$0.
3	☑	5038571114	Brand New SEIKO Watch SPORTURA Chrono Mens	$519.00	$519.00	$519.00	0	1	1		Buy It Now	$4.
4	☑	5029889275	SEIKO MENS SPORTURA TiCN ALARM CHRONO	$518.00	$259.00	$259.00	0	4	2		Buy It Now	$3.
5	☑	5031290052	SEIKO MENS SPORTURA KINETIC CHRONO COC	$510.01	$510.01	$0.01	14	1	1		Regular	$0.
6	☑	5029986547	SEIKO MENS SPORTURA KINETIC CHRONO COC	$455.00	$455.00	$0.01	11	1	1		Regular	$0.
7	☑	5029986626	SEIKO MENS SPORTURA KINETIC CHRONO COC	$450.75	$450.75	$0.01	14	1	1		Regular	$0.
8	☑	5031289899	SEIKO MENS SPORTURA KINETIC CHRONO COC	$441.00	$441.00	$0.01	21	1	1		Regular	$0.
9	☑	5029917981	SEIKO MENS SPORTURA KINETIC CHRONO COC	$440.00	$440.00	$0.01	14	1	1		Regular	$0.
10	☑	5031289931	SEIKO MENS SPORTURA KINETIC CHRONO COC	$438.00	$438.00	$0.01	13	1	1		Regular	$0.
11	☑	5029986595	SEIKO MENS SPORTURA KINETIC CHRONO COC	$435.00	$435.00	$0.01	10	1	1		Regular	$0.
12	☑	5029986726	SEIKO MENS SPORTURA KINETIC CHRONO COC	$425.00	$425.00	$0.01	27	1	1		Regular	$0.
13	☑	5031290077	SEIKO MENS SPORTURA KINETIC CHRONO COC	$420.00	$420.00	$0.01	17	1	1		Regular	$0.
14	☑	5031290092	SEIKO MENS SPORTURA KINETIC CHRONO COC	$420.00	$420.00	$0.01	12	1	1		Regular	$0.
15	☑	5031289965	SEIKO MENS SPORTURA KINETIC CHRONO COC	$418.00	$418.00	$0.01	18	1	1		Regular	$0.
16	☑	5031290010	SEIKO MENS SPORTURA KINETIC CHRONO COC	$418.00	$418.00	$0.01	12	1	1		Regular	$0.
17	☑	5029986674	SEIKO MENS SPORTURA KINETIC CHRONO COC	$415.02	$415.02	$0.01	36	1	1		Regular	$0.
18	☑	5029986575	SEIKO MENS SPORTURA KINETIC CHRONO COC	$415.00	$415.00	$0.01	20	1	1		Regular	$0.
19	☑	5036808029	SEIKO MENS SPORTURA KINETIC CHRONO COC	$410.00	$410.00	$0.01	23	1	1		Regular	$0.
20	☑	5037438728	SEIKO MENS SPORTURA KINETIC CHRONO COC	$410.00	$410.00	$0.01	23	1	1		Regular	$0.
21	☑	5031290061	SEIKO MENS SPORTURA KINETIC CHRONO COC	$408.99	$408.99	$0.01	11	1	1		Regular	$0.

FIGURE 6-12   The Auction tab lets you see the actual listings that make up the report results. Sorting by column makes this a very useful feature.

If you do find irrelevant listings in your results, DeepAnalysis allows you to filter them out and rerun the report. The Filter feature makes DeepAnalysis a truly powerful research tool. You access the filter by using the Include column. Deselect the listings that don't match the kind of item you are researching—only the listings you want have check marks. Then click the Filter This Report button. In the Main Report tab, you'll see the new statistics for all the listings minus those you've filtered out. You can go back to the list of auctions and add in a few more and take out others and run your report again by clicking the Filter This Report button. You can also click Uncheck All and then choose a more selective group by manually checking the Include box next to each listing you want included.

NOTE   *When you save a report, the list of auctions in the Auction tab is also saved. But remember that since eBay archives auctions for only a few months, you won't be able to click through and view the auction once eBay has removed the listing from its main site.*

Seller Tab

The Seller tab shows you a spreadsheet of data organized by seller. While you can't see the sellers' user IDs, this data can help you get a sense of how many sellers are listing in a higher volume (and helps you answer questions like *Do two sellers dominate the category?*) and whether they are getting higher or lower selling prices and STRs. Figure 6-13 shows that DeepAnalysis assigns each seller a unique identification number, so when you sort the list by different criteria, you can see how a particular seller ranks, even though you don't know the identity of that seller.

The ID number always stays the same, allowing you to track a top seller over time—and, for example, if you study listings on eBay.com, you may be able to figure out who the sellers are if they have unique characteristics. You should also be able to identify your own ID to see how your performance compares to other sellers: since you know the number of items you list, your STR, and ASP, just look up your numbers in the chart and write down your DeepAnalysis Seller number.

	Seller	# of Auctions	% of Total Auctions	Auctions w/Sales	Auction Success Rate	% of Total Auctions w/Sale	ASP/Item	ASP/Auction	Total Sa	% of Total Sales	High Bid	Start
1	AC5BC4B45D	1695	25.90 %	1669	98.47 %	34.38 %	$92.15	$92.26	$153,976.9	45.55 %	$150,902.	$20,
2	DB18245041	1177	17.99 %	1171	99.49 %	24.12 %	$74.14	$74.14	$86,823.46	25.68 %	$85,848.4	$4,
3	C9148781AD	121	1.85 %	81	66.94 %	1.67 %	$156.80	$156.80	$12,701.13	3.76 %	$12,329.9	$11,
4	8D2DF0A1CE	235	3.59 %	173	73.62 %	3.56 %	$71.62	$71.62	$12,390.14	3.67 %	$12,390.1	$8,
5	C58E58E150	175	2.67 %	95	54.29 %	1.96 %	$125.85	$125.85	$11,955.29	3.54 %	$11,955.2	$18,
6	6BBB657DAF	1279	19.54 %	819	64.03 %	16.87 %	$14.31	$14.31	$11,716.91	3.47 %	$11,716.9	$12,
7	213EAFD170	64	0.98 %	41	64.06 %	0.84 %	$101.85	$101.85	$4,175.74	1.24 %	$4,554.26	$3,
8	262875EB40	2	0.03 %	2	100.00 %	0.04 %	$1,455.00	$1,455.00	$2,910.00	0.86 %	$2,910.00	$
9	4EFA52E129	183	2.80 %	53	28.96 %	1.09 %	$32.98	$32.98	$1,747.88	0.52 %	$1,747.88	$5,
10	344156A1A0	66	1.01 %	5	7.58 %	0.10 %	$325.00	$325.00	$1,625.00	0.48 %	$0.00	$28,
11	E048AA2272	53	0.81 %	53	100.00 %	1.09 %	$28.04	$28.04	$1,486.01	0.44 %	$1,486.01	
12	B9EB665B5D	18	0.28 %	18	100.00 %	0.37 %	$76.09	$76.09	$1,369.55	0.41 %	$1,369.55	$
13	6697566E94	12	0.18 %	12	100.00 %	0.25 %	$101.22	$101.22	$1,214.62	0.36 %	$1,214.62	
14	FFE08F8E10	22	0.34 %	18	81.82 %	0.37 %	$55.61	$55.61	$1,001.02	0.30 %	$1,001.02	$
15	AFB42B4C76	37	0.57 %	11	29.73 %	0.23 %	$81.93	$81.93	$901.22	0.27 %	$901.22	$3,
16	E8C6B48FCF	24	0.37 %	7	29.17 %	0.14 %	$128.29	$128.29	$898.00	0.27 %	$898.00	$2,
17	1BC1B5797C	8	0.12 %	4	50.00 %	0.08 %	$181.46	$181.46	$725.85	0.21 %	$367.00	$1,
18	1DFD3DE9C9	2	0.03 %	1	50.00 %	0.02 %	$678.00	$678.00	$678.00	0.20 %	$1,287.55	
19	67FE9A468F	25	0.38 %	14	56.00 %	0.29 %	$44.97	$44.97	$629.52	0.19 %	$629.52	$1,
20	D332F26761	42	0.64 %	11	26.19 %	0.23 %	$50.27	$50.27	$552.96	0.16 %	$552.96	$2,
21	39FA236569	12	0.18 %	7	58.33 %	0.14 %	$78.46	$78.46	$549.19	0.16 %	$885.68	$

FIGURE 6-13 The Seller tab shows a list of seller stats that can be sorted by various criteria. This report is sorted by Total Sales.

Column headings are hyperlinked so you can sort the list according to the following:

Seller	Number Of Auctions	Percentage Of Total Auctions
Auctions With Sales	Auction Success Rate	Percentage Of Total Auctions With Sale
ASP Per Item	Asp Per Auction	Total Sales
Percentage Of Total Sales	High Bid	Start Price
Number Of Bids	Average Number Of Bids	Number Of Items Offered
Number Of Items Sold	Percentage Of Items Sold	

Being able to sort sellers by different criteria can be helpful in better understanding a category. For example, how many auctions does the number one seller in a category list? What is her sell-through rate? How many high-volume sellers are there? What is the best STR average in the category (does anybody get 100 percent sell-through)? These are questions sellers often want to know, and DeepAnalysis can help you answer them.

$ALES STRATEGY *Archive reports for your records. Because DeepAnalysis currently looks only at the latest four weeks' worth of data, conduct searches on a regular basis and save the results. I recommend saving reports once a week. Bright Builders hopes eBay will allow it to let customers combine saved reports in a forthcoming release, so be on the lookout for this functionality.*

Keyword Tab

The Keyword tab shows you a spreadsheet of data organized by *keywords*, which are the words used in listing titles, as shown in Figure 6-14. Just scrolling through the list of words used may be helpful in giving you ideas for keywords to use in *your* listing titles.

$ALES STRATEGY *Use the Keyword report to help you with Basic Listing Strategy #5: Uncover the most effective keywords, covered in Chapter 8.*

Saving Reports

You can save reports, and it's recommended you do this regularly, by choosing File | Save As, or by clicking the floppy disk icon at the top of the page. DeepAnalysis will save the report as a *.da2* file that can be opened at any time.

	Keyword	# of Auctions	% of Total Auctions	Auctions w/Sales	Auction Success Rate	% of Total Auctions w/Sale	ASP/Item	ASP/Auct ▽	Total Sales	% of Total Sales	High Bid	Start
1	SLVR	1	0.02 %	1	100.00 %	0.02 %	$2,660.00	$2,660.00	$2,660.00	0.79 %	$2,660.00	$
2	18K	2	0.03 %	1	50.00 %	0.02 %	$678.00	$678.00	$678.00	0.20 %	$1,287.55	
3	995	3	0.05 %	1	33.33 %	0.02 %	$519.00	$519.00	$519.00	0.15 %	$0.00	$1.
4	LASALLE	3	0.05 %	2	66.67 %	0.04 %	$440.25	$440.25	$880.50	0.26 %	$1,490.05	
5	SNL015	24	0.37 %	22	91.67 %	0.45 %	$419.08	$419.08	$9,219.85	2.73 %	$8,700.85	$1.
6	COCKPIT	35	0.53 %	34	97.14 %	0.70 %	$413.26	$413.26	$14,050.99	4.16 %	$14,050.9	
7	SNL017	14	0.21 %	13	92.86 %	0.27 %	$411.55	$411.55	$5,350.14	1.58 %	$5,350.14	
8	USA	1	0.02 %	1	100.00 %	0.02 %	$358.85	$358.85	$358.85	0.11 %	$0.00	$
9	SHIPPED	1	0.02 %	1	100.00 %	0.02 %	$358.85	$358.85	$358.85	0.11 %	$0.00	$
10	SNL025	3	0.05 %	3	100.00 %	0.06 %	$352.28	$352.28	$1,056.85	0.31 %	$0.00	$1,
11	675	5	0.08 %	2	40.00 %	0.04 %	$349.00	$349.00	$698.00	0.21 %	$0.00	$1.
12	SNL012	16	0.24 %	6	37.50 %	0.12 %	$319.81	$319.81	$1,918.88	0.57 %	$293.88	$10.
13	SPORTURA	137	2.09 %	121	88.32 %	2.49 %	$301.71	$304.20	$36,808.38	10.89 %	$35,253.3	$11.
14	14	2	0.03 %	1	50.00 %	0.02 %	$300.00	$300.00	$300.00	0.09 %	$504.49	$
15	KARAT	2	0.03 %	1	50.00 %	0.02 %	$300.00	$300.00	$300.00	0.09 %	$504.49	$
16	SNL023	5	0.08 %	5	100.00 %	0.10 %	$297.60	$297.60	$1,488.01	0.44 %	$1,488.01	
17	NUGGET	8	0.12 %	3	37.50 %	0.06 %	$285.02	$285.02	$855.05	0.25 %	$1,314.54	$2.
18	SNL009	15	0.23 %	15	100.00 %	0.31 %	$280.40	$280.40	$4,206.02	1.24 %	$4,206.02	
19	10KT	2	0.03 %	1	50.00 %	0.02 %	$280.05	$280.05	$280.05	0.08 %	$280.05	$
20	8IN	2	0.03 %	1	50.00 %	0.02 %	$280.05	$280.05	$280.05	0.08 %	$280.05	$
21	LONG	2	0.03 %	1	50.00 %	0.02 %	$280.05	$280.05	$280.05	0.08 %	$280.05	$

FIGURE 6-14   This Keyword report shows the keywords for listings of *seiko mens watch* in order of ASP per auction. You can sort by other criteria including STR (Auction Success Rate) and number of auctions.

How to Search

As mentioned, DeepAnalysis offers three main Research tools (shown in Figure 6-2). eBay Auction allows you to search by keywords or category or both; eBay Category allows you to search by category (this tool may be gone by the time you read this, since it is redundant); and eBay Seller allows you to analyze your own auctions.

eBay Auction (Keyword and Category Searching)

In the research form (shown in Figure 6-2), type in a search term in the Keywords field. Select the number of auctions from which you'd like to draw data and select a time period. If you wish to narrow the search, you can select a minimum and maximum price and an eBay category number; and you can choose to include eBay Store items in search results.

Once you have outlined your search criteria, click the Start button to start your search.

To clear the form, click the Clear button with the pink eraser icon. This allows you to start over with a new search.

Rather than searching by keyword, you may wish to search an entire category. If so, clear the form, type in your category number, narrow the search by price or to include eBay Store items, and click the Start button. If you don't know the eBay category number, you can click the icon to the right of the eBay Category Number box to browse categories.

You can search by category and keyword using the same form.

eBay Category

This tool is redundant and may be gone by the time you read this book. If you want to search by category, use the eBay Auction tool, as I discussed in the previous section. Bright Builders does not support eBay Category, and you should not use it.

eBay Seller (Analyzing Your Own Sales)

eBay Seller allows you to view a summary of your own auction data. You must know the user ID and password of the account you are searching, effectively restricting the Seller search to your own account(s). This is a restriction eBay has placed on all vendors who license its data.

Tracking your sales data over time can help you gauge your sales progress. You can see all of the data as presented in other DeepAnalysis reports: total auctions, total sales in dollars and volume, ASP per item and per auction, and STR. The report summarizes your data by such criteria as auction type and start and end days.

Save these reports regularly to measure your sales over time. This feature can be useful for sellers with multiple user IDs to compare performance by ID.

Wrapping Up

DeepAnalysis has some quirks, but can also be a very powerful tool. I would prefer to see it as a hosted service to make it faster and more stable. It's a disadvantage if you are only getting a subset of all relevant listings in your research results.

Be sure and make use of DeepAnalysis' filter tool to exclude irrelevant listings from your research results. This is a feature I hope other tools adopt. The ability to sort data in Auction, Seller, and Keyword reports is extremely powerful. You can spend a lot of time studying category data, sorting by various criteria to look for patterns and draw conclusions about effective keywords, competitors, and the like. DeepAnalysis shines in the Seller Tab reports and can provide you with the best information about your competitors among all the eBay-licensed services.

Utilize the resources DeepAnalysis has created, such as FAQs, training, and guides, to make sure you use the tools correctly and thus make better decisions in your eBay business.

Chapter 7

Tracking Shoppers' Movement with Sellathon

One of the most common questions asked by sellers (after "What should I sell?") is "How do I get people to find what I'm selling?" As a seller, your goal is to attract as many shoppers to your items as possible. As you research this topic, you'll quickly learn that everybody shops differently. When consumers go to eBay, some search and some browse. Some shoppers sort items by price, while others peruse auctions that are ending soon, hoping to grab a last-minute bargain. Some shoppers bookmark certain sellers and go directly to their eBay Stores, while others are clicking through eBay from search engines like Google.

Sellers market and advertise their eBay businesses in many ways, including these:

- Search engine optimization (making sure listings show up in search results on sites like Google)
- Paid search using programs like Google AdWords and Yahoo! Search Marketing
- E-mail marketing, often to customers who have purchased from them previously

If you knew how people were finding your items, you could take action to attract even more shoppers. The most savvy eBay sellers are doing just that, and you can, too.

eBay Traffic Reports (Chapter 3) give you some information about buyer shopping behavior, and if you have a Featured or Anchor Store, you'll have access to some pretty comprehensive tracking programs. But for most sellers, it's a bit of a mystery as to why an auction counter shows that one auction listing receives 10 views, while another listing receives 1000 views.

The most successful PowerSellers I interviewed for this book—and the most confident in their approach to eBay selling—were those who took the time to study reports generated by eBay Traffic Reports, Sellathon, and auction-management services, and applied the knowledge they gained to their business to improve sales.

Sellathon's ViewTracker tool gives *all* eBay sellers (not just those with Featured and Anchor stores) the ability to track comprehensive information about the traffic coming to their listings. You can find out from where visitors are coming, whether from Google, eBay search, eBay browse, your own site, or some other method; what search terms visitors entered to find your listing; and how often—and when—they click through to your listings. In later chapters, we'll look at how you can apply this information to your listing and marketing strategies to help you make more money.

Sellathon ViewTracker is one of the most innovative tools introduced for general eBay users, and it is just one of many tools for eBayers that does not go through eBay's API or Developers Program, which eBay created to help it work with companies and individuals that create software for eBay. You can read more about eBay's Developers Program in Chapter 3.

Nonapproved eBay Tools

A company might not join eBay's Developers Program for several reasons. First, it costs money. Second, eBay imposes strict requirements and rules on its developers. Some developers believe they would have to remove valuable functionality from their tools to follow eBay's requirements. Other developers may simply want to cash in on the eBay craze without wanting to be accountable for quality products and services.

You should *always* use extreme caution when signing up for any service on the Internet, and in the case of third-party tools for eBay, this advice holds true, too. With eBay-approved tools such as those covered in Chapter 4, you know that eBay is aware of the tool, though eBay does not guarantee its integrity. (Note that there are differences in eBay vendors—Certified Providers go through a rigorous vetting process, while non-certified vendors do not.)

With tools that haven't been approved by eBay, you are completely on your own. Although you should be extremely careful, you don't necessarily need to avoid all of these tools.

Sellathon is a case in point. It is not a member of eBay Developers Program. Logging into Sellathon does not require your eBay password. Many eBay sellers are using the service and are completely satisfied with the result. So for the sake of providing readers with the most information possible, we'll take a look at tools that are targeted at eBay sellers but operate independently of eBay.

TIP   *Always create a new user name and password when using third-party services; never use the same password you use on eBay, and don't use the same password on multiples sites.*

7

Risks in Dealing with Unknown Auction Services

When using any new company, you need to do your homework to make sure it can provide you with the best possible service. Ask your colleagues, read industry discussion boards, get references from the company, do a search using a service like www.whois.sc to find out how long the company has been around, and speak directly to other customers. In dealing with eBay service providers with whom you are unfamiliar, you may encounter some of the following risks.

- **Poor customer service**   If you experience problems and can't get them fixed, you will lose money if you can't get your listings launched on eBay. Good customer service will save you time, too. Check to see if a company has a discussion forum where customers can report problems and help each other with problems.

- **Insecure site**   You need to determine whether the service provider is keeping your data safe, including your financial information.

- **Poor site stability**   If the service provider has technical issues, this may affect your listings. Make sure it has the financial and technical wherewithal to keep its site stable.

- **Poor management and financial resources**   If your service provider goes out of business, you will have to scramble to find a replacement, and your investment of time and money in the service will be lost.

- **Scams**   Anyone can set up a site, make it look legitimate, and collect personal financial information as part of identity theft scams.

- **Account hijacking**   There's always the possibility that a site can be made to look like it offers helpful eBay tools, but is actually looking for you to reveal your eBay password so unsavory characters can hijack it.

Traffic Data: An Introduction to "Analytics"

While most eBay sellers are familiar with sell-through rates (STRs) and average selling prices (ASPs), most people are not familiar with the term *analytics* (sometimes referred to as *emetrics*). Analytics measure the performance of a website in terms of traffic, transactions, and usability. Before we talk about how Sellathon ViewTracker tracks traffic to eBay listings, you should understand the principles behind traffic-measuring tools.

If you have your own website, perhaps you've looked at your log files to try and figure out where visitors to your site came from, what pages visitors are perusing while on your site, and what time of day is the busiest. Webmasters have everything from simple tools to sophisticated software to help them track such data. Why? To help them answer questions to improve marketing and website usability.

> **NOTE**   *Website usability measures how people navigate and use your site. If people find it difficult to read the text, full of distracting flashing advertisements, and impossible to find what they are looking for, your site has low usability. Jakob Nielsen is the guru of usability and defines it on his website at www.useit.com/alertbox/20030825.html.*

Analytics tools help you measure traffic to your website. But how does this information help you in your quest to make more money on eBay? Analytics tools such as Sellathon ViewTracker can give you answers to the following kinds of questions:

- Which ads are driving traffic to my listings or eBay Store?
- Do my e-mail marketing campaigns result in bidding and purchases?
- Are visitors coming from search engines like Google and Yahoo! or from shopping search engines like Froogle, Shopzilla, and Shopping.com?
- Can I improve the usability and navigation on my eBay Store and listings?
- Can I do a better job of cross-promoting my listings?
- How can I improve conversion rates to turn visitors into bidders and buyers?

Sellathon provides information to help you answer these questions, and it also lets you run tests and analyze data to learn more. Knowing what works and what doesn't can help you figure out where to make improvements to increase sales.

Study Traffic to Increase Your Sales

When I attended an eTail conference in Boston, I found that the largest retailers on the web were all concerned about the same issues and were looking at information found in analytics tools to help them address those issues. While many of the companies were household brands that had been around long before the Internet, they were seeking answers to the same questions any eBay seller would want to know—that is, how do I increase my sales and decrease my marketing costs?

According to some of these large online retailers, the keys to successful e-commerce include the following:

- Improve search and navigation on your site.
- Test your marketing, promotional, and design campaigns.
- Measure and analyze site metrics.
- Collect customer e-mail addresses and send useful information and promotions to those customers.

Information from analytics tools can help you in these areas, and while analytics tools for eBay are different from those for e-commerce sites, the principles are the same. The tools tell you where your traffic is coming from so you can improve your marketing. They also tell you about visitors' behavior to help you improve your site's usability and navigation. Analytics continues to play a prominent role at many conferences; eTail now devotes an entire day of its conference to web analytics.

Conversion Rates vs. Sell-through Rates

Large online retailers are obsessed with improving *conversion rates*. When a visitor comes to an e-commerce website, the company wants to convert him or her from a visitor into a buyer. While this is somewhat similar to the STRs we've been talking about for eBay sellers, there are important differences. E-commerce websites calculate conversion rates by comparing the number of *shoppers* to *sales*, while eBay sellers measure STRs based on number of *listings* to *sales*.

If, for example, 1000 shoppers come to your e-commerce-enabled website, and 20 of them order something, that is a 2 percent conversion rate (20 divided by 1000). The average conversion rate for the e-commerce industry is about 2 to 3 percent. On eBay, if you have 100 listings, and 50 of those listings end with a sale, that's a 50 percent STR. While it would be nice if 1 million people viewed your item, to calculate the STR, it only matters how many people placed winning bids on listings. The eBay STR depends on whether a listing sold on eBay, not on how many people visited the listing.

With a website, if your conversion rates are falling, it doesn't make sense to pump more and more money into getting people to your site, since they aren't buying once they get there. That's part of the reason online retailers track this number so carefully.

Measuring eBay Conversion Rates

eBay sellers may find it useful to measure conversion rates. You can start tracking how many *unique* visitors click through to a listing and compare it to the bidding/buying activity to calculate your own conversion rate. Having a good auction description and presentation should earn you a good conversion rate.

Be careful how you calculate eBay conversion rates, however. You need to know how many *unique* visits your auction gets, not the *total* number of visits. (For example, if you have an eBay listing and you get one bid, and your counter reads 100, it could be that one person clicked 100 times and bid once, rather than that 100 people clicked one time each and only one of them bid. Part of the excitement of auctions is seeing whether anyone is bidding against you, and bidders frequently visit auction listings to see if they have been outbid.)

Sellathon can help you track whether those 100 hits came from one computer or from 100 different computers, though it's not a perfect science (see the next section, "Pitfalls to Analyzing Traffic Data"). Unfortunately, no tool calculates the actual conversion rate for you; you have to do this manually and exclude repeat visits from your counts.

Measuring conversion rates for eBay auctions allows you to compare one group of your listings to another group, so you can test certain listing strategies. However, I like to use STRs, not conversion rates, to measure my overall performance on eBay because STRs have a more direct relationship to fees (I can calculate the listing fees based on the number of listings, while the cost of bringing visitors varies widely) and because STR has been traditionally easier to measure (I know with complete certainty how many listings I have, while the number of unique visitors is generally an estimate).

> TIP *If you have an off-eBay website, track the referring URL (method of arrival) for all traffic coming to that site. Note how many people are coming from your eBay About Me page and other eBay pages. Knowing the number of people coming to your site from eBay will help you measure the effectiveness of eBay as a marketing tool for your non-eBay business.*

Pitfalls to Analyzing Traffic Data

Analytics tools—whether they are designed for e-commerce sites or eBay listings—can differentiate users only by their IP address (Internet Protocol address). This means that, for example, if someone logs in from home on Monday evening and from work on Tuesday morning, each visit will be counted as a unique visitor. The software is not smart enough to know the same person is visiting from two different locations.

In addition, a corporation may have one IP address for all of its employees, while some Internet service providers (ISPs) assign a different IP address every time a person connects to the Internet (AOL does this). Nearly all their users share the same small number of IP blocks, so it's nearly impossible to track unique AOL users.

All these anomalies can throw off your counts of repeat versus unique traffic. The best thing to do is track the data over time and look for trends.

If you are interested in reading more about analytics, a UK-based provider of analytics software for e-commerce websites has written a number of useful articles at www.thinkmetrics .com/articles-about-web-analytics.php. ThinkMetrics articles talk about some of the pitfalls of analyzing traffic data.

Analytics Tools and Resources for E-commerce Websites

Those readers who have their own e-commerce websites might be interested in using non-eBay analytics tools. Two of the most well-known analytics tools for measuring traffic to a website are Omniture's SiteCatalyst (www.omniture.com), which powers the eBay Traffic Reports, and WebTrends (www.webtrends.com). Others services include CoreMetrics (www.coremetrics .com), WebSideStory (www.websidestory.com), ForeSee Results (wwwforeseeresults.com), and Hitwise (www.hitwise.com). The tools these companies provide are strictly for e-commerce sites, not for measuring traffic on eBay.

Key things to measure on a website include traffic, conversion rates, repeat visitors, repeat sales, page "stickiness," and referral information (where traffic is coming from). Analytics tools help you learn about shopper behavior so you can fine-tune your marketing campaigns and improve the navigation and usability of your website design. For example, perhaps customers are abandoning the shopping process on one particular page that could be redesigned to be more user-friendly.

Lots of resources are available to learn more about measuring your traffic and applying the information to your business. If you are selling on eBay exclusively, you many not find it necessary to use these resources. But if you have your own e-commerce site, you should use a tool to track traffic and measure key performance indicators. You can find resources on the following sites.

- **Web Analytics Association (www.webanalyticsassociation.org)**   Association of vendors, marketers, consultants, and trainers involved in the field of web analytics.

- **WebAnalyticsDemystified.com (www.webanalyticsdemystified.com/link_list .asp)**   A page of links to vendors, articles, and more.

- *Buyer's Guide to Web Analytics* **(www.marketingsherpa.com)**   MarketingSherpa .com's guide to buying analytics services, available at the MarketingSherpa Store.

- **Future Now, Inc. (www.futurenowinc.com)**   Web analytics gurus Bryan and Jeffrey Eisenberg's website tells you more about analytics and their services.

7

Why Stickiness Matters

Stickiness refers to how long visitors stay on a website or on a particular web page. If there is compelling content, visitors will stay longer. E-commerce site owners like sticky pages because they feel that the longer a visitor stays, the more likely they are to order something and the more likely they will be to return in the future.

Sellathon ViewTracker

Sellathon (www.sellathon.com) launched its ViewTracker service in October 2003 to provide eBay sellers with traffic data—the same kind of data webmasters use to measure traffic to their own websites. These analytics tools aid in making decisions about website usability and marketing strategies.

Sellathon founder Wayne Yeager said when he decided to sell some of his unwanted gear on eBay in 2002, he was immediately struck by the lack of visitor data and other marketing information available to eBay sellers. As a longtime web entrepreneur and someone who had come to depend on web analytics, Yeager decided to build the tool he wanted to use.

Sellathon's tool was revolutionary when it first launched. At that time, eBay provided no traffic data at all to its sellers, not even storeowners. Some auction-management services such as ChannelAdvisor provided analytics tools for high-volume sellers, but nothing was available for the general eBay seller.

Sellathon generates unique codes that you insert in your eBay listings. These codes allow the ViewTracker tool to track your traffic and generate reports. Sellathon's ViewTracker tool lets sellers see in real-time when visitors arrive, the words they searched to find the listing, which categories they searched in, and how they sorted the results. The tool also allows sellers to see visitors' personal search preferences, whether or not they placed a bid, if they're watching the auction from their My eBay page, and where they live.

The benefit of using analytics tools like Sellathon is it allows sellers to measure the effectiveness of their marketing and advertising campaigns and see which keywords buyers use to shop for items. You can draw conclusions from this kind of traffic data and apply them to your listing and marketing strategies immediately.

Since an eBay seller can insert code into only their own listings, Sellathon customers can track statistics only for their own eBay listings. Data cannot be used for detailed competitive research, but this also means you don't have to worry that your competitors can track *your* auctions.

How Sellathon Works

When you sign up to use the ViewTracker counter, you learn to create a snippet of HTML code that you copy and paste into your auction descriptions (or auction template). The code will not be visible in your listing but causes a counter to appear at the bottom of your auction, as shown in Figure 7-1.

FIGURE 7-1   When you place Sellathon ViewTracker's code in your listing description, you can choose the style of counter you wish to display.

Every time someone visits your listing, it sends data about that visit to your ViewTracker account. ViewTracker then organizes data it tracks into two major sections—Highlights and Details—which you can view to learn more about the traffic visiting your listings.

Sellathon's ViewTracker provides information about each visitor to help you know where the person came from, when they came, if they arrived by searching or browsing, what search terms were used in a search, what search preferences visitors selected, and more. Sellers commonly use Sellathon ViewTracker to measure the effectiveness of all aspects of their listing and marketing techniques, including such things as what keywords to include in titles, when to end an auction, and what features to use in their listings.

The information ViewTracker provides is not only interesting, it can tell you things you can use to improve your presentation and marketing strategies. For instance, if data reveals that many people are limiting their searching only to sellers that accept PayPal, this will help you in any future decisions about whether to keep offering PayPal as a payment option on your listings. You can use ViewTracker to review search terms to see what keywords are most important to include in your listing titles. You'll soon see that you can apply traffic data to your listing and marketing activities in many ways to increase your eBay sales.

Sellathon ViewTracker Navigation

ViewTracker has a simple design and is easy to navigate. At the top right after logging in is a summary containing your name and how long you have been a member, the type of license you have and when it expires, and your Archives status (how long your expired auctions information will be stored on Sellathon's servers). You can purchase an upgrade to extend the archive period by clicking the Upgrade link. (This is recommended.)

Directly under the summary section, you will see a menu bar, and under that are three sections: a traffic graph, a folder menu, and a folder summary, as shown in Figure 7-2.

Organizing with Folders

Sellathon organizes your listings into folders. This not only helps you organize listings—for example, active (live) auctions versus ended (expired) auctions—but it lets you create your own custom folders. Figure 7-3 shows ViewTracker's default General folder containing Live, Expired, and Archive subfolders, and custom folders I created called SKU 99, Store Items, and Auctions.

You can view data from individual auction listings, but you can also view data from all the auction listings in a particular folder. If you create custom folders for certain types of listings, you can compare those types of listings as a whole by comparing the folder data. For example, you might create a folder for all your toy train auctions with a Buy It Now option and another folder for all your toy train auctions that don't use a Buy It Now option. If all other things are equal (same duration, same starting price, same title and description, and so on), you can compare the data from each of the folders to try and gauge which type of listing is most effective.

NOTE   *When you set up custom folders, you must create separate codes for each folder—see the "For Advanced Users: Managing Custom Folders" section a bit later in the chapter.*

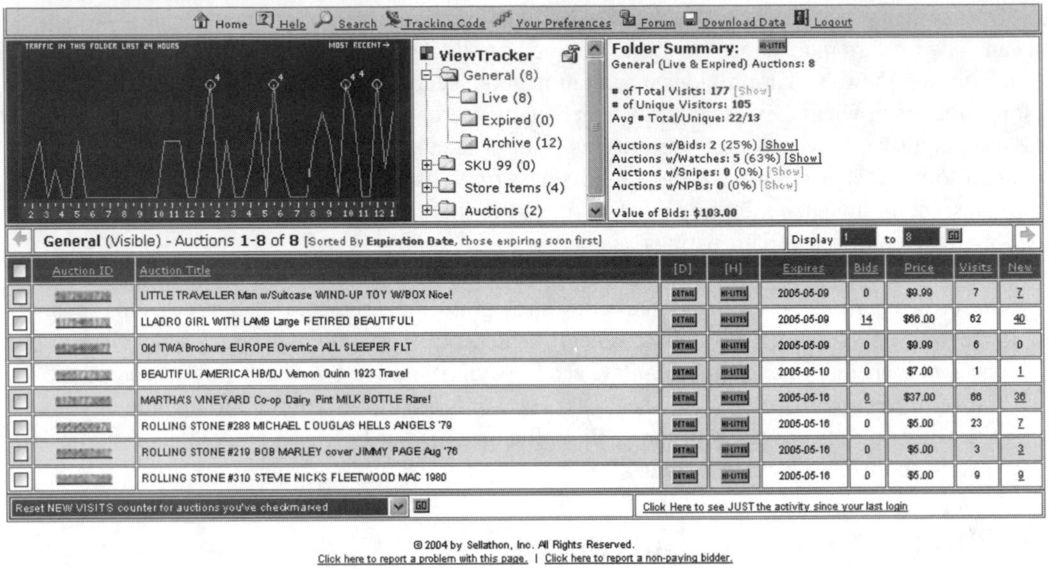

FIGURE 7-2   Sellathon ViewTracker stores listings in folders and allows you to see statistics about a particular auction or all the auctions in a folder.

ViewTracker Menu Bar

The ViewTracker menu bar appears on every page on the ViewTracker website (see Figure 7-2). The menu bar has the following navigation buttons:

- **Home**   Takes you to the home page (the first page you see at login).
- **Help**   Takes you to the Help section for the specific page you're viewing.

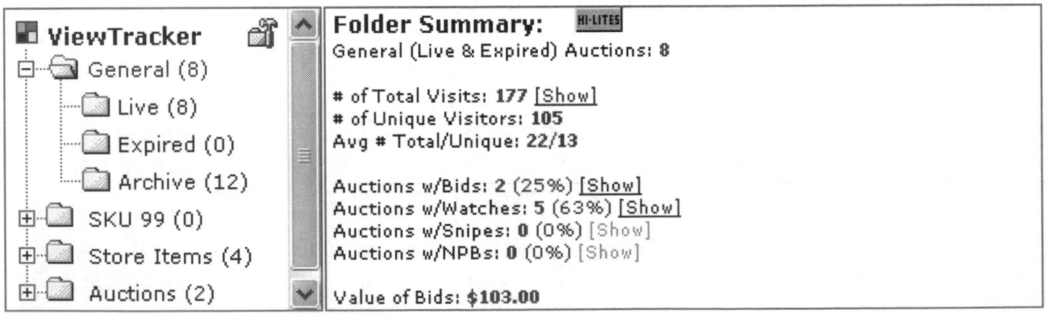

FIGURE 7-3   Folders help you organize different types of listings so you can compare data from each group.

- **Search**   Takes you to the Search page, which allows you to search through all your results using several different methods.
- **Tracking Code**   Takes you to the page where you can copy your Tracking Code and decide which version of the ViewTracker counter you want to use.
- **Your Preferences**   Takes you to the page where your personal information and user preferences are stored.
- **Forum**   Takes you to the Sellathon message boards (anyone can visit the boards, but you must register in order to post a message).
- **Download Data**   Takes you to the Download page, where you can decide which auctions and information fields to include in your CSV download. CSV is a comma-delimited file format that lets you import data into spreadsheet and database applications.
- **Logout**   Logs you out of ViewTracker.

ViewTracker Traffic Graph

The traffic graph shows the most recent 24-hour traffic to your eBay listings, as shown in Figure 7-2. Click a folder, and the traffic graph will change to show traffic to listings in that folder.

ViewTracker Folders

ViewTracker places listings into a set of default folders (General, Live, Expired, and Archive—see Figure 7-3). Clicking a folder will bring up listings in that folder as well as a summary data section that tells you information such as how many total visits came to all of the listings in the folder. You can click any of the listings to see it on the eBay site.

You can go to the ViewTracker Folder Management Page by clicking the small hammer icon within the folder section. Use this page if you want to add, remove, or rename folders, or move listings to a new folder.

ViewTracker Folder Summary

This section, shown in Figure 7-3, shows a list of statistics describing the listings in a particular folder. You can see at a glance how many listings you have running, the total number of visits, total number of unique visitors, and bidding information, such as how many auctions have bids and the number of auctions with watches. (Conveniently, Sellathon always gives raw numbers and percentages.)

NOTE   *You can click ViewTracker in the folder section to go back to summary information about auctions in all of your folders.*

First Things First: Create Tracking Codes

ViewTracker does not require that you enter your eBay password. It allows you, the seller, to place a code in your listings that allows ViewTracker to track the traffic coming to your listings.

Meet a Vendor: Sellathon Inc.

Wayne Yeager founded Sellathon and launched its ViewTracker service in 2003. Wayne said the number one thing his customers are now doing with ViewTracker is optimization: finding the best titles, best days and times to list, best categories to list in, and so forth. He says,

> Discovering how buyers actually find your items is probably the most revealing and instantly beneficial service that we provide. Plus, it starts you on the path of understanding that eBay is, at its core, a search engine. So once you see for yourself how your potential buyers are using that search engine, you have a pretty good advantage over those sellers who are still basing their listings on guesswork and old wives' tales.

Wayne believes that at the very highest level, "auction metrics" is not hugely different from "web metrics" and that the key concept for online auction sellers is how much are you paying for your visitors versus how much are those visitors worth to you.

Every eBay seller should be tracking the cost of bringing visitors to listings—metrics that include eBay's listing fees, final value fees, and listing upgrade fees (such as bold titles, purple highlights, and so on). According to Wayne,

> The goal should be to get the highest number of interested visitors to your items for the least amount of money. Since listing fees and final value fees are basically sunk costs, the game is to tweak the stuff that's essentially free—your title, your listing times, your description, your photos, your starting price, etcetera—to attract more visitors, more bidders and hopefully, more money.

As for eBay sellers who are so busy they aren't sure data analysis is right for them, Wayne says, "If someone is so busy that they can't spend 10 or 15 minutes a day in strategic thought, then something's broken. It sounds like the business is running them, not the other way around."

Sellathon, Inc.
200 East Reynolds Road, Suite 12
Lexington, KY 40517
www.sellathon.com
Telephone: 859-272-2467
Customer Support: support@sellathon.com

TIP *Put the ViewTracker code in your listings as soon as possible; otherwise, ViewTracker will have no data and will be useless to you. You can add the code to your template so it will automatically appear in each new listing you create.*

To create the tracking code to insert in your eBay listings, click Tracking Code in the menu bar. Then complete the following four steps:

1. Select the type of counter you want to display in your listings.

2. Leave the default setting in place unless you want to create custom folders.

3. Leave the affiliate fields blank unless you participate in the affiliate program.

4. Copy the resulting code into your listing descriptions.

Any time you make a change in steps 1 through 3, the code in step 4 is automatically modified to reflect that change. This allows you to run eBay listings with different ViewTracker codes, which can help you test various selling strategies.

ViewTracker Reports: Highlights Page

The statistics summaries by folder can be quite useful, but to get to the heart of ViewTracker data, look for the Hi-Lites links, which take you to the Highlights page. You can view data by folder or by individual listing.

To view data by folder, look at the top Folder Summary section, where you will see a Hi-Lites link. Clicking this link will take you to the report page, which has three tabs: Visitor Data, Arrival Methods, and Search Terms.

You can also view data by individual listing. When you are viewing a folder, you'll see the individual listings at the bottom of the page. The fifth column contains Hi-Lites links. Click the Hi-Lites button next to a listing, and you will be taken to the report page for this listing.

Visitor Data Tab

The Visitor Data tab (the default view when clicking the Hi-Lites link) displays six sections. Figure 7-4 shows the first five sections.

- ■ **Hourly Visitors** Shows you when traffic is coming to your listings.
- ■ **Most Active Date** Shows you traffic data by date.
- ■ **Comparative Analysis** Compares certain metrics of listings in the folder you are viewing with listings in all live auctions. Metrics include number of unique visitors and number of repeat visitors.
- ■ **Most Active Day of the Week** Shows you at a glance on which day of the week most traffic arrives.
- ■ **Top 10 Visitors** Shows you the IP address of the top visitors to your listings in the folder selected.
- ■ **Top 5 Browsers, Operating Systems & Resolutions** Shows you which browsers, operating systems, and resolutions visitors to your listings are using.

7

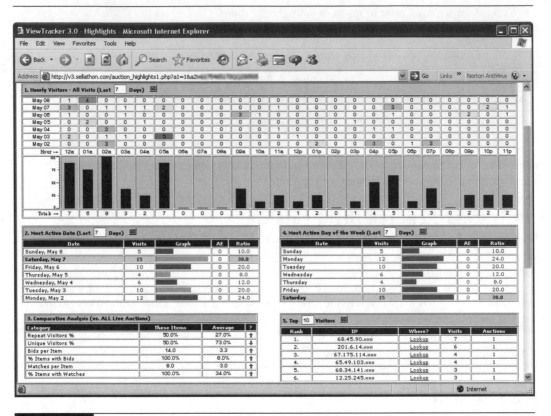

FIGURE 7-4   The Visitor Data tab in Sellathon's Highlights page shows you detailed statistics about traffic to your listings.

$ALES STRATEGY   *Use the Visitor Data tab in the Highlights page to help you with Basic Listing Strategy #1: Find the best time to end an auction (Chapter 8). You can view traffic by hour and by date.*

Many sellers believe they get the most bidding activity in the last minutes of an auction. Therefore, they want their auctions to end when there the most people are online. On a folder or individual listing Highlights page, you can see reports of when your auction(s) got the most visits: one report is by date, and the other is by day of the week.

Take into account when your listings ended when looking at this data, since it can affect the results. (This is because eBay sorts results by ending time.) For example, if your auction ended on a Sunday evening, and that's when your auction got the most traffic, you should run another test. Try seeing whether Sunday evening is still the most popular time to visit your listings if they end on a Wednesday.

Arrival Methods Tab

You can see at a glance whether most visitors to your listings were searching a category, searching all of eBay, had the listing stored in their My eBay, came from a cross-promotion, and much more. Figure 7-5 shows the detailed information revealed to sellers about how eBay shoppers are finding their listings, much of which eBay itself does not make available to sellers. You can quantify what percentage of visits were sorted by auctions ending first versus newly listed or by price, for example.

$ALES STRATEGY *Use Sellathon's Arrival Methods tab on the Highlights page to help you with your marketing strategies. Knowing where traffic is coming from can help you with Marketing Strategy #3: Improve your advertising and publicity (Chapter 10).*

| FIGURE 7-5 | The Arrival Methods Tab in Sellathon's Highlights page shows sellers exactly how shoppers are finding their listings on eBay. |

For example, ViewTracker has a method of arrival called Direct Link Via Email. You can monitor how this number changes after you send out an e-mail marketing newsletter that links directly to your listings to try and gauge the success of the e-mail campaign. Using this example, you could also measure traffic by date in the Visitor Data tab to see if traffic increased on the day you sent out the newsletter. We'll talk about more options for measuring the success of your marketing campaigns in Chapter 10.

Six sections appear in the Arrivals Methods tab:

- **Top 5 Methods Of Arrival**   Shows where most traffic to your listings is coming from. In Figure 7-5, you can see the number one method of arrival for this auction was Searching All Of eBay, and the number two method of arrival was Searching Category.

- **All Methods Of Arrival**   Shows where all traffic to your listings is coming from.

- **Top 5 Most Popular Categories Browsed**   Shows which categories visitors were *browsing* when they found your listings. In Figure 7-5, you'll see the category numbers listed; click the lookup to see the actual name of the category.

- **Top 5 Most Popular Categories Searched**   Shows which categories visitors were *searching* when they found your listings.

- **Most Popular Sorting Methods**   Shows how visitors had sorted eBay listings results when they found your listings (that is, newly listed versus ending today).

- **The 5 Most Common Page #s Users Found**   When eBay shoppers browse or search, they are presented with search results that most often than not exceed one page in length. ViewTracker can tell which page of the search results your listing was on when the visitor found your listing.

> **$ALES STRATEGY**   *Use the Top 5 Most Popular Categories Browsed and Top 5 Most Popular Categories Searched sections in Sellathon's Arrival Methods tab to help you with Basic Listing Strategy #4: Locate the best category (Chapter 8).*

Search Terms Tab

The Search Terms tab contains two sections, as shown in Figure 7-6. The first section, Search Type, shows you whether visitors who found your listings by searching were searching Titles Only, or were searching Titles & Descriptions. Note that eBay's default search method is Titles Only.

The second section, Top 10 Search Terms Used To Find Your Auction(s), contains the actual search terms, or keywords, visitors entered when they conducted the search that led them to your listings. You should expand to find all of the search terms visitors used and try to include as many as possible in your listings, saving the most critical for listing titles and remembering to put the others in the description—without violating eBay's Keyword Spamming policy, of course, which was explained in Chapter 2.

It takes a bit more effort to figure out the words people are using to search for items like yours but are *not* finding you because you are not including those words in your listings. Run some tests that vary the titles of your auctions, like substituting the plural of a word instead of the singular, or using synonyms (*vintage* versus *old* versus *antique*) and see which ones do better.

FIGURE 7-6 Sellers of all levels will find the Search Terms tab to be one of the most useful in helping them improve listing titles to drive more traffic to their auctions.

Sellathon created a new service in the summer of 2005 called SellerPower (www.sellerpower .com). Sellers enter a word such as *duck*, and SellerPower comes back with search terms related to that word. You can choose the most popular search terms, depending on what you are selling, of course (you would choose a different set of words depending on if you were selling duck decoys or rubber duckies). Sticking with the duck example, SellerPower comes back with a list of search terms when you enter the term *duck*; here are the top ten:

- duck
- rubber ducks
- rubber duckie
- ducky
- ducks
- duck bathroom
- Oregon Ducks
- duck shower curtain

Learn from Others: Data Tops Circuit City's Shopping List

Tim Reilly heads up Circuit City's Direct Fulfillment & Trading Circuit program, which liquidates items on eBay for the Circuit City retail chain. Tim uses a number of tools to help him measure and improve the performance of his eBay liquidation program.

Circuit City is a leading specialty retailer of brand-name consumer electronics, personal computers, and entertainment software, with 612 Circuit City Superstores and five mall-based stores in the U.S. and a website at www.circuitcity.com. It has been selling items on eBay since May 2004.

Tim said the Trading Circuit Team uses a program called AuctionIntelligence* from Certes to help them measure the success of Circuit City's liquidation program on eBay and to understand their share of the market in key categories, identify their top competitors, and find ways to improve listing strategies.

The team uses Sellathon ViewTracker to get information on what is driving visits and views, though Tim said it would be much more useful if it captured the eBay user ID, not just a partial IP address.

Tim said ViewTracker visitor data helps identify prime times for auctions to close and the best keywords to use in titles. "We are in the process of hiring an 'auction merchandiser' to help with creating the best listings possible—everything from titles, to cross-promotions, to search terms, to look and feel, to listing strategies."

Tim was excited when Sellathon introduced SellerPower in 2005. "SellerPower answers one of my chief complaints about View Tracker's keyword tool—knowing what words people have used to find *my* listings is only somewhat useful, knowing what words they use to find *other* people's listings is much more powerful.

"We expect that Sellathon's ViewTracker and SellerPower applications will play a huge role in helping us get the maximum visibility of our auctions."

---

*This book does not profile AuctionIntelligence by request of Certes, who said it is not actively marketing the service and is supporting only current customers.

 rubber duckies

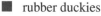 duck hunting

SellerPower draws upon the auctions containing ViewTracker codes used by sellers who are trying out Sellathon's 30-day free-trial offer. It creates a database of the most popular keywords and search phrases used by eBay visitors to those free-trial ViewTracker auctions.

So while SellerPower does not draw from every single eBay auction—only from those listings placed by sellers trying out Sellathon—the search terms are real, since those auctions with ViewTracker's code are capturing real-live eBay-shopping traffic patterns. Use SellerPower as a directory of words to consider trying in your eBay titles, and measure the results with Sellathon ViewTracker.

Figure 7-6 is interesting because it reveals that a number of shoppers used the word *with* in their keyword searches. As any eBay seller knows, the title field is valuable real estate—a seller has only 55 characters to describe an item and put in the most important keywords he or she thinks a shopper will use to find an item. (This is confirmed on the same Sellathon report. Look again at Figure 7-6 and see that 37 out of 38 searchers used Title only searches.)

This seller could easily have decided to leave out the word *with*—even in this context—and replace it with something she thought was more important. In this case, it looks like the word *with* was even more important than the word *retired*, at least in terms of raw numbers. Only two searches used the word *retired* as a keyword, while three searches used the word *with*.

The actual title of this auction was, "Lladro Girl with Lamb Large Retired Beautiful!" Knowing that no one searched the term *beautiful* might make this seller look for more targeted words in future listings. You could make a case that the word *beautiful* was what inspired people to visit the auction, but why guess—run tests with and without such superlatives, and use Sellathon to see which listings do better.

$ALES STRATEGY *Use Sellathon's Search Terms tab in the Highlights page to help you with Basic Listing Strategy #5: Uncover the most effective keywords (Chapter 8). You can also use it to help you formulate keywords if you participate in paid-search marketing, covered in Marketing Strategy #3: Improve your advertising and publicity in Chapter 10.*

ViewTracker Reports: Detailed Visitors Log Pages

ViewTracker Highlights pages summarize a lot of information, but to dig into the details, go to the Detailed Visitors Log pages. You can get there by clicking a folder, then clicking the Detail button of the listing you want to review.

Figure 7-7 shows the Detailed Visitors Log page for an auction of a milk bottle from the Martha's Vineyard Co-op Dairy. It shows the last 10 visits to the listing. At the top, it summarizes information so you can see that this listing had 69 visitors, 37 unique visitors, 6 bids, and 10 watches (users click Watch this Item, and the item appears in their My eBay page). It also shows that the average time spent viewing the listing was 23 seconds, and Sellathon detects 0 snipes have been placed on the auction.

Advanced Users: How Sellathon Knows Length of Visits

When you're browsing the Internet, changing from one URL to the next is an event that can usually be detected by the JavaScript command `onUnload`. Before new content can be loaded, the old content has to be unloaded. Sellathon's script checks for that command, and when it detects an `onUnload`, it notifies Sellathon of the time. By comparing the time when the page was loaded with the time the page was unloaded, Sellathon knows the amount of time a visitor spent on the page.

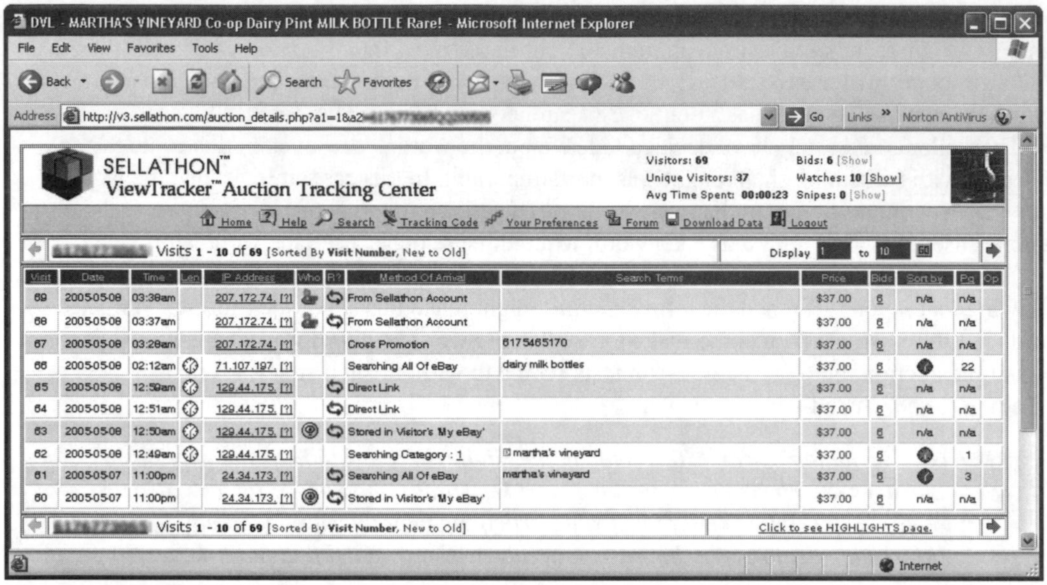

FIGURE 7-7   Sellathon ViewTracker's Detailed Visitors Log page allows you to see each visit to your auction and when and how they arrived there.

Several columns of information appear in the Detailed Visitors Log page:

■ **Visit**   Visit number.

■ **Date**   Date of visit (you can set your time zone in the preferences section).

■ **Time**   Time of visit.

■ **Len**   Length of time page was viewed; a clock icon indicates ViewTracker was able to gather this information—place your mouse over the clock, and a small box pops up with the length of time the item was displayed on the visitor's screen (maximum time is 10 minutes).

■ **IP address**   IP address of the visitor minus the last four sets of numbers to protect the privacy of the visitor. Clicking the IP Address shows you all the visits that this IP address has made to this item, and clicking the question mark (?) icon will cause a box to pop up with an indication of the geographic location of the visitor.

■ **Who**   Tracks flags that eBay sends of some type (watch placed, high bidder, auction owner, losing bidder, and so on). You can use this to see which visits are yours, and which visitors are watching your auctions in their eBay account. One of the icons indicates that the visitor placed a snipe bid on the auction.

■ **R?**   The blue and red arrows indicate a repeat, not a unique, visitor.

- **Method Of Arrival**   Where the visitor came from (for example, visitor number 67 came from a cross-promotion link, while visitors 64 and 65 came from a direct link to this listing).

- **Search Terms**   What search terms were used to find the auction. If the visitor searched titles and descriptions instead of titles only, a small *D* will appear to the left of the search terms. You can see that visitor number 66 entered the search term *dairy milk bottles* to find this listing.

- **Price**   Indicates the price of the auction when the visitor arrived at the listing.

- **Bids**   Indicates number of bids the auction had received when the visitor arrived.

- **Sort By**   How the visitor sorted the results.

- **Pg**   The page number on which the item was found.

- **Op**   eBay options—ways visitor sorted and/or searched using eBay's special options, such as show Item Near a Specific Zip Code, or Show Gift Items.

You can click the Help icon when viewing the Detailed Visitors Log page and scroll down to get an explanation of the column heads and the types of data included in each column.

7

Learn from Others: Afternoon Delight—Shopping from Work

Tim Reilly is in a fairly unique position compared to other eBay sellers: he has access to sales data from Circuit City's website. Tim reviews the traffic and sales reports from CircuitCity.com to see when people are shopping online.

Tim said that while people like to point to 7 P.M. to 11 P.M. Eastern Time as the best time to end listings, because that is the highest traffic time, the CircuitCity.com hourly sales reports showed that lunch time (11 A.M. to 4 P.M. ET) is also a popular shopping time. He ran tests to see whether data from new-product sales on the retailer's own website would translate into liquidation items on eBay, and he used Sellathon and sales reports to measure the effects of midday auction ending times.

The results revealed that people shopping at lunch are not "browsing," they are "shopping," with higher incremental bid amounts per bid due to using eBay's Proxy Bid feature. (With proxy bids, when you place a bid on eBay, you enter the maximum amount you'd be willing to pay for the item. The eBay system places bids on your behalf whenever you are outbid, using only as much of your bid as is necessary. Your proxy bid is kept private from other users.)

"We are starting to look a level deeper at the trends to determine if certain products do better at different times, etc. It'll take a while to get enough data to make a good determination, but we'll get there." Tim said he uses reporting tools in all of the services he uses, like Kyozou and MyStoreCredit.com, to help him determine their effectiveness and his ROI from using them.

Tim plans to continue to grow Circuit City's eBay liquidation program with a third and possibly a fourth distribution center, a facelift to his eBay Store, and some other innovative programs, which, of course, he'll analyze with data-tracking tools.

$ALES STRATEGY *Look in ViewTracker's Method of Arrival column for the words* Product Finder. *If you find a visitor who used Product Finder to locate your listing, you can hold your mouse over the codes in the Search Terms column and a pop-up box appears to give you more information. This can help you with Basic Listing Strategy #4: Locate the best category (Chapter 8), which includes whether or not to use Item Specifics in your listings. You can also scroll over the OP column, which reveals whether shoppers used search and sort options such as Show Items from a Specific Seller.*

For Advanced Users: Managing Custom Folders

You can create custom folders in ViewTracker. Let's say you want to analyze traffic by product SKU number or some other criteria.

You can have ViewTracker sort auctions into custom folders by going to Your Preferences and looking in the Smart ViewTracker Options section. You can choose to have ViewTracker sort auctions into folders by the following criteria:

- eBay Category
- Auction Starting Date
- Auction Ending Date
- Words in Auction Title
- Auction vs. Store Items

Figure 7-8 shows the Smart ViewTracker Option section in Your Preferences. Sorting listings by eBay category or by auction versus store items can be very useful. You might want to compare the performance of the categories in which you sell, for example, or compare traffic to your auction listings versus your store listings.

First you must create the custom folders. Do this by going to the ViewTracker Folder Management Page by clicking the small hammer icon within the folder section seen in Figure 7-2 (you can see a close-up view of the folder section in Figure 7-3).

Once you have created the customer folder, you must create a special Tracking Code. Sellathon recommends only experienced users try this feature. I agree—wait until you have used Sellathon ViewTracker enough to feel like you have moved beyond the beginner stage. But definitely use it to test different approaches to your listings, such as choosing the most effective category for your listings.

We saw earlier how to create Tracking Codes by clicking on Tracking Code in the menu bar. In step 2, instead of choosing the default selection, Do Not Override My Default Folder Settings, select the second radio button, Experienced Users Only: Override The Default Folder Settings On My User Preferences Page And Place Auctions Containing This Tracking Code In The Following Folder.

```
SMART VIEWTRACKER™ OPTIONS:

When ViewTracker™ starts, load...
  ⦿ ViewTracker™ Data Summary
  ○ Main ViewTracker™ Page with:
      ☐ LIVE auctions
      ☐ EXPIRED auctions
    from [General ▼] folder.
  ○ ViewTracker™ Highlights with:
      ☐ LIVE auctions
      ☐ EXPIRED auctions
    from [General ▼] folder.

ViewTracker's™ "Smart Sort" feature
can automatically sort new incoming
auctions into appropriate folders...
  ○ By eBay® Category
  ○ By Auction Starting Date
  ○ By Auction Ending Date
  ○ By Words in Auction Title
      [   Word Sorting Rules   ]
  ○ Auction vs Store Items
  ⦿ Do not automatically sort
```

FIGURE 7-8   Go into Your Preferences to have ViewTracker sort your listings into folders organized by criteria such as category or auction ending date, or to stop it from automatically sorting your listings.

You'll then be asked to select the folder from the pull-down menu, so find the custom folder you created for this purpose and select it. As soon as you choose the right folder, your tracking code will be dynamically altered to reflect that change.

Now when you insert the Tracking Code in your listings, use the custom code only for the auctions you want placed in your custom folder. Any auction containing this code will be placed in the folder you selected from the drop-down menu when you created your code and will override any settings you have chosen on the Your Preferences page.

If you have created five custom folders for your five product lines, for example, remember to use the correct corresponding code when placing the ViewTracker code in your listings. In other words, each folder should have its own code, but you can use the same code in all of the listings of a given folder.

Using Folders to Manage Multiple eBay User IDs

You can use ViewTracker folders to manage multiple eBay user IDs. Most sellers use at least two eBay user IDs for various reasons (one for buying, one for selling; or one ID for each product line or category in which they sell). I recommend you set up special user IDs to test out various selling strategies. Some tests you conduct work better with two comparable IDs than with using one user ID.

ViewTracker doesn't have an automatic option to sort by user ID because eBay doesn't broadcast that information. It's up to you to set up custom folders, and then use different ViewTracker codes for each user ID as explained earlier.

Understanding ViewTracker's Tracking Methodology

Sellathon's servers receive auction data only at the moment a visitor views your auction. This means your auctions won't show up in ViewTracker at all until someone has actually gone onto eBay and clicked your listing to view it.

This also means that when you look at ViewTracker data for an auction that is showing up, the data on the Highlights and Detailed Visitors Log pages may not be completely up-to-date.

TIP   *Before looking at ViewTracker reports for active listings, make sure you have viewed each of your active listings to refresh the data. You need to do this only once for closed listings, since you care about traffic to your listings only while they are active.*

Let's say you know you have a bid on an auction, but the bid isn't showing up on ViewTracker. Sellathon's servers have no way of knowing the status of the auction until the next visitor comes along and views your auction, unless the bidder goes back and views the listing after placing the bid. Always go into your auctions and view them yourself before doing in-depth analysis on your listings. This can be an inconvenience or a major headache, and it's something I hope that Sellathon will come up with a solution for before long.

TIP   *Sellathon has a community forum where you can ask questions. Recent discussions include strategies on applying Sellathon data to improve sales, how to figure out the most popular time of day for listings, and technical questions about ViewTracker codes and how to download ViewTracker data. To access the forum, go to Sellathon's home page and click Community at the top of the page.*

Downloading Data

You can download ViewTracker data in CSV files and import the data into spreadsheet programs. This allows you to generate your own custom reports with just the information you want and track data over time so you can look for seasonal patterns and category trends, for example.

On the menu bar, click Download Data. This link takes you to the Download Data page, where you can decide which auctions and information fields to include in your CSV download. (CSV is a comma-delimited file format that lets you import data into spreadsheet and database applications.)

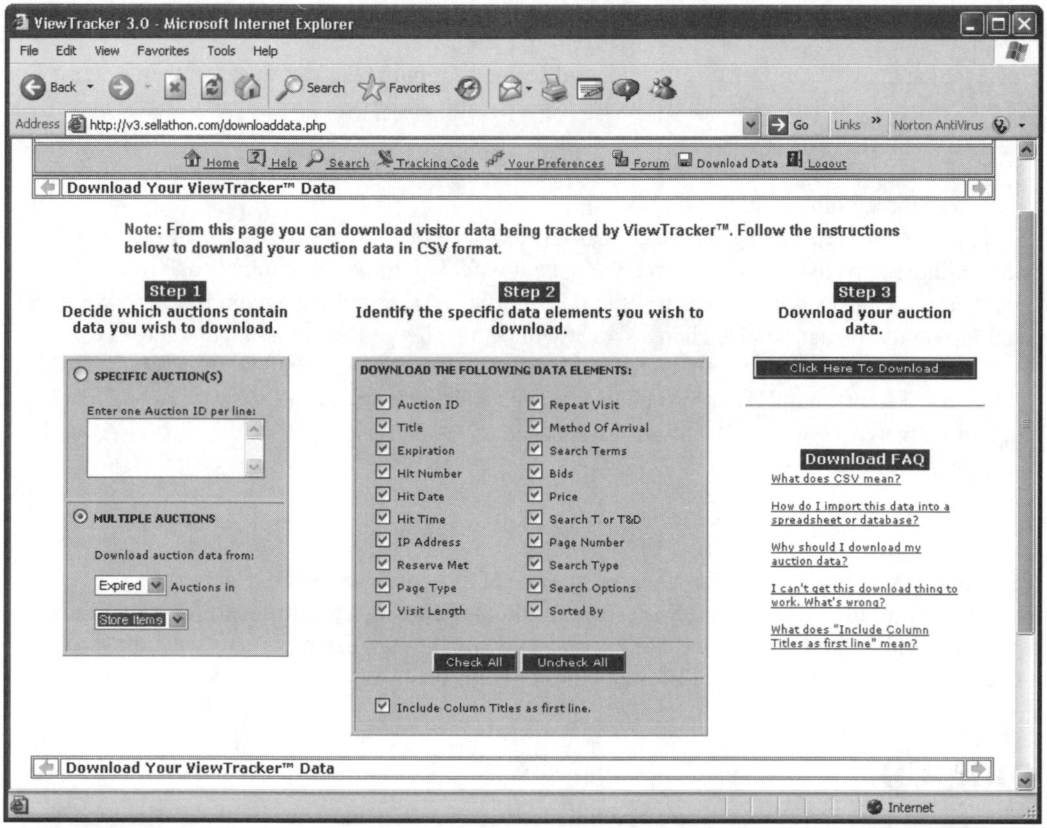

FIGURE 7-9 Tell ViewTracker which listings you want to download, which fields you want to include, and then click the Download button.

Figure 7-9 shows step 1 of the download procedure, where you can specify which listings you want to download (one listing, all listings, all expired listings, or all live listings) and from which folder (all folders or one particular folder). In step 2, you can indicate which fields you want to include in the download, and then initiate the download procedure in step 3. Once you have downloaded the data, you can open the file in your application.

If you're new at downloading ViewTracker data, leave Include Column Titles As First Line checked (in step 2). Then when you open the data in a spreadsheet application such as Microsoft Excel, the column names will appear at the top of each column (Date, Time, IP Address, and so on) so you know exactly what the data in each column is.

Traffic-Tracking Reports from Auction-Management Services

We looked at analytics tools for measuring traffic and shopping behavior at e-commerce sites, and we looked at Sellathon, an analytics tool specifically designed to track eBay traffic and shopper behavior.

eBay Traffic Reports and Sellathon's ViewTracker tool are the only eBay-centric analytics tools worth mentioning as of this writing.

However, auction-management services (AMS) have many reporting tools for the eBay seller. Hundreds of listing tools are out there, so it would be impossible to list each one. You should ask *your* AMS if it provides tools to track traffic and shopping behavior. If your AMS is geared to multi-channel selling, chances are it will be tracking traffic across all marketplaces.

You can look for auction-management services in several places, including eBay Solutions Directory (http://solutions.ebay.com) and Auction Software Review (www .auctionsoftwarereview.com), a subscription-based review service.

Sellathon archives data only for a certain amount of time, so it behooves you to save your data to your own computer on a regular basis. You might also consider printing certain ViewTracker reports and keeping them in a binder. For example, you might organize reports by category, so you can refer to them as you are listing different types of items on eBay.

Wrapping Up

A whole new generation of reporting capabilities for eBay sellers has opened up. Sellers who see the value in the kinds of information analytics tools provide continue to experiment on ways to apply it to their own businesses, pushing the envelope to give them a competitive edge.

Expect to see more tools, more features, and more options in the area of traffic-tracking tools. We'll talk in more detail about how to apply traffic data information to your listings and strategies in the next three chapters, and we'll meet some PowerSellers who are spending hours every week reviewing data and using it to improve their businesses.

Part III

Putting eBay Data to Work

Chapter 8

Basic Listing Strategies: Make More Money on Every Transaction

Some people are convinced that Sunday evenings are the best time to end an eBay auction. Others believe weekday afternoons are the best times. Others think it doesn't make a bit of difference to your selling price what day or time your auction ends.

Think of the amazing selection of items you can purchase on eBay—from iPods to Lionel trains, McCoy pottery to Chanel pocketbooks, commercial stoves to Toyota trucks—and you can begin to understand why it's difficult to make generalizations about when is the best time to end an auction on eBay. Now imagine that you could use a resource to see which ending days and times were most effective in the last few weeks for the type of items you are selling, or whether ending day had any effect at all. Imagine that you could use tools to track this information over time for your own eBay listings. You could confirm your own gut feelings, and you could see whether ending dates and times made a difference depending on what kinds of items you were selling.

The tools reviewed in Chapters 3–7—from eBay reports to market-data tools to traffic-tracking software—can help you better understand the dynamics of eBay and help you predict future buyer behavior. Every decision you make about your eBay business can be aided by the information you mine from eBay's market data and what you learn about your own past sales performance. You can use this information to increase traffic to your listings, increase sell-through rates (STRs), and earn more money.

In this chapter, we review basic listing strategies, such as learning when to end an auction and uncovering the most effective keywords to include in your listing title. You'll learn how to improve your listings to increase traffic, bids, sell-through, and selling prices.

Making better decisions about basic and advanced listing features will help you increase selling prices and STRs. We'll review the five Basic Listing Strategies in this chapter:

- Find the best time to end an auction.
- Determine optimal auction duration.
- Choose the most profitable starting price.
- Locate the best category.
- Uncover the most effective keywords.

We will discuss the various approaches to optimizing your listings. Then we'll review the tools we discussed in previous chapters and learn which ones work best in determining the techniques to use in your listings.

Start with a Strategy Game Plan

You should create a "game plan" for applying what you learn in this book to your business operations. Read this chapter and make sure you understand the basics. You may believe you have already perfected some of the listing strategies discussed in this chapter, so concentrate on those areas you think you can improve right away. But don't assume you can't improve your current methods. It's amazing how fine-tuning even minor elements of an auction listing can net significant returns.

We'll see how Silver, Gold, Platinum, and Titanium PowerSellers are using market-data tools, eBay Sales and Traffic reports, and traffic-tracking tools to study the data and improve their listings. Silver PowerSeller Bobby Minnich (bobby131313) spends 10 to 12 hours a week studying his data. But it's *applying* what he learns from the data that sets this seller apart. He uses the data to improve his listings, and he can see the payoff in reports (and in his bank account).

The point of reviewing market and historic sales data is to determine whether you can improve your sales, and it should become a routine part of your activities. Only you can decide which reports are most important and how often you should review them. Realistically, you can't study each piece of data on a daily basis or you will get mired in details. However, don't think reviewing data is not a good investment of your time. It's typical for PowerSellers who use eBay-data tools to think of the hours they spend each week reviewing data as a good investment.

Take a step back after reading this chapter, try some techniques, and decide which reports to review daily, weekly, monthly, quarterly, or annually. You may want to analyze and test all five Basic Listing Strategies immediately and decide to review them again each quarter. You may find certain reports useful on a daily basis, such as regularly reviewing effective keywords, and decide to research and run additional tests when you are evaluating a new product line.

Having a game plan that you can revise as you go along ensures that you apply what you've learned to your business to increase your sales.

8

#1 Find the Best Time to End an Auction

From eBay's earliest years, sellers have tried to determine the best day and time to end an auction. Sellers tend to end their auctions when the largest numbers of buyers are online perusing listings.

eBay sorts search results by *time ending soonest*, as you can see in Figure 8-1. Most shoppers will not scroll through all search results pages for the 2446 auctions returned in the results in this search. Having your items ending within minutes of when the most shoppers are searching brings your listings to the top of the search results and is an ideal way to be seen.

While a search returns items in order of time ending soonest, the default for browsing is actually *newly listed*. Whenever you search or browse, you can sort results different from the default view, but it's important to understand how most potential buyers are viewing listings.

eBay sales are cyclical according to time of year, day of the week, and time of day. Summers are traditionally slower months, as for the retail trade in general. Medved QuoteTracker (www .medved.net/cgi-bin/cal.exe?EIND) tracks eBay auction counts. Figure 8-2 shows auction listings for the year 2004. The data in this chart shows the number of items listed on eBay (not the number of bids or sales). Other factors affect the number of listings, especially eBay promotions, such as Free Listing Days, which were discussed in Chapter 2.

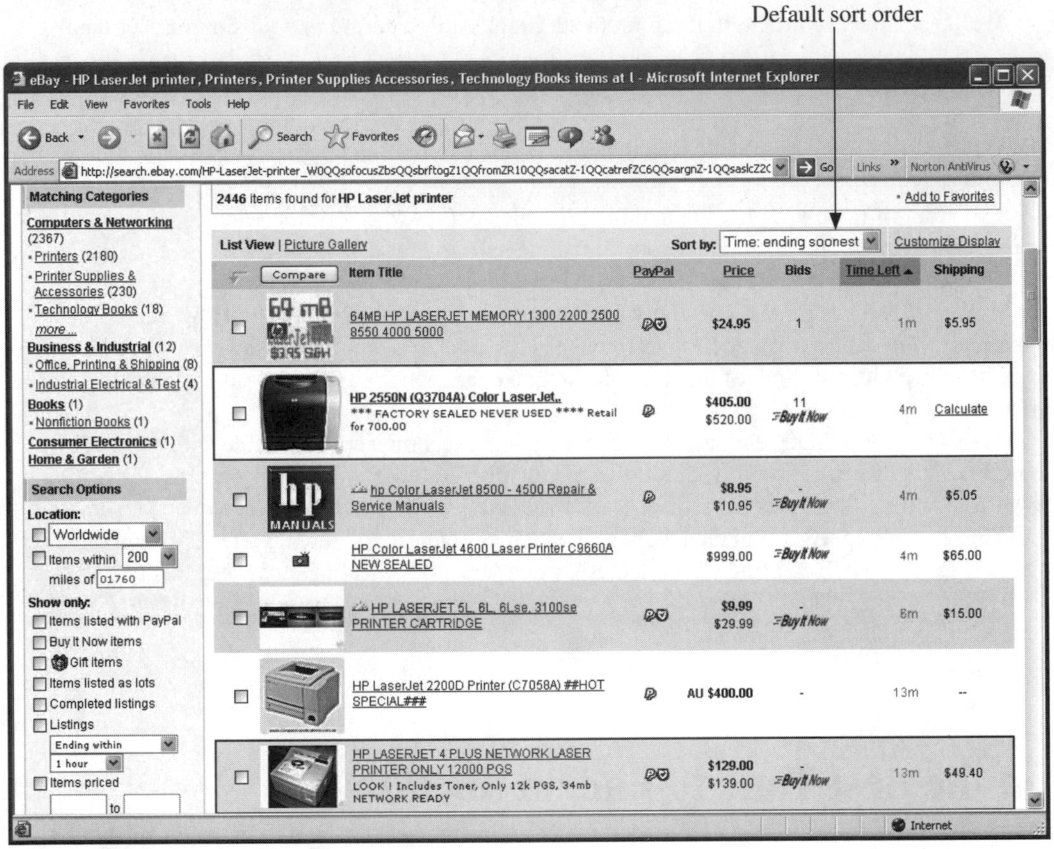

Default sort order

FIGURE 8-1   eBay sorts search results by time ending soonest.

NOTE   *Some people believe the day an auction ends is irrelevant. If you agree, it's still worth reading this section of the chapter and reviewing data for yourself. The data these tools reveal for your listings may surprise you.*

AuctionBytes has conducted surveys since 1999 to determine which day auction sellers consider the best day to end an eBay auction. In those surveys, Sunday consistently came in first, and Wednesdays and Fridays appeared to be the most unpopular days. In 2005, 7.4 percent of respondents said day of the week doesn't matter. Table 8-1 shows the full results from the study going back to 1999.

The multi-year study shown in Table 8-1 measures sellers' perceptions across all categories. The survey is a good indicator of the perceptions of one population of sellers, but is not reflective of buyers' perceptions and may even be self-perpetuating. That's why it's best to test your assumptions using data-tools.

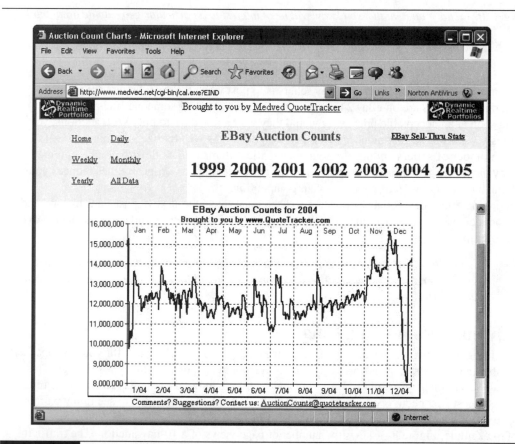

FIGURE 8-2 Medved QuoteTracker shows the seasonal nature of eBay listings, though it does not reflect actual sales.

	Sunday	Monday	Tuesday	Wednesday	Thursday	Friday	Saturday
Dec 99	41	15	6	4	5	11	18
Feb 01	52	18	1	5	8	3	11
Jan 02	60	9	4	4	10	3	9
Mar 03	64	11	4	3	7	3	8
Feb 04	57.5	9.5	5	4	7	2	7
Feb 05	56.8	11.5	4.4	3.8	7.3	2.6	6.2

TABLE 8-1 AuctionBytes surveys of eBay Sellers show many believe Sunday is the best day to end an auction, the most popular day for six years running

TIP
If you have an item that you know will be of interest to a particular geographic area, think about when those shoppers are most likely to be online. This applies to demographics, too. Stay-at-home parents, office workers, and students may all have widely different schedules. Look at your traffic data to pinpoint these trends.

Common wisdom among many eBay sellers is to post when the most buyers are online. But in reality, buyers are on eBay 24 hours a day, 7 days a week. If someone finds an auction ending soon at an acceptable price, why would they wait a few days to bid? With auctions, you obviously want the largest number of bidders so your items will realize a higher price. But a large number of sellers ending auctions for identical items dilutes the advantage you may have by having large numbers of buyers. In other words, selling at non-peak times reduces your potential customers, but it also reduces your competition.

Examine eBay market data by product and category, look at your own past sales history, and then conduct test auctions. Results can vary depending on many factors and can also change over time, so keep testing.

TIP
AuctionBytes created a calendar tool to help you figure out what days to start an auction based on ending day and auction duration. The calendar can be found online at http:// auctionbytes.com/Calendar.

Study the Ending-Time Data

When trying to determine the most-trafficked time of day or day of the week for your listings, remember that the first day and last day get a boost from the exposure eBay gives listings. This is because eBay displays results of browsing and searching in order of "newly listed" and "time ending soonest," respectively. Look at the middle days of a listing life-span to see if any patterns emerge about when people are looking at your listings.

For example, Figure 8-3 shows the number of page views of a 10-day auction. The traffic to the listing was highest on the day the auction was scheduled to end—Sunday. The next highest trafficked day was Tuesday. This seller should run similar auctions that end on another day of the week and compare sales to determine whether Sunday is still the most popular day for the listing.

You can review your own sales history to look for trends. eBay reports and Sellathon reports can help, such as eBay's Traffic Reports' Page Views Report shown in Figure 8-3. If you need to, go back to Chapter 3 to the section on eBay Sales Reports Plus to review the Sales By Format report, which shows you metrics by ending days for your sales. Sellathon's ViewTracker (Chapter 7) reveals traffic (when people came to your listings) by date and time of day in the Visitor Data report in the Highlights pages.

Research using eBay market data tools (Chapters 4–6) can help you determine when is the best time to end an auction for a product or category. Terapeak offers an hourly analysis report for finding the optimal time of day. DeepAnalysis has an Ending Day section on its Report page that shows usage, STRs and average selling prices (ASPs) based on the day of the week an auction ended. Andale Counters Pro also lets you see traffic to your listings by hour and day.

Figure 8-4 shows an example of a report from DeepAnalysis with key metrics by ending day for a search on *salad spinner* in the Home & Garden category.

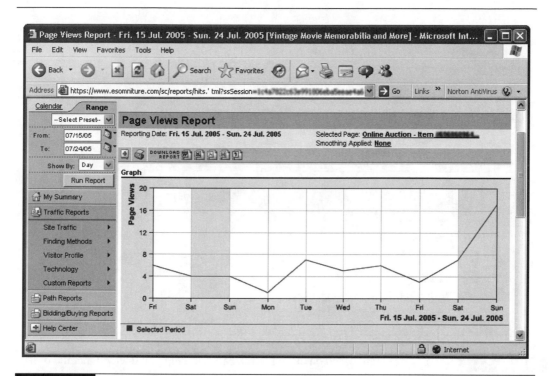

| FIGURE 8-3 | Data tools like this eBay Traffic Report can tell you which days get the most traffic to your auctions, but keep in mind that the ending day (in this case, Sunday) is always likely to get the most traffic because of the way eBay sorts search results. |

Notice several interesting points about the auctions in the report shown in Figure 8-4:

■ Most auctions ended Sunday and Monday (38 and 37, respectively); the day with the least number of auctions ending was Saturday (23).

■ The STR (Auction Success Rate) was highest for auctions ending on Wednesday (69 percent).

■ The ASP was highest for auctions ending on Friday ($15.66) and lowest for auctions ending on Monday.

Based on this chart, it looks like Wednesday was a pretty good day for ending auctions for salad spinners—it had a 69 percent sell-through and a fairly high ASP. But don't forget to look at the actual listings making up these results (in this case—using DeepAnalysis—click the Auction tab). See if any unusual listings might have influenced the results you see in this report. And, of course, you should keep an eye on all categories in which you are selling to look for trends— things change fast on eBay, and what's true today may not be true tomorrow.

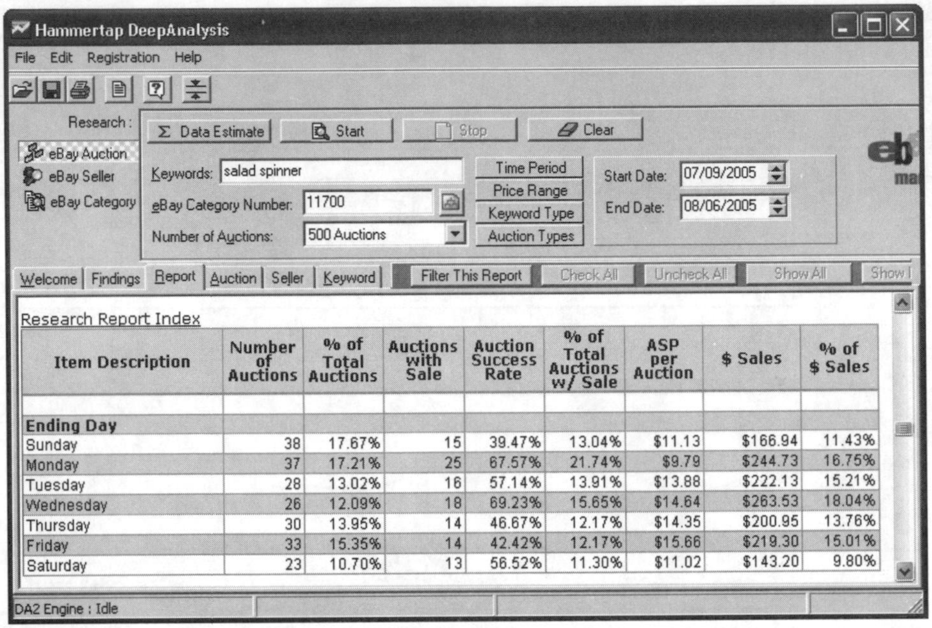

Item Description	Number of Auctions	% of Total Auctions	Auctions with Sale	Auction Success Rate	% of Total Auctions w/ Sale	ASP per Auction	$ Sales	% of $ Sales
Ending Day								
Sunday	38	17.67%	15	39.47%	13.04%	$11.13	$166.94	11.43%
Monday	37	17.21%	25	67.57%	21.74%	$9.79	$244.73	16.75%
Tuesday	28	13.02%	16	57.14%	13.91%	$13.88	$222.13	15.21%
Wednesday	26	12.09%	18	69.23%	15.65%	$14.64	$263.53	18.04%
Thursday	30	13.95%	14	46.67%	12.17%	$14.35	$200.95	13.76%
Friday	33	15.35%	14	42.42%	12.17%	$15.66	$219.30	15.01%
Saturday	23	10.70%	13	56.52%	11.30%	$11.02	$143.20	9.80%

FIGURE 8-4   Reports like these based on eBay market data can help you decide what the best ending days are for *your* auctions.

#2 Determine Optimal Auction Duration

Of all the issues addressed in this chapter, auction duration is the issue most associated with the type of item you are selling. Though various schools of thought surround the optimal auction duration, smart sellers will do their own research to test their assumptions.

Some Background on Auction Duration

eBay charges insertion fees based on the starting price of a listing, and sellers have the option of making listings run 3, 5, 7, or 10 days (there is an extra fee for running 10-day listings). In October 2003, eBay instituted 1-day auctions with certain restrictions—sellers were required to have either a minimum feedback rating of 10 or be ID Verified. (By 2005, you must have either a feedback score of 10, or a feedback score of 5 with a PayPal account, and you must accept PayPal as a payment method on the listing.) In October 2004, eBay banned 1-day auctions from eBay Motors listings.

eBay and sellers have different motives when it comes to auction duration. Both want to sell items quickly, of course. But many sellers believe the longer an item is on eBay, the more exposure it will get, leading to a higher selling price. eBay believes customers should be able to get items as quickly as possible and hopes to make the difference in possibly lower prices with added volume from quickly turning listings.

Practicals vs. Collectibles

Putting yourself in your buyers' place can help you determine what duration is best for the type of item you are selling. Imagine that you need to purchase a new cable for your computer. You find an auction that ends in five days with a starting bid of $3.99 and another listing with a Buy It Now price of $5.99. Would you wait five days to see if you could get the cable for $2.00 cheaper? Not only do you have to wait for the auction listing to end, but you may not even win the auction and you'll have to start all over again. All this time, your computer cable is broken.

This example demonstrates that for "practical" items, you may be better off running shorter duration listings. (You may also consider using Buy It Now, and we'll discuss this strategy in Chapter 9.)

Now imagine you are a pottery collector, and you find an auction for a very uncommon piece you are eager to add to your collection. In this case, you have fewer options for acquiring the piece (you can't go down to the local department store, for example). If this is the only auction for this particular item, you probably won't mind waiting for the auction to end. A 10-day duration may benefit the seller so she has a longer time to attract as many collectors as possible who may get into a bidding war and drive up the price as a result.

Consumers and collectors shop in different ways on eBay. A consumer is looking for a commodity and weighs price and availability in the buying decision. A collector hunts and is willing to pay more and wait longer for a special piece.

Determining what you're selling and how long a buyer may be willing to wait for your auction to end should factor into your decision on auction duration.

The Case for 1-Day Auctions

When eBay introduced 1-day auctions, it said sellers had cited three issues in requesting the duration: holiday sales, the nature of some time-sensitive merchandise (such as event tickets), and the need to get around the 10-item listing limit. (eBay sellers may post up to 10 identical items; they must go to a multi-item listing, also known as Dutch auctions, if they want to sell more than 10 identical items at once.)

Here is a summary of eBay's case for 1-day auctions:

■ The seller is offering tickets, travel, tee times, food, and other time-sensitive products.

■ The seller wants to offer auctions related to holiday shopping or marketing events (such as one-day-only product releases).

■ The seller wants to list 70 identical listings over a week instead of 20 (given the 10-listing limit rule).

■ The seller wants to increase the excitement associated with the listing by leveraging the increased bidding that often happens at the beginning and end of an auction.

One-day auctions are also used by savvy eBay sellers who see high bidding activity on certain items and want to take advantage of this by putting similar items in the mix with auctions that end before those belonging to their competitors.

TIP   *Remember the effect that Buy It Now (BIN) auctions have on duration data, as mentioned in Chapter 4. When a multi-day BIN auction is purchased through a BIN bid, eBay counts the number of days that have passed, not the duration set by the seller. So if a 7-day BIN auction is purchased through BIN in three days, eBay will count that as a 3-day listing in the market-data statistics.*

Currency (and Lag) of eBay's Search Index

eBay periodically cycles through the auctions listed and gets information on new listings, high bid, current number of bids, and other information, and it adds this information to the database used to search the marketplace. Until the listing is included in the general index, a potential bidder has limited ways of knowing of the auction's existence. (A search by seller or item number would display the items, but a general search would not.)

In the past, it might take hours or even a day or more to have a listing be included in the main search. This is why many sellers prefer longer duration auctions and may even avoid 1-day listings. However, eBay's indexing has improved dramatically over the years. In most cases, listings will be indexed and included in a search within 5 minutes. Of course, from time to time, this can vary and depends on a number of factors, including the volume of new and relisted items that are posted on the site at any given time.

Items *can* be viewed immediately once they have been listed if you have the item number or do a search by seller and click View Seller's Items, but this doesn't help much, since you are trying to attract the attention of millions of eBay shoppers who don't know you.

Study the Duration Data

When trying to determine the optimal duration for your listings, you can do research using eBay market data tools (Chapters 4–6) and review your own sales history to look for trends—eBay reports (Chapter 3) and Sellathon reports (Chapter 7) can help.

Figure 8-5 shows a Terapeak report called Successful Listing Duration Lengths for a search for *iPod accessories* on eBay. The report shows the listings of each duration (1-day, 3-day, and so on) and of those, how many sold. In this particular report, 3- and 5-day auctions are shown as the least utilized, but they had the highest STRs.

Unfortunately, BIN auctions muddy the data waters a bit; so, for example, a 7-day BIN auction purchased on the fifth day of its lifespan is counted as a 5-day listing. It's also worth noting that because so few 10-day auctions are listed in the results, you can't assume a 10-day auction would have a low STR. You should always look at *all* the data and not rely solely on one report to draw your conclusions; ASP is another important metric to take into account.

In our example with iPod accessories, auctions with a shorter duration were more successful for a number of reasons. (We talked about consumers who want instant gratification when shopping for practicals versus collectibles, for example.) Always look at the behind-the-search results, and conduct tests of your own to see if you experience any significant differences with differing durations if you are selling these types of items. You can create custom codes in Sellathon to insert in each type of auction (3-day versus 7-day, for example), and let Sellathon reports help you determine whether there is any effect. Remember to keep everything else the same in the test auctions so you isolate the effect duration has on your sales.

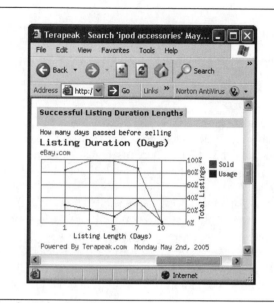

   Terapeak tracks duration lengths and sell-through (STRs).

#3 Choose the Most Profitable Starting Price

Many newbies start selling on eBay by listing their auctions at starting prices that are too high. They fail to understand the psychology of buying that plays such a big factor in auctions.

Auction shoppers are attracted to listings with a low starting price. Once shoppers have bid on an auction, they are vested in the auction and will generally follow it throughout the duration to see if they have won. They may get extremely competitive and view the bidding like a game they want to win. This can lead to bidding frenzy and—sellers hope—to higher selling prices. Remember that bidders have fun trying to get a bargain and outbid other shoppers.

Jay and Marie Senese are one the most famous couples selling on eBay. They sell under the eBay user ID JayandMarie (formerly onecentcds@aol.com). They start most of their auctions at a starting bid of 1 cent, with no reserve. This strategy helped them become the first sellers to reach 100,000 feedback ratings in 2002, and the first to reach 200,000 feedback points in 2004. They obviously believe in the low starting price strategy on eBay auctions, and of course, a low starting price means lower listing fees, too.

Pricing Low to Attract Bids

Another factor that helps low-priced auctions achieve higher prices is the fact that buyers value the popularity of listings. Buyers who see two auctions for the same item may believe that the listing with many bids is somehow better. They often assume that other bidders have compared the two auctions and found one better than the other.

Learn from Others: A Freezer Heats Up at 99 Cents

Some sellers of high-value items embrace the low starting-price philosophy. Titanium PowerSeller ACityDiscount sells restaurant equipment in the Business & Industrial category on eBay. About 95 percent of all ACityDiscount auctions for used items have a starting price of 99 cents on eBay.

ACityDiscount was liquidating some inventory for a national restaurant chain. One of the items was a large commercial walk-in combo cooler/freezer. ACityDiscount listed the freezer on eBay at a fixed price of $10,000, where it sat, unsold, for three months. With one month left to sell the item, ACityDiscount changed the listing to a 99-cent auction, and it ended the bidding at $10,000.

Sometimes listing an item at a fixed price is a type of test; you can find out if it sells or not. But it does takes nerves of steel to list a $10,000 item for 99 cents, because with online auctions—just as in live auctions—there are no guarantees that you'll get the selling price you hope to achieve. (We'll talk about setting a Reserve Price in Chapter 9.)

ACityDiscount had lots of experience with selling on eBay, and a good reputation. They knew that effective keywords, good photos, descriptions, and feedback all help auctions achieve a good ending price.

Conduct a search on eBay and scan the search results. See if your eye is drawn to the Number Of Bids column. Do you find you are more likely to view an auction with 20 bids than one with 0 bids? Does it make you wonder what's so special about the item that has garnered more bids?

Getting people to bid on your auction can increase its popularity, and some believe one of the best ways to get people to bid on an item early is to have it priced at a very low starting point. But for every rule, there are exceptions. For high-end goods, some sellers believe shoppers sort items by order of highest price to help them view the "best" items without having to scroll through many pages of search results. Sellathon reports (Chapter 7) let you see how searchers sort their searches.

> **TIP** *eBay has a tiered fee structure for listing fees. At the time of this writing, it costs 25 cents to list an item with a starting price of 99 cents or less, and it costs 35 cents to list an item with a starting price between $1.00 and $9.99. If you were thinking of listing auctions at $1.00, save yourself a dime and start them at 99 cents.*

Starting Prices: Auction vs. Fixed Price Format

Setting a starting price on an auction is much different than setting a price on a fixed price item. In choosing whether to sell something in an auction format or fixed price, the seller evaluates several factors, which we discuss more in the next chapter for Advanced Listing Strategy #2—Choose Auction-style listings versus Fixed Price format.

If you think an item is relatively common and easy to find, its value is well known and there may be few bidders, you may be disappointed with the results if you auction it off at a low starting price. You can use eBay market data to help you determine whether an item is rare or not. (Just because you haven't seen it before doesn't mean it's rare.)

Using Fixed Price format, you obviously choose a price that gives you enough room to cover your costs and make a profit. But the higher the price, the longer it may take to sell, if it sells at all. That's why testing prices of Fixed Price listings is just as important as testing the starting price of auction listings. You don't want your goods getting dusty waiting to sell, but you want to make as much profit as you can.

When Cost Doesn't Matter: eBay as a Marketing Campaign

If you are using eBay as a customer-acquisition tool, you will likely take a different approach to setting prices.

Large sellers who have their own e-commerce site may use eBay as an advertising tool, using the site to get new customers, whom they hope will purchase from their e-commerce site in the future. In this case, you might be willing to sell a certain amount of items on eBay at a reduced margin or even below cost, thinking of it as a marketing expense. If this is the case, it's even more important than ever to measure the results to see if your eBay campaign is a success.

Some sellers also use auctions as loss leaders, setting prices extremely low, but hoping through cross-promotional efforts they can get the buyer to purchase other complementary items at the same time. Factor this into your price-setting strategy, and measure the results to see if it is working or not. We talk more about cross promotions and other marketing strategies in Chapter 10.

The 99-cent/NR Starting Price Strategy

Since so many experienced sellers use the 99-cent/NR (99-cent/no reserve) starting-price strategy, you may be wondering if this might be right for your auctions. It can be difficult to take the risk on a high-priced item—if you are wrong, the cost of mistakes can be steep. However, if it makes you more money on future sales over the long term, it can be a worthwhile investment.

NOTE   *If you are selling high-value items and are considering testing a low starting price strategy, you might want to set a Reserve Price. We'll talk more about this in Chapter 9.*

While the 99-cent/NR strategy works well for some sellers and some items, it might not be the best strategy for you or your items. Review market data and your own past sales, and run some tests to see which pricing strategy works best for you.

Before you list auctions with a low starting price, make sure your auctions can be found. Listing in the right category and using effective keywords helps to ensure potential buyers can find your listing. If you do everything right, but misspell a keyword so only one person finds your auction by chance, that person will get a great bargain and you will be out of luck. eBay shoppers are savvy, and some even use tools to find typos, so always list carefully, especially with low starting prices.

NOTE   *Fatfingers (www.fatfingers.com) is a service designed to help you check for misspellings in eBay auctions. The service works with many of the international eBay sites as well.*

Study the Price Data

The ACityDiscount example cited earlier in this chapter is a dramatic example of the effect of starting prices on sales. But you should conduct routine tests to see what effect different starting prices have on your listings. Sellathon's ViewTracker reports (Chapter 7) can help you track the effects of starting prices, and you can look at eBay market data (Chapters 4–6) to look for patterns and see what other sellers are doing.

The Auction tab in DeepAnalysis (Chapter 6) has a column called Starting Price. You can sort by Starting Price and review the auctions with high starting prices and with low starting prices to see which ones realized the highest ASPs and STRs. You can also sort the column by ASP and see which strategy the best auctions used in realizing higher selling prices.

TIP   *Starting prices are usually much higher for Fixed Price listings (Buy It Now) than for auction listings, so take this into account when reviewing data reports.*

Figure 8-6 shows the DeepAnalysis Auction tab report for a search on *salad spinner* in the Home & Garden category after results were sorted by starting price, highest priced items first. The listings show the importance of comparing apples to apples: the auction with the highest starting price was a lot of Tupperware items; the next item was a commercial salad spinner. You would want to find the items on the list most like yours, and study only their starting and ending prices to get background for your listings.

Sort by Starting Price

DeepAnalysis lets you sort search results in order of starting price to help you figure out what other sellers are doing and how those auctions performed.

#4 Locate the Best Category

The key to success on eBay is making sure your items can be found. For situations in which buyers are browsing categories as opposed to searching for items by keywords, placing an item in the right category is crucial. Some eBay shoppers set up favorite categories on My eBay that they check regularly for new items of interest.

It's easy to choose a category for certain kinds of items, but sometimes the choice is not so clear. If you are selling a piece of Disney pottery, for example, would you place it in the Collectibles category (several could apply), or would you put it in the Pottery & Glass category? Or would you put it in both categories?

What about a book on auto repair? Should you place it in the Books category, or should you place it in the Cars, Parts & Vehicles category?

eBay sellers have used Completed Item searches for years to help them decide in which category to place their auction listings. Some of the tools outlined in earlier chapters can help sellers make informed category decisions.

eBay's Item Specifics and Product Finder

Along with browsing and searching, in some categories, Product Finder is available instead of a deep subcategory hierarchy. That's because eBay has been introducing Item Specifics and in some cases has rolled up categories (covered in Chapter 2). The Books category, for example, contains a Fiction subcategory (along with other sister subcategories), with no additional subcategories under Fiction. Instead, sellers fill out the Item Specifics fields to describe the item's attributes, such as category, format, and condition.

Figure 8-7 shows a search for *television* in the Consumer Electronics, Televisions subcategory—note in the left column the Televisions Finder, where you can narrow down results by TV Type, Display Technology, Screen Size, Brand, and High Definition.

Some sellers evaluate the use of Product Finder/Item Specifics tools by looking at reports from Sellathon. If they determine that shoppers aren't using Product Finder, they may not invest the time in filling out Item Specific fields. Just be aware that eBay is pushing Item Specific attributes, making it increasingly important for sellers to fill out Item Specifics fields when listing items in the categories that offer them.

Double Your Fun: Listing in Two Categories

eBay allows sellers to list in two categories. For an item with cross-appeal, this may be an effective strategy to increase the chance your items will be found by browsing shoppers. Decide whether the strategy is worth testing in your situation—insertion fees on an item listed in two categories are doubled.

eBay prohibits listing items in inappropriate/irrelevant categories. (eBay reserves the right to move your listing to a different category if it believes your listing is incorrectly categorized.) Some restrictions apply to listing in two categories, including Real Estate listings, eBay Motors listings, and Multiple Item Auctions (http://pages.ebay.com/help/sell/l2c.html).

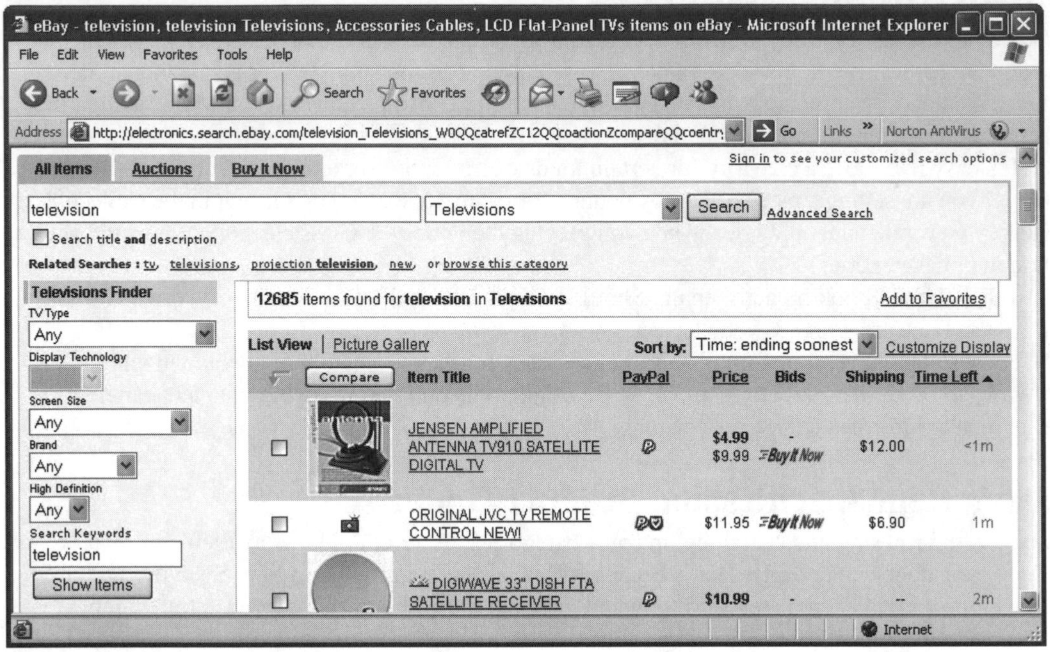

FIGURE 8-7   In some categories, such as Consumer Electronics, eBay's Product Finder helps buyers find what they are looking for by narrowing down their searches by attributes.

eBay Search Expansions: Saved by the Category

eBay came up with "search expansions" to help shoppers find items when searching by keywords. In the past, shoppers who typed in a general description into eBay's Search box wouldn't find the relevant listings if they did not include appropriate keywords in the title (you'd search for TV and you wouldn't get television, for example).

With eBay's search expansions, when someone uses the Search box to find a particular type of item, eBay will show results for listings that have those keywords in the title but will also show all items in a relevant category that it has mapped to the keyword.

To explain how this works, eBay uses the example of a shopper who enters the keywords *action figure* into the Search box. eBay uses search expansions to include all items with the words *action figure* in the title, as well as all items in the Toys & Hobbies, Action Figures subcategory. And if the shopper types in *Superman action figure*, eBay will show all listings with *Superman action figure* in the title *and* all the listings with *Superman* in the title that are in the Action Figures subcategory. This means if you don't get the keywords just right in your title, you might be saved if you put your listing under the right category.

8

NOTE
Until you as a seller can look up and see what keywords are mapped to which categories, it's best to stick to your current title-keyword strategy; don't abandon the practice of adding synonyms in your title if you think it draws more visitors.

Study the Category Data

To help you choose categories for an item that has cross-appeal, see how many items are listed in each applicable category using eBay market data tools (Chapters 4–6). Be sure and check STRs and ASPs: a dearth of a particular item in one category could net you higher prices because of less competition, or it could mean shoppers just don't look in that category for the item you are selling and it would be best to avoid.

Sellathon ViewTracker reports (Chapter 7) tell you how many visitors found your items searching eBay, searching a category, browsing a category, and other information. These statistics are enormously helpful and will help you learn the importance of choosing the right category. You can run tests and measure traffic and methods of arrival (how shoppers found your listings) to refine your category selection process further. Figure 8-8 shows a Sellathon Arrival Methods report for a collectible milk bottle auction.

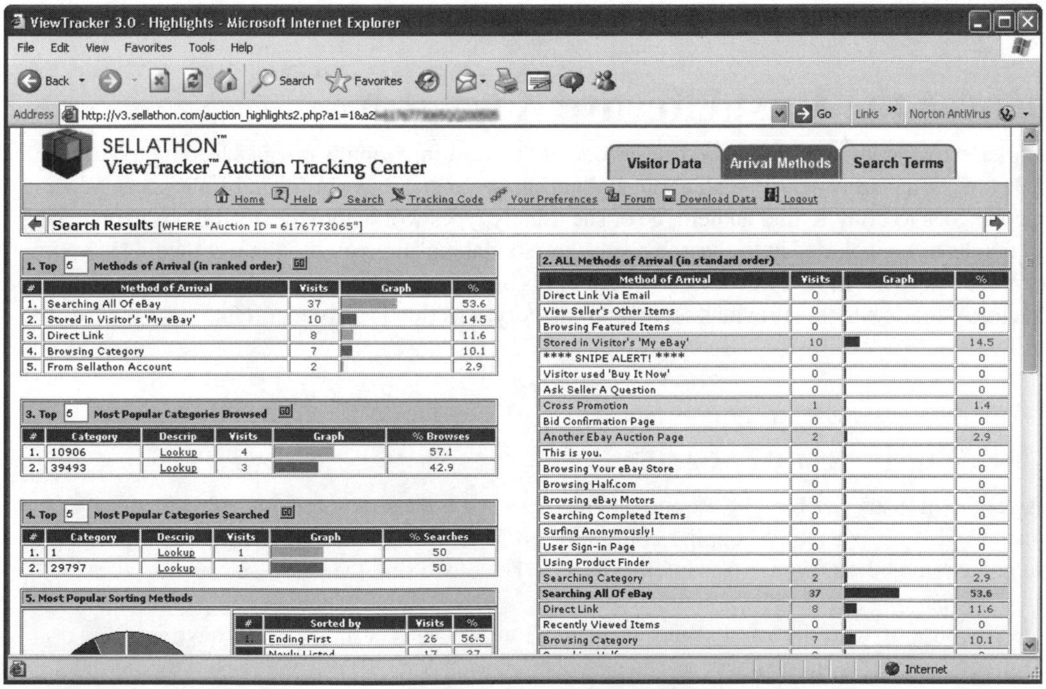

FIGURE 8-8   Sellathon gives you statistics about how many visitors browsed and searched which categories—good information that also allows you to compare results for two identical items placed in different categories.

The report reveals the following interesting points:

- 10 percent of visitors browsed a category before visiting this auction.
- The two most popular categories browsed were numbers 10906 and 39493.
- The most popular categories searched were 1 (collectibles) and 29797.
- More than half of visitors to this auction searched all of eBay.

These statistics would be even more valuable if you were comparing two identical auctions posted in two different categories—and of course you would want to compare the selling price for those two items as well.

You can also study reports from Sellathon to see how many visitors find your listings through Product Finder (the Item Specifics tool). The Sellathon Details page for a listing has a column called Method Of Arrival. If the visitor used eBay's Product Finder tool to locate your item, it will be indicated in this column. The next column (Search Term) will indicate the Item Specifics attribute the visitor used. This will tell you whether the time you spent filling out Item Specifics in your listings was a good investment.

> **TIP**   *One PowerSeller said he does research on the fly. If he lists something he's never sold before and it gets no bids, he'll consider changing categories during the auction, or he might add a category. eBay allows these changes if there are no bidders, so give it a try.*

#5 Uncover the Most Effective Keywords

Using effective keywords in auction titles is one of the most important strategies leading to success in eBay auctions. eBay selling is all about making sure your auctions are found by shoppers. When someone goes to eBay to find an item, he or she usually types words into the Search box. You want your results to be included in the search results list, so making sure you use the right words in your title is critical to success. Of course, some shoppers browse, particularly window-shoppers and collectors—that's why the previous section on category selection is also important.

The "Business" of Search

An entire industry has built up around the Internet search. Internet searching is big business—just ask Google, Yahoo!, Shopping.com, Shop.com, BizRate (Shopzilla.com), and other search engines. Businesses want Internet users to be able to find their products and services, and they pay big bucks to help them do it.

Keeping up with the latest search strategies and services is crucial if you have an eBay Store and operate your own e-commerce website. One of the best resources on the field of Internet search is Danny Sullivan's SearchEngineWatch.com (www.searchenginewatch .com), where you will also find Chris Sherman's excellent free e-mail newsletter, *SearchDay*.

CAUTION   *Remember that keyword spamming is against eBay's rules. Chapter 2 includes an explanation of eBay's "Search Manipulation and Keyword Spamming" policy. Do not put words into your title that are popular but have nothing to do with what you are selling.*

Why Keywords Are Critical

Sellathon tracks eBay shopping patterns with its ViewTracker software (Chapter 7). Sellathon CEO Wayne Yeager said that his research reveals a rule of thumb that applies to eBay in the aggregate, as shown in Figure 8-9.

Wayne said that some items tend to be found almost exclusively by browsing, while others are found almost exclusively through searches. He said that a lot of variation exists from category to category and even from item to item.

eBay CEO Meg Whitman told analysts that when she joined the company in 1998, more people browsed eBay than searched it, but by 2005, more searchers than browsers used eBay. Meg's statement and Wayne's research confirms that having the right keywords and being in the right category are both crucial to success on eBay. But don't rely on their research to tell you what is right for your listings—do your own research using data tools to find out for yourself how buyers are finding *your* listings.

Searching Title vs. Title and Description

eBay provides 55 characters in the Title field. This means sellers have only 55 characters to describe their item and include effective keywords. This can be challenging.

The default search on eBay searches only titles. But shoppers can manually check a box so that eBay searches the title *and* the description field for the search term. This means sellers need to include the most crucial keywords in the title field, but can also hedge their bets by including important keywords, synonyms, and misspellings in the auction description as well.

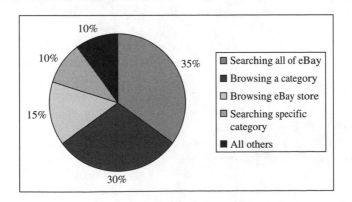

 FIGURE 8-9   Sellathon rule of thumb for finding method.

Many of the tools covered in earlier chapters have ways to help you determine which keywords are most effective for the item you are selling. You can look at eBay market data for your category, and you can study your own past auctions.

Platinum PowerSeller David Yaskulka (BlueberryBoutique) sells fashion items on eBay and uses tools, including eBay reports, to keep an eye on what terms people are searching in his categories. He discovered that some words are more popular when buyers are looking for ties than other words—for example, shoppers may be using the word *designer* more than *handmade* when conducting searches, so he adjusts his listing titles accordingly. Some sellers spend hours analyzing the effectiveness of keywords in their titles.

TIP   *Study the keywords used to find your auctions in Title and Description searches to help you identify popular keywords you should be including in your titles. (Most searches are Title Only searches.) Sellathon and eBay Traffic Reports (Finding Methods report) provide keyword information.*

There's no question that brand and designer names work wonders when included in listing titles (when appropriate). But don't forget generic words, too.

Silver PowerSeller Bobby Minnich said he is amazed to find that many eBayers who are selling Lionel trains fail to include the word *train* in their titles. Using Sellathon data, he found

Learn from Others: "Designing" eBay Keywords

Designer items are hot on eBay. Julia Wilkinson, author of the book *Top 100 Simplified Tips & Tricks: eBay* and the e-mail newsletter *Yard Salers and eBayers* (www.aolmemorabilia .com/yab), sells a lot of clothing and accessories on eBay.

Julia keeps track of the best-selling designers. Surprisingly, she says some decent brands *don't* sell well on eBay. She scours shops and yard sales for hot items, keeping her designer list in mind.

What Julia and most experienced eBay sellers know is that popular designer items have a tremendous advantage on eBay: the designer name makes a great keyword for your auction title.

Julia says designer Lilly Pulitzer items do phenomenally well on eBay, and of course she always includes *Lilly Pulitzer* in her auction titles when selling the designer's clothing and accessories. But look at the name—it's very easy for sellers to misspell the words *Lilly* and *Pulitzer*. Here's Julia's trick: she figures out the common misspellings and includes those in her auction title if possible. By including misspellings, she attracts bids from buyers who aren't sure how to spell a designer's name.

You can use data tools to look at the keywords people are using to find your items. You can run some test auctions where you intentionally include common misspellings in the listing titles, and see if they bring you bidders.

You should include designer and brand names in your auction titles, and when possible, capitalize on buyer typos and misspellings by including misspellings as well.

the most common search terms used by shoppers looking for the toys are *Lionel train*. By leaving out the word *train* in the title, some sellers are missing out on potential bidders and buyers.

> **TIP** *eBay has a Subtitle feature (for an additional charge to sellers) that shows up on the search results pages to help describe your item and make it stand out. But eBay's search tool does not index subtitles. This means keywords included in the subtitle will* not *be searchable by shoppers.*

There's only one way to know whether you should be including generic words, and which ones, in your titles—look at keyword reports from market-data tools and traffic-reporting tools, and test, test, test.

> **TIP** *eBay allows shoppers to exclude words from searches, and Sellathon ViewTracker reveals this information. Go to the Search Terms column on the Details Page and look for a red minus sign. Roll your cursor over this icon to display the excluded words. Commonly, shoppers exclude popular designers or brands when they are looking specifically for another designer, so they don't have to scroll through irrelevant listings.*

Study the Keyword Data

The best way to uncover effective keywords is to study reports from eBay (Chapter 3) and Sellathon (Chapter 7) to see how visitors are finding your listings. eBay Traffic Reports identify keywords used by shoppers to find your listings. Go to your eBay Traffic Reports and under Finding Methods, go to Search Keywords Reports. You'll see an example in Figure 8-10. A huge drawback, however, is that you can't isolate the report to any particular listing. eBay reports the keywords used to find your store and *all* of your listings.

This is where Sellathon ViewTracker has the advantage. Sellathon's Highlights pages contain a Search Terms tab, where you will find the Top 10 Search Terms Used To Find Your Auctions, as shown in Chapter 7. To get more specific, go to the listing you are interested in and click the Details page, where you will find Search Terms—these are the actual search terms used by visitors to find that listing. A letter *D* will appear if the searcher used Titles And Descriptions search instead of Titles only. Sellathon's SellerPower.com tool and Deep Analysis' Keyword Report can also be helpful.

You should also stay informed by reviewing hot lists, talking to vendors and other sellers, and reading about what's going on in your industry. If you are a top seller in an eBay category, you should also have access to the Category Manager at eBay—talk to her regularly and foster that relationship. Attracting shoppers to your auctions through effective keywords—without spamming—is critical.

How the Tools Stack Up

We covered a number of tools in Chapters 3–7 that can be used to gather information and analyze eBay data. There is no one-size-fits-all tool, nor is there one tool that can do everything you need to make the best decisions about basic listing strategies.

Andale, Terapeak, and DeepAnalysis offer solutions for mining eBay data. eBay Sales Reports Plus allow you to look at your own sales performance, as do some of the auction-management services—particularly those geared for high-volume sellers. And eBay Traffic Reports and Sellathon offer analytics solutions that show you how traffic came to your listings and allow you to test various approaches to listing strategies.

The tools are best used in combination—make sure you have something that allows you to look at eBay products and categories as well as a tool that helps you measure traffic and learn where visitors are coming from. Through a careful review of data and by running test auctions, you can figure out what works for you—from the best time to end your auctions to uncovering the most effective keywords.

Here's a summary of some of the tools you can use to help you formulate your Basic Listing Strategies. Go back to previous chapters to review the tools in more detail.

eBay's Completed Item Search

Use eBay's closed listings to help you identify the most successful listing strategies employed by eBay sellers. Wading through eBay's Completed Item Search is a manual process, however, so it's impossible to look at data on a category level. Narrow down the search as much as possible and then try to identify the strategies the most successful listings used to get bids. (We reviewed how to search eBay's Completed Item Search in Chapter 3.)

eBay Sales Reports Plus & Traffic Reports

eBay Sales Reports Plus has a Sales By Format report to help you with Basic Listing Strategies using your *own* data to guide you. Compare your performance by ending time and duration. The Sales By Category report breaks out your sales by category. And eBay Stores Traffic Reports identify keywords shoppers used to find your listings. Figure 8-10 shows the keywords entered by shoppers into eBay's Search box to find a particular eBay Store for a certain month. Also, by revealing which listings received the most traffic, you can use eBay's Traffic Reports to help you test various listing strategies.

Andale

Andale's Price Finder Tool has charts that can help you improve your Basic Listing Strategies using data from eBay's closed listings. (Don't rely on its Smart Andale Search—you should conduct an All Items Data Search to avoid limiting search results too narrowly.)

You can see in Figure 8-11 that Andale makes recommendations for you with regard to all Basic Listing Strategies. However, I prefer to delve into the data behind the recommendations to see how the recommendations are being made. Using the How To Sell feature reveals the details.

Terapeak

Terapeak offers several reports under the Research tab to help you formulate better Basic Listing Strategies. The reports compare metrics from eBay's closed listings so you can see which strategies achieved the highest STRs and ASPs. The Hourly Analysis report helps you find best time of day;

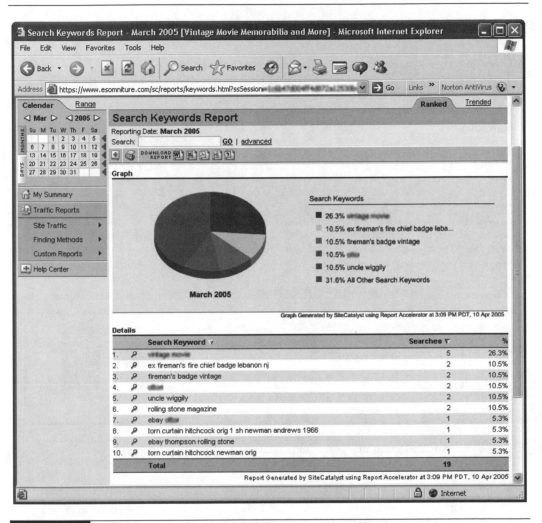

FIGURE 8-10 eBay Stores Traffic Reports shows keywords used by shoppers to get to your store.

the Successful Listing Duration Lengths report identify optimal listing duration; Sub-Category Revenue & Seller Breakdown and the Pricing reports identify most profitable starting prices.

Terapeak also has custom keyword reports to help sellers identify keyword trends. Contact Terapeak for more information and pricing.

DeepAnalysis

DeepAnalysis Research Reports allow you to compare STRs and ASPs for products and categories from eBay closed-item data to help you formulate listing strategies. The Ending Day section

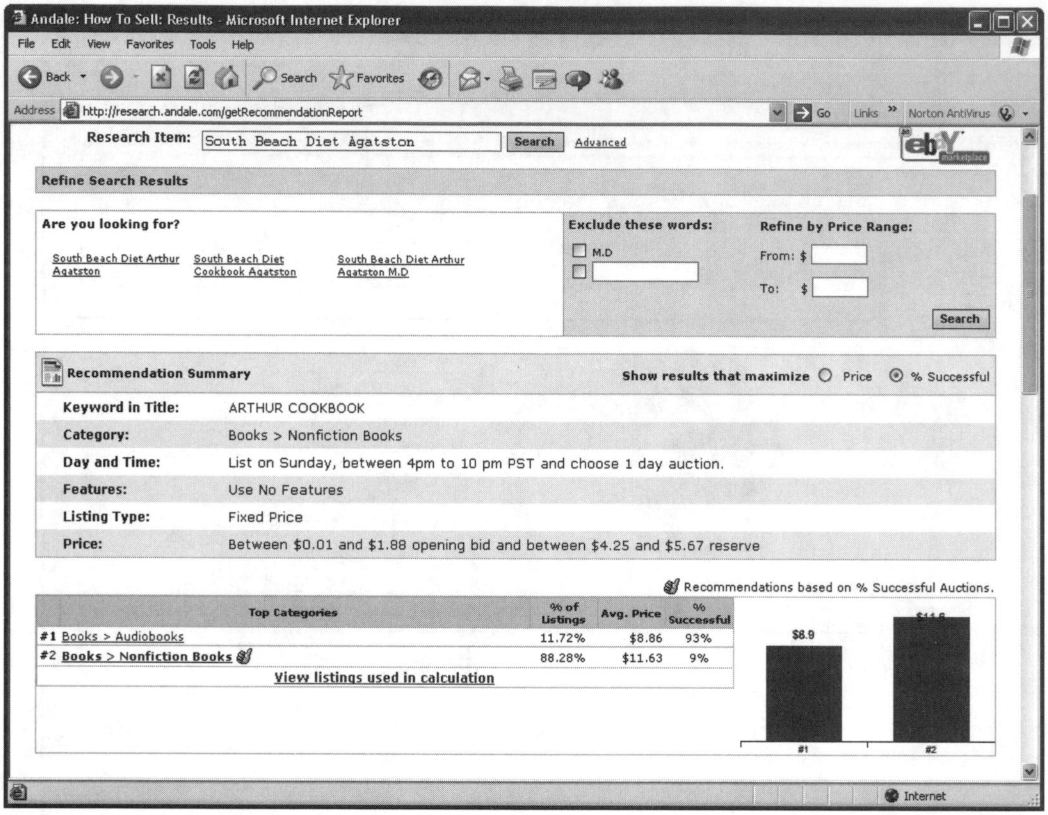

FIGURE 8-11   Andale Report makes recommendations about listing strategies.

helps you compare auction ending times (see Figure 8-12), and the Duration sections help you find optimal duration for regular and Buy It Now auctions. The Keyword Report can help you find effective keywords for your listing titles.

Sellathon

Sellathon's traffic data can help you determine the best time to end your auctions—use the Visitor Data tab in the Highlights page. You can also see which categories are most popular for *your* listings (as compared to market-data tools that look at eBay data as a whole).

Sellathon's Search Terms tab in the Highlights page tells you what keywords visitors used to find your auctions, and this can help you figure out the most effective keywords for your listing titles. You can also see on the Search Terms tab how many people used Titles Only searches compared to Titles & Descriptions. Also try using SellerPower.com.

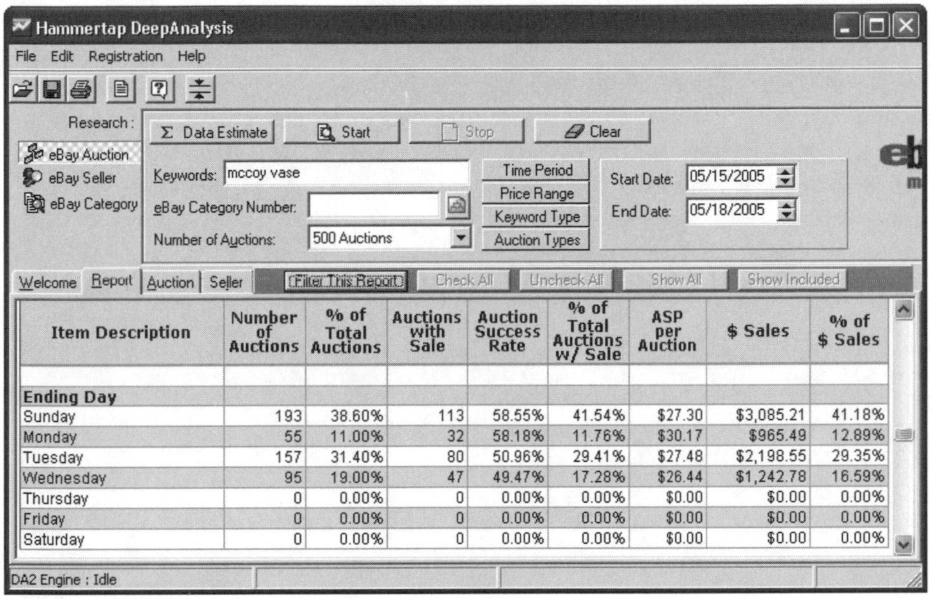

Item Description	Number of Auctions	% of Total Auctions	Auctions with Sale	Auction Success Rate	% of Total Auctions w/ Sale	ASP per Auction	$ Sales	% of $ Sales
Ending Day								
Sunday	193	38.60%	113	58.55%	41.54%	$27.30	$3,085.21	41.18%
Monday	55	11.00%	32	58.18%	11.76%	$30.17	$965.49	12.89%
Tuesday	157	31.40%	80	50.96%	29.41%	$27.48	$2,198.55	29.35%
Wednesday	95	19.00%	47	49.47%	17.28%	$26.44	$1,242.78	16.59%
Thursday	0	0.00%	0	0.00%	0.00%	$0.00	$0.00	0.00%
Friday	0	0.00%	0	0.00%	0.00%	$0.00	$0.00	0.00%
Saturday	0	0.00%	0	0.00%	0.00%	$0.00	$0.00	0.00%

FIGURE 8-12 DeepAnalysis Ending Day report shows metrics such as usage, ASP, and STRs for your search or category research.

Wrapping Up

Data tools reviewed in Chapters 3–7 can help you formulate better basic listing strategies. Once you decide which tools you want to use, you can delve into the reports in more detail.

Optimizing your listings is one of the most productive uses of your time. While components such as auction duration and choosing a category may seem extremely basic, if a change enables more eBay shoppers to find *your* listings among the millions of items listed on the site every day, it can make you more money. And on eBay, pennies, dimes, and dollars really add up.

Chapter 9

Advanced Listing Strategies: Grow Your Business

You can save time and money if you avoid listing items that won't sell—or that won't sell at a price you need to achieve to make a profit. You can make money if you identify items that are more profitable than what you are currently selling. In this chapter, we'll hear from one of eBay's earliest PowerSellers who tells us how he did just that by using reports that analyzed different types of fishing equipment that he was considering adding to his product line.

You'll also learn how to apply eBay data to Advanced Listing Strategies, including how to evaluate products to sell on eBay. Advanced Listing Strategies are the secrets behind many of eBay's most successful sellers, who use them to refine their business models and make their businesses more profitable.

Every eBay seller wants his listings to stand out from the crowd. Sellers can do this by the products they choose to sell, how they sell them, and the policies and services they offer. eBay offers several optional features to help, such as Bold, Featured, Gallery, and so on; and third-party services offer advanced features, such as audio and video. Since these features cost you money, it's wise to find out whether they are effective before you use them. Spending $2 to increase the selling price by 50 cents is not a good investment. But spending $2 and getting an extra $20 is a great return on your investment.

This chapter will help you learn to make wise decisions about Advanced Listing Strategies:

- Research what to sell.
- Choose auction-style listings versus Fixed Price format.
- Analyze effectiveness of reserve price.
- Evaluate optional features and upgrades.
- Refine your offer and policies.

#1 Research What to Sell

Some of eBay's biggest sellers got their start by buying and selling items related to their interests, hobby, or passion. Items such as clothes, CDs, movies, books, sporting equipment, collectibles, and memorabilia are good examples of such items.

It is advantageous to sell what you know. It's easy to put yourself in your buyer's place and create auctions that are attractive to them. You may have inside knowledge of how to get inventory and know what a good price is for resale. You know what flaws and problems you might encounter, and your interest in what you sell can make the job easier because you enjoy what you do.

But what if you want to expand your offerings, or—if you haven't been selling seriously on eBay yet—where do you begin if you have no idea what to sell? And how do you know whether a particular item or product line will sell well and whether it will make you money on eBay?

Finding Out What's Hot

You can start by using some brainstorming techniques to get ideas about good items to sell on eBay. Some of the tools discussed in this book provide ways to generate reports of items that are selling well on eBay. You can also find lists of popular items outside of eBay.

Use common sense with a dash of skepticism when looking at "hot lists." Some lists may be compiled by manufacturers or retailers who want to sell you items based on their own product line or inventory.

Following are some suggested sources to find out what's currently hot and help you sell the hottest items on eBay.

Industry Sources

Industry trade publications and websites may publish hot lists or talk about trends that give you hints about popular styles or new technology. You can find lots of information from your local public or college library as well—go to the reference desk and make friends with the librarian. Librarians love to research new topics and can point you in the right direction. And, of course, you can learn a lot from search engines like Google and Yahoo!

Industry trade shows are also great places to do research and connect with suppliers and distributors. You can get ideas on what might be hot this season (or next) or establish relationships with vendors who are trying to liquidate last season's inventory.

As an example, I went to Yahoo! (www.yahoo.com), clicked the Directory tab, and did a search for *Toy Manufacturers Association*. I discovered a link to the Toy Industry Association (www.toy-tia.org), which is a terrific resource for anyone selling toys. Try doing searches like this to uncover resources in your industry.

eBay Lists

eBay's Seller Central section has resources under "What's Hot" to help users get ideas for what items and categories are selling well. (We reviewed these in Chapter 3.)

Hot Items By Category shows a PDF file for the latest month containing categories for which demand is growing faster than supply and where bid-to-item ratios are relatively high.

eBay Pulse can give you some general ideas of what items are in high demand on eBay. (You can also get to eBay Pulse directly by going to http://pulse.ebay.com/.) You can use the lists on the main page, or use the pull-down Category menu at the top of the page to filter the lists to show content for specific categories on eBay. Figure 9-1 shows the eBay Pulse page for popular searches for consumer electronics. *iPods* and *iPod* appeared at the top of the list on May 10, 2005.

You can also review the Merchandising Calendar on eBay Seller Central to see what promotions eBay is planning to feature on the eBay home page. The featured placement sends more traffic to these products, helping boost sales.

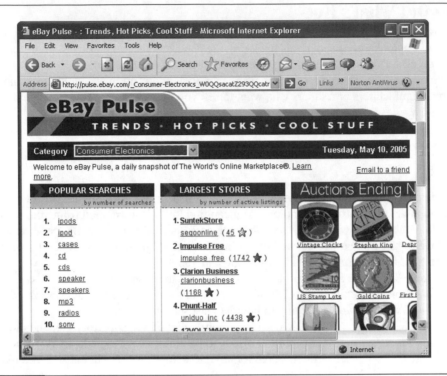

FIGURE 9-1   The eBay Pulse page displays popular searches at the category level.

Learn from Others: Blueberry Boutique Draws the "Shades"

eBay Platinum PowerSeller Blueberry Boutique (www.blueberryboutique.net) is the number one seller on eBay of shirts and ties and also sells jewelry, designer sunglasses, and other fashion items. CEO David Yaskulka, who owns the company with his wife, Debbie, says he uses eBay market data to identify new products and improve his listing strategy all the time.

David reviews most searched for phrases in his categories to keep an eye on what consumers are looking for. This helps him identify new product lines and also helps him fine-tune his listing strategy. He uses three methods to help him find out what eBay consumers are searching for: he reviews eBay Traffic Reports, monitors the discussion boards in the Clothing category, and talks regularly with his eBay category manager.

David monitors the most-searched words and phrases that shoppers enter into eBay's search engines. At one point, David noticed an upsurge in shoppers searching for the words *Blinde sunglasses*. He was unfamiliar with this brand, so he contacted his supplier to find out more about them; he began selling these Italian sunglasses to satisfy the growing demand on eBay.

Hot Lists from Other Marketplaces

TIAS.com has been publishing a monthly Hot List of antiques and collectibles since June 2002. These top 10 lists are based on hundreds of thousands of searches by people using the online search engines at the following marketplaces:

- TIAS.com (www.tias.com) is one of the Web's largest online antique and collectible malls, with 800 merchants and about 190,000 unique customers a day.

- AntiqueArts.com (www.antiquearts.com) specializes in high-end antiques and art.

- Kovels.com (www.kovels.com) is a free online price guide to antiques and collectibles from noted experts Ralph and Terry Kovel.

TIAS hot lists can be viewed online in the TIAS newsletter archives—just search for *Hot List* at www.tias.com/newsletter. Keep in mind that these searches are what people were looking for, not necessarily what they were buying. In many cases, people will search for items when they are just trying to determine the value of a specific item that they have in their possession. And keep in mind that people were searching for these items on TIAS, not eBay; it's an *indicator* of possible demand on eBay in the antiques and collectibles categories.

Hot Lists from Shopping Search Engines

Shopping search engine services allow visitors to enter a product and find that product for sale across multiple e-commerce sites. They are a sort of Yahoo! or Google for e-commerce sites. Many of them show the most popular searches or products.

Shopping.com conducts millions of shopping searches each week. The site publishes a Consumer Demand Index (CDI) that reveals emerging trends and highlights the hottest products (www.shopping.com/cdi). Figure 9-2 shows the top-ranking keyword searches for the word *Headphones*.

Other shopping search engines have popular searches features—sometimes you have to dig around their sites to find them. Here are some examples, though they may change over time.

BizRate.com lists What's Hot and Popular Products on its home page (www.bizrate.com). NexTag has popular searches on the category pages (www.nextag.com). BrilliantShopper.com has a popular products feature on its home page (www.brilliantshopper.com). Froogle has a feature that lists "A few of the items recently found with Froogle" on its home page (www.froogle.com). PriceGrabber has a list of popular categories and the top items within those categories (www.pricegrabber.com).

You might find other ways to use shopping search engines in your research. Entering a search term or drilling down into a product category can give you ideas and can be educational about what other brands are out there on other e-commerce sites.

Lists Generated by Data-Analysis Tools

Andale and Terapeak provide lists of what's hot on eBay based on licensed eBay market data. They examine eBay categories, looking for minimum revenue and bids and for growth in the amount of bidding in these categories. See Chapters 4 and 5 to learn how to access these lists.

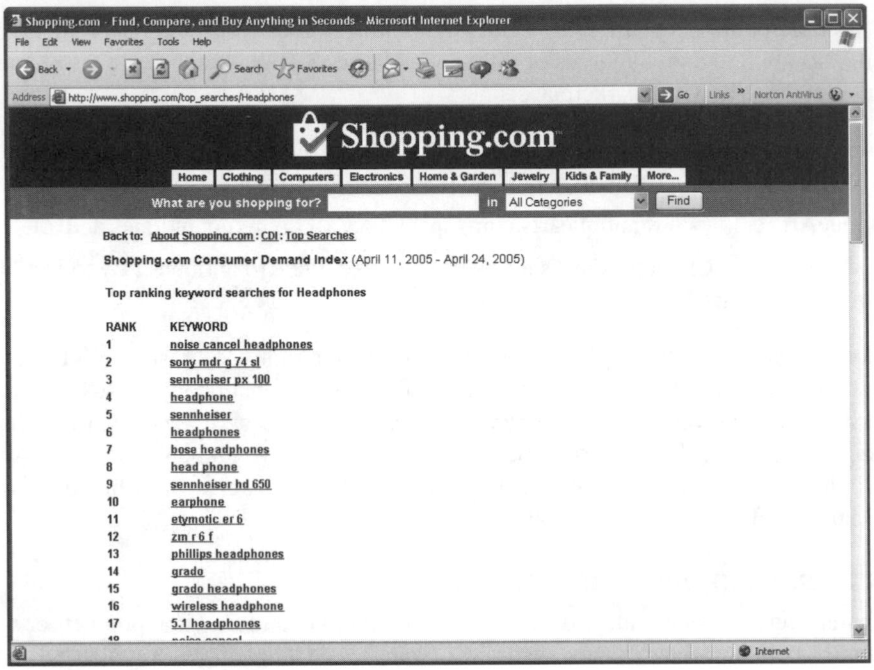

FIGURE 9-2   Shopping.com's Consumer Demand Index displays top-ranking keyword searches—in this case, for *Headphones*.

Learn from Others: Jimwarden Goes Fishing for Inventory

Jim Miller joined eBay in 1997 and credits his daughter with helping him find hot items like Beanie Babies, Hit Clips, and Mighty Beanz to sell on eBay. He became one of the first eBay PowerSellers in 1998 (eBay user ID Jimwarden). His website is at www.jimwarden.com.

Jim is a Silver PowerSeller and sells fishing tackle on eBay. His distributor offers a broad range of products, so Jim started using Terapeak to see which items had the best sell-through rates (STRs) and average selling prices (ASPs).

"I have been selling the Mio 136 Auto Navigation system fairly successfully," Jim said. "They also have a Mio 168 model that I hadn't gotten around to listing. Terapeak research showed me that the Mio 168 had a much higher sell-through rate with many more units being sold than the Mio 136 model."

eBay market data provided information to Jim that helped him narrow down his choices. He hopes to make more money selling the Mio 168 model. And by using a market-data tool to figure out which items to sell, Jim will have more time to do "real-life" fishing.

Factors to Consider When Evaluating Products

Don't assume that you should look at hot lists and then start selling those items on eBay. The lists are intended to get you brainstorming on what is popular with buyers or browsers. You need to do a lot of work before you hang your hat on a particular product. Here are some questions you need to consider before listing potential hot items:

- Will it be profitable to sell the product? What are the costs? You need to factor in *all* the costs of selling the item. What are the selling prices on eBay?

- Does the product have staying power? Many items found on hot lists are short-lived fads or, especially in the case of consumer electronics and computers, can become obsolete with the next technology release.

- Have you considered the importance of brand? Just because music players are hot doesn't mean Brand X will sell well.

- Have you considered the competition? Remember that thousands of people are looking at these same lists and may be looking to jump in and start selling on eBay.

- Do you sell what you know and know what you sell? Make sure you become an expert in whatever area you are considering selling. Knowing what product features are important to buyers will help you create better listings.

Study the Research Data

You can use What's Hot lists to generate ideas. Take the time to study the potential for new products using market-data tools from Chapters 4–6 (which also have What's Hot lists). When you evaluate new products, use tools from Andale, Terapeak, and DeepAnalysis to help you research the STRs and ASPs of the products you are considering. These tools can help you understand the category as a whole and let you study the success of individual brands as well. eBay shoppers are finicky, and you don't want to be stuck with a warehouse (or basement) full of duds.

#2 Choose Auction-Style Listings vs. Fixed Price Format

When Pierre Omidyar created eBay (called AuctionWeb at the time) in September 1995, the only way you could sell an item was by using the auction format. eBay has grown incredibly since those days and has become much more complex. Sellers can choose to list in an auction-style format, an auction format with Buy It Now, a Fixed Price format, or a Fixed Price eBay Store format. eBay reports that all Fixed Price formats make up about a third of the gross merchandise volume (value of all goods sold) on its site.

It's extremely important that you find out which format is most effective for your items. Top eBay PowerSellers know that choosing the right format for an item can make the difference in making a sale or having a dud listing, and even more important is finding the right combination of listing formats to optimize your sales.

Figure 9-3 shows how eBay Stores Reports Plus Sales By Format report breaks out your monthly sales by auction, fixed price, and store inventory, and gives you the ASP per item by format.

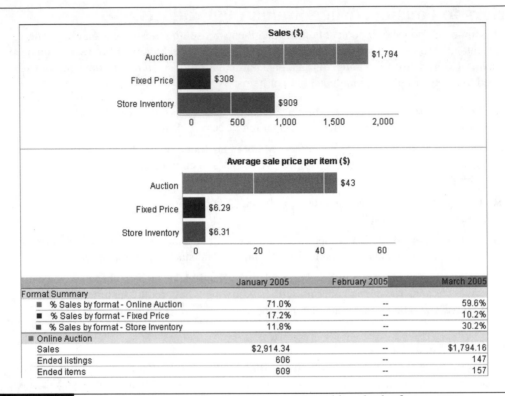

	January 2005	February 2005	March 2005
Format Summary			
■ % Sales by format - Online Auction	71.0%	--	59.6%
■ % Sales by format - Fixed Price	17.2%	--	10.2%
■ % Sales by format - Store Inventory	11.8%	--	30.2%
■ Online Auction			
Sales	$2,914.34	--	$1,794.16
Ended listings	606	--	147
Ended items	609	--	157

FIGURE 9-3   eBay Sales Reports Plus show you your monthly sales by format.

TIP

Make frequent backups of all of your data. Under the charts in Figure 9-3 is a table of the most recent three months of sales data. In March, eBay lost this seller's data for February (you can see that column is blank). If you download your data, not only can you create customized spreadsheets, but you'll also have a backup.

When I was looking for Wusthof knives on eBay, I noticed a seller who listed the same item in several different formats: an auction with a low starting bid and long duration to get eyeballs; a few auctions with higher starting bids and shorter duration to satisfy those wanting quicker gratification, and a ton of Buy It Now auctions to get those who want the items immediately. That seller could satisfy me no matter what my mood—patient bargain-hunter, gambler, or impatient shopper. (This selling strategy works only when you have multiple quantities of the same item, of course.)

Three Ways to Sell Items at a Fixed Price

eBay offers three ways to sell items at a fixed price:

Auctions with Buy It Now   Shoppers can either buy the item instantly at the Buy It Now price, or they can place a bid on the item at the starting bid price. If someone purchases using Buy It Now, the listing is ended. If someone bids on the item instead of making a Buy It Now purchase, the listing changes to a straight auction format. The Buy It Now feature is available only when no bids have been received for the item or until the reserve price is met. The item will appear in regular eBay browsing and search results.

Fixed Price Format   Buyers can purchase your item immediately at the price you set, but they cannot bid on your item. The Buy It Now price is always available; it will not disappear. You can sell quantities of one item or more per listing. The item will appear in regular eBay browsing and search results.

Store Item   Sellers wanting to sell in the store format must have a store, for which there is a minimum monthly subscription fee. Buyers can purchase your item immediately at the price you set, but they cannot bid on your item. You can sell quantities of one item or more per listing. The item will *not* appear in regular eBay browsing and search results—it will appear only in store searches, your eBay Store, and in cross-merchandising for your other listings. (Sellers choose to sell in store format for a variety of reasons, including much lower listing fees.)

9

Rare vs. Common Items

In choosing whether to sell something in an auction or Fixed Price format, the seller usually evaluates several factors:

- Is the item rare or a limited-edition?
- Is the value of the item unknown?
- Is the item used?
- Is the item likely to be sought after for some other reason?

If you answer yes to any of these questions, the auction format may be the best way to sell the item. Because bidders have no idea of your asking price, they are stimulated by other bidding on your property and may bid more than you would have asked.

If you think an item is relatively common and easy to find, its value is well known, and it may have few bidders, you may want to sell the item for a fixed price, use a Buy It Now price, or place the item in your eBay Store.

Research for Identification

Online communities are great for networking, but you can also use them to help you do research. Sometimes you may want to sell an item you don't know anything about, which makes it difficult to describe its best features. Perhaps you don't even know what the item is or its age—this is common in the field of collectibles. But just because you've never seen it before does not mean it is rare or valuable, so do your homework before you offer an item. Once you know what the item is, you can plug it into the data tools to estimate its rarity and worth.

Try finding communities that can help you identify items. Use proper "netiquette"—people are more likely to help you if you are polite and are contributing to the conversation. You can also try using appraisal services for antiques, collectibles, or memorabilia. Here are some helpful links.

- **eBay Community Hub (links to discussion boards and eBay groups)**   http://hub .ebay.com/community
- **OTWA (Online Traders Web Alliance)**   www.otwa.com/community
- **AuctionBytes Forums**   www.auctionbytes.com/forum/phpBB/index.php
- **Yahoo Groups**   http://groups.yahoo.com
- **Google Groups**   http://groups.google.com
- **Association of Online Appraisers (links to online appraisal services)**   www .aoaonline.org/
- **Appraisers Association of America**   www.appraisersassoc.org

Just because you consider an item to be a "collectible" doesn't mean it's rare or sought after. Many's the time a dealer purchases an item that he has never seen before, but discovers to his disappointment that there are 50 items just like it listed on eBay. Always test your assumptions by checking eBay market data.

The Stores Effect: Auctions as a Marketing Tool

If you own an eBay Store, you may have a different approach to selling and listing than an eBay seller who does not own a store. This has to do with the fact that auctions can be used to drive traffic to stores.

The main eBay search tool searches only the core platform (meaning non-store items). Search results consist only of auction and fixed-price listings—it does not return store items unless fewer than 21 search items are returned, but even then, only up to 30 store items are displayed.

Because most eBay shoppers use the main Search box to find items, they are not necessarily finding store items. So smart storeowners have developed a strategy to run auction and fixed-price listings that will drive traffic to their store items.

In addition, some sellers use eBay auctions as a customer-acquisition tool, hoping they can get their eBay customers to purchase directly from their e-commerce site for future purchases. They view eBay costs as a marketing expense. In this case, sellers might run more auctions than store listings, since auctions are found with eBay.com searches. If you have a website, go ahead and include links to it in places where eBay allows it, such as your About Me page and in your e-mail signature line.

Once a customer has completed the transaction, some eBay sellers send a follow-up thank-you e-mail asking whether the customer would like to sign up for their opt-in e-mail newsletter. Good judgment should be used, however, since eBay buyers are sensitive to spam and are quick to report real and perceived violators of eBay policy. We talk more about this in Chapter 10.

NOTE   *eBay auction and Fixed Price listings on the core platform can be 1, 3, 5, 7, or 10 days in duration and are searchable with the eBay.com Search box. The core platform excludes eBay Stores listings, which must be a minimum of 30-days in duration and are searchable only on the eBay Stores search box, with a few exceptions noted previously.*

Learn from Others: ACityDiscount Looks at the Big Picture

Titanium Powerseller John Stack of ACityDiscount (www.acitydiscount.com) says when he analyzes his sales performance, some reports show that Fixed Price listings on eBay (not including store items) are unprofitable. But, he continues listing them—and for good reason.

ACityDiscount sells new and used restaurant equipment, and they use three listing formats: auctions, Fixed Price, and store listings. The company lists all used items in an auction format starting at 99 cents, with No Reserve. The company sells a certain percentage of goods in a Fixed Price format. The rest of the new inventory goes into the eBay Store.

When John looks at the three listing formats separately, he finds that auctions do very well, with a nearly 100 percent STR and a good ASP. His Fixed Price listings average only about a 10 percent STR, and items in his store sell well and are profitable.

Anyone looking at the results of each format—auction, Fixed Price, and stores—separately might think ACityDiscount should get rid of the Fixed Price listings. But John knows that those Fixed Price listings are what drives traffic to his store.

ACityDiscount makes tremendous use of cross-promotional techniques to show visitors to any one listing all the other relevant listings the company has up for sale on eBay. (We'll talk more about cross-promotional techniques in Chapter 10.)

The following illustration shows an ACityDiscount 7-day Fixed Price listing for a 30-quart pizza dough mixer. When you scroll down within the item description, you'll see a list of seven other pizza dough mixers; some are different sizes or have different features. If you click through on one of the listings for a 20-quart mixer, you'll see that it's an eBay Store listing and 10 of those items are available for sale.

(continued)

John Stack knows that buyers who use the main search box on eBay to find pizza dough mixers won't find those store listings, but they will find his auction and Fixed Price listings on the core platform using the eBay.com Search box. So he drives traffic to his store by leading shoppers through and helping them find the item they are looking for.

Remember that it costs as low as 2 cents to list an item in eBay Stores, compared to a minimum of 30 cents for auction listings. So there is an incentive to list items in an eBay Store to save money on listing fees, but buyers have to be able to find those store items.

John said as his company has grown, he has started to view eBay posting fees as an advertising expense for the new equipment that is listed in the stores. That's why he says it's important for him to look at his sales performance on eBay as a whole, and not look at the results of each format separately.

Study the Format Data

You can use market-data tools from Chapters 4–6 to find out whether auctions or Fixed Price listings get a higher STR and ASP. Make sure you are comparing apples to apples. If you are selling last year's items and looking at data for this year's models, you might see a big difference in which format you should choose.

You can also run tests of several quantities of the same item to see which does best—auctions, Buy It Now auctions, Fixed Price, or eBay Store items. Look at eBay reports, including eBay Traffic Reports' Most Popular Pages section, and Sellathon's ViewTracker to examine the results of your tests.

#3 Analyze Effectiveness of Reserve Price

A Reserve Price on eBay is like insurance for the seller. The feature is optional (and a fee is charged for using it). The Reserve Price is the lowest price for which a seller is willing to sell an item, but it's higher than the starting bid.

To win an auction with a Reserve Price, a bidder must meet or exceed the Reserve Price and have the highest bid. If a bidder's maximum bid meets or exceeds the reserve, the bid will be automatically raised to meet the reserve. If no bidders meet the Reserve Price, neither the seller nor the high bidder is under any further obligation to complete the transaction.

Why use Reserve Price when you can just start the bidding at the lowest price for which you are willing to sell an item? Sellers say buyer behavior, or the psychology of auctions, attract buyers to listings with a lower price. Once they have bid on an auction, those buyers are then vested in that auction and will follow it throughout the duration.

One PowerSeller, commenting in a 2003 article on Reserve Price auctions, explained that he uses reserves because he doesn't believe bids are high enough on eBay. Because each type of item has its own dynamic, the strategy for selling one type of item is not the same as for selling another—such as electronics and toys, for example. Even within the same category, differences in strategies are important to note.

The problems with reserves are that they cost money if the item doesn't sell, and buyers don't like them—they believe Reserve Prices disrupt the fun of bidding. So sellers must weigh the benefits of knowing they won't sell the item at a loss if they use Reserve Price, versus the possibility the item won't sell at all or won't go as high as it might if it did not have a Reserve Price.

The use of Reserve Prices varies widely by category and is used more frequently for higher value items. Therefore, it pays to do your research and conduct your own tests before using this option.

Study Reserve Price Data

You can use market-data tools to see if auctions that used the Reserve Price feature netted a higher or lower ASP and STR, but study the numbers carefully. Take into account the fees levied on your auction if it closes without a winning bid—these can be expensive tests to run, so start cautiously.

DeepAnalysis offers a Feature Analysis report in the Report tab. The first line item in the report is Reserve Price. It contains usage, STR, ASP, and percentage of dollar sales made up by auctions using Reserve Price. You can compare these numbers to the category average.

You can also click the Auction tab in DeepAnalysis to see the listings that make up the search results; check the Reserve Met category to see the listings in which Reserve Price was not met. Study those auctions to see if you can learn from them. (You can see an example of this report in Chapter 6.)

Terapeak's Listing Features report in the Report tab tells you what percentage of listings used at least the Reserve Price feature.

9

Andale's Price Finder tool offers a Listing Type report that gives you usage, STR, and ASP for auctions with no reserve and auctions with reserve.

#4 Evaluate Optional Features and Upgrades

eBay offers sellers a variety of features to make their listings stand out from those of other sellers. In addition, third-party tools offer features like adding audio or video to your listings. Most of these features cost extra money, so it's important to know which ones work and whether they will increase traffic and bidding to your listings.

Sometimes it helps to put yourself in your buyers' place. Ask yourself, if you were shopping, what would draw your attention to listings? Next, look at what other sellers are using. The tools in Chapters 4–6 can help you determine which eBay features sellers are using, and you can also peruse Completed Item search results.

Look at the features used and compare the ASP and STRs with listings that did not use those features (remember to compare apples to apples). This will help you learn whether those features helped increase selling prices.

Finally, look at the costs of the features and determine the cost versus benefit. If spending $1 can help you earn an additional $20, that's a good return. Spending an additional $1 to earn an additional $1.20 may not be worth it if your STRs are low.

What the Experts Say

eBay's Gallery feature displays a thumbnail photo of an item in the search results, so buyers don't have to click a listing to see whether the item is what they are looking for. Scot Wingo, president and CEO of ChannelAdvisor Corporation, and author of *eBay Strategies*, said that according to his company's research, Gallery is by far the most effective upgrade offered by eBay. In fact, he recommends Gallery for any item that is worth more than $10 and is not a commodity item.

As always, follow up with your own studies. Examine eBay market data in your category, and run tests of your own listings to see how auctions perform for identical items, some using Gallery and some not using Gallery. Buyer behavior can vary by category, so it's always wise to test your assumptions.

Study the Features Data

The tools in Chapters 4–6 can help you measure which eBay features are being used. While you can't assume other sellers know the best features to use, you will be competing with their listings, so you should know what they are using.

CAUTION   *Use caution when comparing listings with special features and those without them. Sellers are more likely to spend money on upgrades when they are offering high-value items, so you may not be comparing apples to apples. I might spend extra to use Gallery on a brand-new "iPod New In Box," but I wouldn't use Gallery on a listing for a used iPod in poor condition. Look at the listings to get a reality check.*

Learn from Others: Wake Up and Smell the Coffee

It didn't surprise me when I learned that Skip McGrath (user ID mcgrrrrr) of Auction-Sellers-Resource.com (www.auction-sellers-resource.com) regularly runs tests on his auctions.

Skip wanted to find out whether a service called Seller's Voice would be a good investment. Seller's Voice is an audio service for eBay. When someone opens an eBay listing that uses Seller's Voice, they hear the seller talking, providing information about themselves and the product for sale.

To test the service, Skip listed eight auctions of Starbucks collectibles; on four listings, he used Seller's Voice, and the other four, he did not include the feature. Everything else was the same, including the starting price, duration, and ending day and time. Here's a table showing a comparison of listings using the feature and those not using the feature:

Auction Item	Price without Seller's Voice	Price with Seller's Voice
Seattle Destination Series Starbucks Mug	$9.99 (1)	$19.05 (4)
Miami Destination Series Starbucks Mug	$14.05 (2)	$16.55 (4)
Seattle Series One Starbucks Mug	$19.10 (3)	$26.77 (7)
Starbucks Pike Place Bearista Bear	$14.99 (1)	$26.03 (5)

The number of bids is in parentheses next to the selling price. The test shows that auctions with Seller's Voice received more bids and a higher selling price than identical items without Seller's Voice.

Skip then calculated the monthly cost of using Seller's Voice, and determined that he easily made up the cost of an entire month's service in just those four auctions.

This is a great example of how you can run tests yourself. Remember that just because Skip's test showed Seller's Voice would be a good investment for his coffee mug auctions does not mean the service would be right for *your* auctions. Instead, this example highlights the importance of testing a feature before committing to using it.

When you do consider services, be sure to look at the big picture and factor in the costs of using the features. (Also factor in the setup time in your calculations; labor is a valid cost whether or not you are doing it yourself or have employees.)

9

Since some features—such as audio and video—are not widely used, you may not find a way to measure results using market-data tools, but this does not mean those features wouldn't be a good investment. In these cases, you'll have to rely on testing the features for yourself—you can use Sellathon's ViewTracker to help you track the results of test auctions.

You can also do Completed Listings searches, look at the items that sold with the highest prices, and see if they used any special features.

> **TIP** *eBay occasionally runs sales on certain features, giving you an opportunity to try them at a reduced cost (or for free). This would be a good time to run tests, but be aware that results may be skewed from all of the other sellers who are also taking advantage of these sales. Monitor competitive listings to measure the effect of sales on your own test results.*

#5 Refine Your Offer and Policies

If you've ever bought something on eBay, you know how important presentation can be. Good photos and professional-looking descriptions can make you more comfortable dealing with a seller. If an eBay shopper buys an item from you, he must send you the money and rely on your honesty to deliver the item. Increasing the confidence and level of trust can help you get more bidders and increase your selling price. And your presentation and policies may be the deciding factor when a buyer chooses you over another seller of an identical item.

Components of an eBay Listing

Experienced eBay sellers know that the most important components of a good eBay auction listing include these:

- Title
- Photos
- Template
- Description of the item
- Return policy
- Shipping and handling policy
- Information about any additional fees or services

Take a look at the listing in Figure 9-4 from eBay seller joeleighs, whose company is 3Balls Golf (www.3balls.com), a golf retailer. This will give you an idea of some of the ways you can present information.

3Balls Golf provides two boxes for shipping information—one for domestic rates and one for international shipments. The text is large and easy to read.

Knowing that customers can often get the shipping and handling fees wrong, and what a hassle this can cause you, means it makes sense to make it as easy as possible for visitors to find and interpret your information. Tweaking the way you present information to your buyers is worth it and can save you money, time, and aggravation.

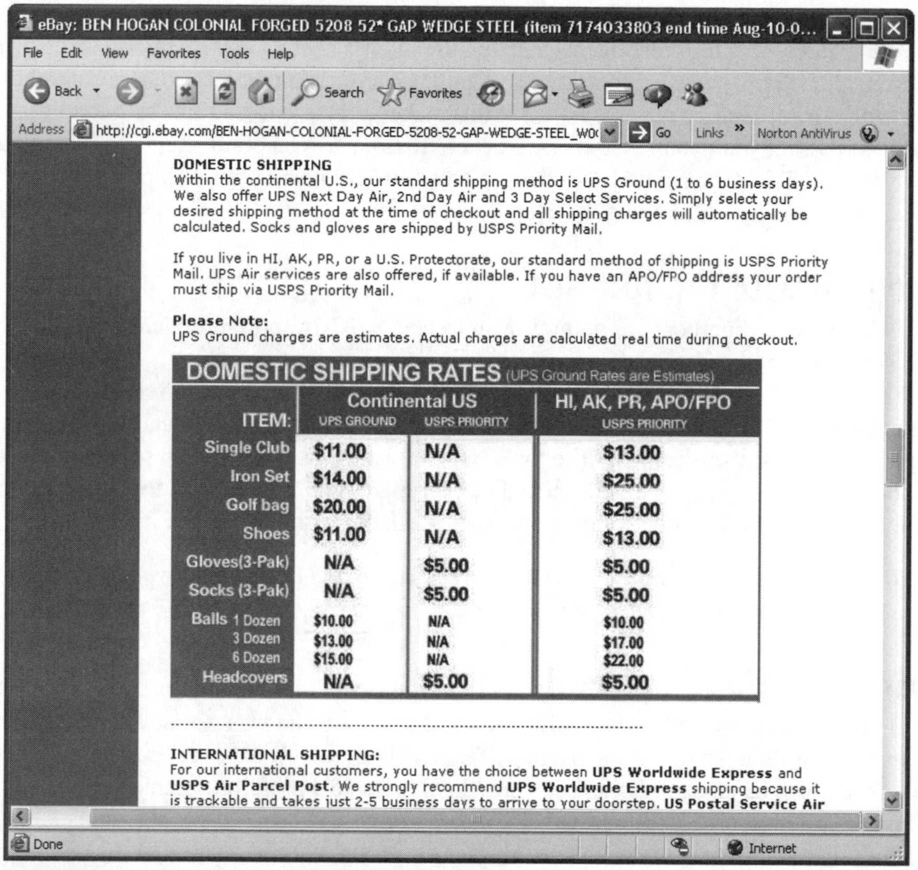
eBay: BEN HOGAN COLONIAL FORGED 5208 52* GAP WEDGE STEEL (item 7174033803 end time Aug-10-0...
File Edit View Favorites Tools Help
Back Search Favorites
Address http://cgi.ebay.com/BEN-HOGAN-COLONIAL-FORGED-5208-52-GAP-WEDGE-STEEL_W0
Go Links Norton AntiVirus
DOMESTIC SHIPPING
Within the continental U.S., our standard shipping method is UPS Ground (1 to 6 business days). We also offer UPS Next Day Air, 2nd Day Air and 3 Day Select Services. Simply select your desired shipping method at the time of checkout and all shipping charges will automatically be calculated. Socks and gloves are shipped by USPS Priority Mail.
If you live in HI, AK, PR, or a U.S. Protectorate, our standard method of shipping is USPS Priority Mail. UPS Air services are also offered, if available. If you have an APO/FPO address your order must ship via USPS Priority Mail.
Please Note:
UPS Ground charges are estimates. Actual charges are calculated real time during checkout.
DOMESTIC SHIPPING RATES (UPS Ground Rates are Estimates)
ITEM: Continental US UPS GROUND USPS PRIORITY HI, AK, PR, APO/FPO USPS PRIORITY
Single Club $11.00 N/A $13.00
Iron Set $14.00 N/A $25.00
Golf bag $20.00 N/A $25.00
Shoes $11.00 N/A $13.00
Gloves(3-Pak) N/A $5.00 $5.00
Socks (3-Pak) N/A $5.00 $5.00
Balls 1 Dozen $10.00 N/A $10.00
3 Dozen $13.00 N/A $17.00
6 Dozen $15.00 N/A $22.00
Headcovers N/A $5.00 $5.00
INTERNATIONAL SHIPPING:
For our international customers, you have the choice between UPS Worldwide Express and USPS Air Parcel Post. We strongly recommend UPS Worldwide Express shipping because it is trackable and takes just 2-5 business days to arrive to your doorstep. US Postal Service Air
Done
Internet

FIGURE 9-4 Golf retailer 3Balls Golf uses large, clear boxes to convey shipping information to potential buyers to reduce confusion (and subsequent customer-service problems).

TIP *Studying feedback comments and e-mail questions from buyers and potential buyers can point to areas that need testing. If shoppers keep asking you about your refund policy even though you spell it out in your Terms Of Service in the auction description, test new wording or new placement. Measure the average number of questions you get before you make the change, and compare them with the number of questions you get after the change.*

Test, Test, Test

Marketers religiously test the effectiveness of their copy—the words used to describe in ads what they are selling and why buyers should shop from them. You should also test the effectiveness of your copy, your photos, and everything about your listings.

Some components of your listing will change from auction to auction, depending on what you are selling, and some will stay the same. Generally, eBay sellers have the same return policy, at least for all like items. Testing components that you use in every listing can be a good investment.

Try listing some items with a generous return policy (if you are prepared to honor it), and list others with a more restrictive policy—see if this makes a difference. (This can get a little tricky, since you don't want your customers to get confused, and you don't want to get confused yourself about which items have which policies.) This is where having two comparable eBay user IDs can help you test different strategies.

Keeping Up with the Joneses

Knowing what your competitors are doing is also tremendously important (even better than matching your competitors' policies is having *better* policies than they have).

While tools like DeepAnalysis and Terapeak don't generally tell you what return policies sellers are using, you can use them to identify the top sellers in your category and see what they are doing by going into their listings. (The tools will not list the user IDs of top sellers, but if you use the tools regularly to track competition and market share, you may be able to identify them.)

You should also monitor your competitors—we'll talk more about that in Chapter 11.

NOTE   *To search by seller on eBay, go to Advanced Search and click Find Items—Items By Seller. Enter the seller's user ID in the Search box.*

Shipping and Handling Policies

If you find yourself at a cocktail party of eBay buyers and sellers and want to see fireworks, just start a conversation about shipping and handling fees and policies. eBayers feel passionately about this issue. On the one hand, some believe it's only right to make a profit on shipping and handling, comparing eBay to mail-order catalogs. Others believe eBay sellers should not charge handling fees at all and should charge exactly what the shipping costs are without marking it up one penny.

Discord exists even among sellers. Sellers complain of competitors who list items at a lower price and have much higher shipping and handling charges to make up the difference. The buyers are attracted to the selling price, and often don't bother to read the fine print to see what the shipping and handling charges are. They may assume the auction for $9.99 is a better deal than the one for $14.99. It might be true, but if a $9 shipping and handling fee is added to the first listing, a $2 shipping and handling fee for the second listing makes the second one the better deal. It's surprising how many buyers fail to look at important details like these fees.

Amazon has learned to tap into a buyer phenomenon to increase its sales: the love of free shipping. But while it may work for Amazon, most eBay sellers I talk to balk at the idea of offering free shipping.

This is a prime example of a policy you need to carefully research and test, and having the right formula can add to your bottom line. Be sure to test all of your policies routinely and fine-tune your offers to get the most traffic, bids, and highest selling prices possible. Sometimes a small change can make a big difference to your bottom line.

Study the Policies Data

Market-data tools don't give you the ability to compare the effects of different polices or quality of photos and copy. You will have to do more manual searching, such as going through Completed Item searches on eBay to identify the best-selling items and whether any patterns emerge about what makes them different from less successful auctions.

You can also run tests to see whether offers and policies—such as offering free domestic shipping—will net you a higher ASP and STR. Sellathon can help you track the effects, but it's tricky to isolate the effect of a policy.

Experiment with the best policies and offers you can make in your listings, and see what works best for you. Buyer attitudes can vary depending on the item, category, and personal preferences. Whatever you do, make sure you present the information clearly in your listing description.

How the Tools Stack Up

Use a combination of tools to make the best decisions about advanced listing strategies. You can mine eBay data using Andale, Terapeak, and DeepAnalysis. You can look at your own sales performance using eBay Sales Reports Plus or by using auction-management services. And you can study visitor traffic to your listings using eBay Traffic Reports or tools such as Sellathon ViewTracker, which allows you to test and measure various approaches to advanced listing strategies.

By looking at eBay data and testing various approaches, you can improve your advanced listing strategies, from learning what to sell to refining your offer and policies.

As far as learning what works best in terms of special services or optimal policies, such as whether to offer a refund policy, you will need to run tests and then measure and compare the results. You can run simple tests or run a series of tests to add special codes in each type of listing to make it easier to track the results.

Here's a summary of some of the tools you can use to help you formulate your Advanced Listing Strategies. Go back to previous chapters to review the tools in more detail.

eBay's Completed Listings Search

It's difficult to use eBay's closed listings to identify strategies such as what you should sell and which upgrades to use. You can peruse the closed listings of successfully sold items in the product or category in which you're interested; this might show you what successful sellers are doing in terms of policies, or if a particular feature is commonly used by sellers in that category. But in general, there's no efficient way to identify successful advanced listings strategies using eBay's Completed Listings search.

eBay Sales Reports Plus and Traffic Reports

You can use the Sales By Format section of eBay Sales Reports Plus to help you track the performance of auctions versus Fixed Price formats for your own past listings on a monthly basis. You can also test identical items in different formats and measure results using tools like eBay Traffic Reports' Most Popular Pages section.

You can use the Sales By Category section of eBay Sales Reports Plus to help you identify the categories in which you are *already* selling that are performing the weakest or strongest. Take a look at other products in your strongest category—this might help you decide what additional items you want to look into selling.

While eBay Sales Reports Plus doesn't currently track the success of listings by features or Reserve Price, this feature may be added in the future—even by the time you're reading this book.

By revealing which listings received the most traffic, you can use eBay's Traffic Reports to help you test various listing strategies.

Andale

Andale has a What's Hot list to help generate ideas on what to sell. Andale's Price Finder tool has charts generated from eBay's closed listings that show usage of eBay upgrades.

You can see in Figure 9-5 that the report includes usage, ASP, and STRs for auctions using Bold, Highlight, Gallery, Gallery Featured, Featured Plus, and the Gift icon. This report for Bose headphones shows the listings using eBay's optional Gift icon did much better (ASP = $246.80 and 100 percent sell-through) than listings with no features at all (ASP = $208.02 and 68 percent sell-through). (Remember the point I mentioned earlier; it's possible the item with the Gift icon upgrade was a higher-quality/higher-value item to begin with, so check the listings to see if you can find out.)

Andale also breaks down listings by reserve, no reserve, auctions with Buy It Now, and Fixed Price listings. Conduct an All Items Data Search to avoid limiting search results too narrowly.

Use the How To Sell feature to study the details. The charts compare STRs and ASPs based on feature usage so you can decide which upgrades might be most effective.

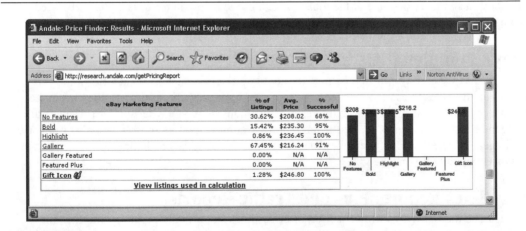

FIGURE 9-5   Andale's report for Bose headphones shows metrics for auctions based on upgrades used.

Terapeak

Terapeak has a Category Hot List that can help you generate ideas on what to sell. Terapeak offers several reports that compare metrics so you can see what approach nets the best STRs and ASPs:

- Terapeak's Listing Type Usage vs Success Rate section in the Research tab tells you what percentage of listings were auctions, multiple items, Fixed Price, eBay Store, or second chance, and what percentage of each successfully sold.

- The Listing Features report in the Research tab shows you how listings with various features performed, including Bold, Highlight, Gift Icon, eBay Picture Services, Featured Plus, Gallery Featured, Second Category, Scheduled, Buy It Now, and Reserve. They show how many listings used the feature and the percentage of items sold. The Selling Features tab in Terapeak allows you to delve deeper into feature usage and performance.

DeepAnalysis

DeepAnalysis Research Reports allow you to compare STRs and ASPs for products and categories from eBay closed-item data to help you formulate listing strategies. The Feature Analysis section in the Report tab measures the success of eBay's optional features such as Gallery, Bold, and Highlight, as well as the Reserve Price feature. The Auction Type section can help you make a decision about format.

Sellathon

While Sellathon doesn't offer specific reports that break down the performance of Advanced Listing Strategies, the tool does allow you to set up tests and print reports by auction types as you define them. This means you can create two types of listings, and by inserting two different codes you can track the traffic that goes to each type of listing to see which type is drawing the most attention.

Testing is one of the only ways to measure subtle changes in your offer or policies, so Sellathon is a vital tool in helping you fine-tune some of your advanced listing strategies.

Wrapping Up

While Advanced Listing Strategies are more difficult to measure than Basic Listing Strategies, the extra effort can be worth your time. Finding new products that have higher STRs and ASPs is every eBay seller's dream. Selling smarter can save you time and add to your bottom line.

Remember that your competitors may be using certain techniques in their listings, but they may not be fine-tuning their strategies and measuring the results. The bottom line is that only you can discover what works best for you.

Chapter 10

Marketing Strategies: Market Like a PowerSeller

When you want to kick your business up a notch, marketing is the way to go. eBay sellers fall into two camps: those who sell exclusively on eBay, and those who sell on multiple channels or marketplaces. Your approach to marketing will vary depending on what kind of seller you are, but every seller should actively market his or her business to drive traffic to listings and increase sales.

The biggest challenge is figuring out which marketing efforts are working most effectively so you know where to spend your time and dollars. You can use eBay data tools to measure the results of your marketing campaigns to determine what works and what doesn't to boost your traffic and sales.

eBay sellers can market their listings and their business in lots of ways: via advertising (online and offline), paid searches, coupons, e-mail marketing, newsletter marketing, and flyers inserted inside packages. Even simple things like posting information on online bulletin boards and including a signature in every post that includes a link to your eBay Store or website is marketing. Or new approaches, such as publishing a blog about the product or market in which you sell, can also prove effective.

It's up to each seller to determine which marketing techniques are worth measuring and how frequently to run new tests. Time and money are valuable resources, so most sellers focus on testing techniques that require a large amount of one or the other to justify these expenditures and get the best return on their investment.

All major marketing efforts are categorized into the five strategies reviewed in this chapter:

- Cross-promote your listings.
- Increase repeat sales.
- Improve your advertising and publicity.
- Enhance your reputation and credibility.
- Expand your presence.

#1 Cross-Promote Your Listings

If you are not cross-promoting your auctions, you are throwing listing fees out the window. When a buyer visits your listing, it makes sense to let the buyer know what else you are offering, particularly if you offer complementary items. Someone looking for women's shoes might want to see matching handbags, for example.

Not long ago eBay sellers had no way to cross-promote their listings. AuctionHelper (www.auctionhelper.com) was the first service to develop such tools, and eBay and other vendors eventually jumped on the cross-promotion bandwagon.

The concept of cross-promotion hit home for a lot of people when eBay introduced its cross-promotional tools for eBay Stores. When someone views one of your store items, four of your other items are promoted to the buyer in a display box, as shown in Figure 10-1.

NOTE *eBay has a strict policy about what you can link to in your listings. Most rules apply to off-eBay links. Be sure you are familiar with and conform to its latest policies, which can be found in the eBay help files at http://pages.ebay.com/help/policies/listing-links.html.*

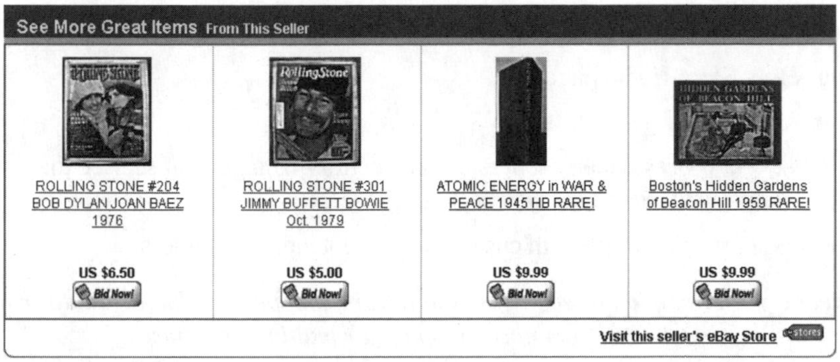

See More Great Items From This Seller

ROLLING STONE #204 BOB DYLAN JOAN BAEZ 1976	ROLLING STONE #301 JIMMY BUFFETT BOWIE Oct. 1979	ATOMIC ENERGY in WAR & PEACE 1945 HB RARE!	Boston's Hidden Gardens of Beacon Hill 1959 RARE!
US $6.50	US $5.00	US $9.99	US $9.99
Bid Now!	Bid Now!	Bid Now!	Bid Now!

Visit this seller's eBay Store

FIGURE 10-1 eBay's cross-promotional tool allows sellers to display photos of four other items at the bottom of the View Item page, so visitors can view more of a seller's listings.

eBay's Cross-Promotions Tool

You can learn about eBay's cross-promotions tool in eBay's Help files. The "Cross-Promoting Your Items Overview" section can be found at http://pages.ebay.com/help/sell/cp-overview.html. You can also find more information at http://pages.ebay.com/sell/crosspromo/.

eBay's cross-promotions appear in the following situations:

- When a buyer bids on your item
- When a buyer wins your item
- When a buyer views your listing (for eBay Store sellers only; non-storeowners can use a non-eBay tool, such as AuctionHelper or Auctiva, discussed a bit later)

As the seller, you can create rules to set up how eBay decides what other listings to cross-promote for each type of listing being viewed. This is where testing is important. You might find shoppers looking at dresses are more likely to click over to other dress styles, or they might be more inclined to look at matching shoes. And it might even vary depending on whether shoppers are still browsing or if they are checking out to pay for their purchase. (You have several opportunities to cross-promote items, including during the checkout process.)

All these factors need to be considered when you set up rules for various cross-promotional tools, and testing and measuring to see which items do the best in real auctions is the best guide you will have.

Other Cross-Promotional Tools

You can use your own cross-promotional techniques. You can keep it simple with some text links pointing to your store, or you can jazz it up with buttons that link to store categories.

You have several opportunities to cross-promote:

■ In your listings (View Item page)

■ On your eBay Store Home page

■ On your About Me page

■ In the Checkout process (many sellers use an auction-management service that takes buyers to their own website for the checkout process)

■ In all e-mail correspondence with customers and potential customers

TIP   *A great cross-promotional technique is to reward shoppers for buying additional items from you, such as offering combined shipping for multiple purchases.*

In addition to your own tools and linking devices, many auction-management services provide cross-promotional tools, including AuctionHelper (www.auctionhelper.com), Vendio (www.vendio.com), and Auctiva (www.auctiva.com). Check with your service provider about tools that may help you not only cross-promote but also measure their effectiveness and help you refine your marketing techniques.

TIP   *Most savvy sellers use auctions to drive traffic to their eBay Stores inventory, since for the most part, store items don't show up in search results, but auction listings do. (Store items have significantly lower listing fees but higher Final Value Fees.)*

Including links to your store categories in auction and store listings is a free, effective way to cross-promote your items. You can study how other sellers cross-promote their offerings—whether it's through hyperlinks or a third-party tool—to get ideas.

PowerSellers Do It Their Way (Cross-Promote, That Is)

eBay sellers are a varied bunch, and many like to manage their businesses in unique ways. Cross-promotional techniques are no exception, and you'll find a lot of different ways to tempt visitors to your listing to click through to another.

eBay Platinum PowerSeller Andrew Evan Green (Taximarket) included the following hyperlinked text at the top of his auction description for an office chair: "Click here to see our complete line of office chairs & furniture in our eBay Store!" Clicking the link brought visitors to the Taximarket Store, with a gallery view of all the other office chairs for sale by Taximarket.

Toward the bottom of Taximarket's auction for the office chair, Andrew included other links to his eBay listings: another link to office chairs, a link to office desks, and a link to telescopes, an item in which Taximarket specializes. By linking to the entire office-chair inventory in his store, Andrew is driving people in the market for an office chair to a wide range of offerings and hoping at least one of his chairs will satisfy a shopper's needs. (It also may give shoppers a sense of security knowing Taximarket has a store and is selling a range of chairs.)

Another eBay PowerSeller, Platinum PowerSeller David Yaskulka of Blueberry Boutique, creates boxed areas with headings to organize links. This is effective since the store sells a lot of designer items; in one box on his About Me page, for example, he includes a heading "Shop by Designer" and lists top designers. Each designer name is hyperlinked, so visitors can click to listings that feature items from that designer.

eBay Titanium PowerSeller ACityDiscount includes a hyperlinked list of store categories in the left column of the store's listing description and puts a list of related items at the bottom of the listing description. Underneath that is a list of eBay Store categories with thumbnail pictures of the types of items found in that store category—for instance, a picture of a dishwasher appears just above the category name Dishwashing Sinks—Tables.

If you are a golfer, it would be hard *not* to click on some of the links to other items on 3balls Golf's stores homepage. Throughout the store's pages on eBay, boxes list items for sale with effective titles like "Stock up now," "This week's hottest sellers," and "3balls Golf Dollar Store." These eye-catching boxes entice customers to click through to other products. In addition, buttons let viewers browse by category and manufacturer.

Learn from Others: Going for Gold with Cross Promotions

Bobby Minnich (Bobby131313) is a Silver PowerSeller and sells coins on eBay. To test and measure his cross-promotional efforts in his eBay Store listings, Bobby has come up with some creative ways to use Sellathon ViewTracker (discussed in Chapter 7).

Within his eBay Store listings, Bobby includes clickable buttons for the types of coins he sells (Quarters, Halves, Dollars, and so on). When someone is perusing his store items, he hopes the shopper will continue to browse his store by clicking these cross-promotional buttons. Bobby links the buttons to his other items using a special code, or keyword, so that when a shopper clicks one, a page showing only Bobby's items in that category appears.

For example, if a shopper clicks the Gold and Silver button in one of Bobby's listings, a search is launched in his eBay Store for the term *uscoinsbullion*. Bobby has all his Gold and Silver coin listings coded with the term *uscoinsbullion* so the shopper finds items relevant to what he or she is looking for.

Bobby deliberately uses terms on these buttons that no searcher would ordinarily type into the eBay Search box. When he looks at Sellathon ViewTracker to see which search terms visitors used, he can differentiate the cross-promo visits. He knows that if 100 visitors found him with the search term *uscoinsbullion*, they must have clicked the Gold and Silver button in one of his other listings. (And using ViewTracker, he can see from which listings they linked.)

This gives him valuable information about the popularity of each of his categories, and it lets him measure results over time, as well as test new templates to see if one is more effective than another.

Bobby has invested a lot of time in learning the way his traffic-tracking program works and how he can use features to give him information to increase his sales and go for the gold.

10

Keep an eye on top sellers. Look beyond your own categories and see what eBay PowerSellers in other categories are doing. You might get some useful ideas you can apply to your own cross-promotional activities. You can find lists of eBay's top sellers on several sites—one is located at www.nortica.com/UserArea/ebay500_15.asp. Periodically peruse these sellers' listings to see if the techniques they use would make sense for your listings. You don't have to be a copycat, but you can keep your eyes open for effective techniques and best practices.

Study the Cross-Promotions Data

You can use tools such as eBay Traffic Reports and Sellathon ViewTracker to determine which listings are most popular, and use those popular listings to drive traffic to other items you are offering.

If you have a Featured or Anchor eBay Store, you have access to path data. This shows you how shoppers are navigating your listings so you can see from where they are coming, how they move from one listing to another, or whether they leave your store after viewing one item. This will help you understand shopper behavior and how visitors are navigating through your listings and can help you improve your cross-promotions. We reviewed eBay's Traffic reports in Chapter 3.

If you have a Basic eBay Store, you should look into tools such as Sellathon ViewTracker, which can track data through eBay's cross-promotions tool (but not through other vendors' cross-promotional tools). ViewTracker will indicate whether someone clicked a listing using eBay's cross-promotions tool and will identify from which auction the visitor came—look on the Details page on ViewTracker, as shown in Figure 10-2. This allows you to run tests and see which cross-promoted items are getting the most hits with which listings.

Visit	Date	Time	Len	IP Address	Who	R?	Method Of Arrival	Search Terms	Price	Bids	Sort by	Pg	Op
36	2005-05-16	12:13am		64.230.16. [?]		↻	Searching Category : 280	"rolling stone"	$5.00	1	●	1	
35	2005-05-16	12:12am		64.230.16. [?]			Searching Category : 280	"rolling stone"	$5.00	1	●	1	
34	2005-05-16	12:09am		68.36.80. [?]		↻	Direct Link		$5.00	0	n/a	n/a	
33	2005-05-16	12:04am		24.167.91. [?]			Searching All Of eBay	rolling stones	$5.00	0	●	1	
32	2005-05-16	12:02am	◐	65.100.200. [?]			Searching All Of eBay	bob marley	$5.00	0	●	1	
31	2005-05-15	11:21pm		200.121.19. [?]			Direct Link		$5.00	0	n/a	n/a	
30	2005-05-15	11:03pm		71.32.2. [?]			Searching All Of eBay	bob marley	$5.00	0	●	1	
29	2005-05-15	08:17pm		68.36.80. [?]		↻	Direct Link		$5.00	0	n/a	n/a	
28	2005-05-15	06:34pm		70.59.200. [?]		↻	Cross Promotion	▨▨▨▨▨	$5.00	0	n/a	n/a	
27	2005-05-15	06:32pm		70.59.200. [?]		↻	Browsing Your eBay Store		$5.00	0	●	1	

FIGURE 10-2   ViewTracker's Details page shows you how visitors got to your listing (Method Of Arrival); here, ViewTracker shows that visitor number 28 came through a cross-promotion link and indicates the listing number of the auction from which they came.

Unfortunately, no tool at this time lets you easily summarize and compare the effectiveness of various cross-promotional techniques. The eBay Traffic Reports Full Paths report consists of a list of each visitor's path through your listings. If the first visitor came to one of your auctions and exited, you can see that information. If a second visitor arrived and moved from one auction to another of your auctions and then exited your listings, you can see that. But nowhere does it summarize this information. You have to peruse the list and look for cross-links.

Your auction-management service may provide information about cross-promotion effectiveness through its reporting tools.

#2 Increase Repeat Sales

On eBay, listing fees are part of the cost of doing business. You get a better return on your investment in listing fees if buyers return to your eBay Store or website and buy from you again. You should do everything you can to get past buyers to purchase from you again.

Brick-and-mortar stores know that if you have purchased from them once, you are more likely to purchase from them again in the future—if the customer has had a good experience, of course. So these stores send their customers reminders, and they generally get a better response than sending mass mailings to people who may never have shopped at the store before. (Marketing to previous customers is a customer *retention* cost, as opposed to marketing to get new customers, which would be a customer *acquisition* cost.)

Most large retailers keep customer lists, and they periodically send customers flyers or letters to inform them of sales. But on the Internet, sending e-mails is often viewed as spam. That's why it's critical that you be very careful when implementing this marketing strategy.

You can remind past eBay buyers about your current listings and upcoming sales in several ways:

- Opt-in e-mail marketing, including e-mail newsletters
- Coupon services (a form of opt-in e-mail marketing)
- Flyers or coupons inserted inside packages sent to customers
- Direct mail, such as a postcard sent through the U.S. Postal Service
- RSS (Really Simple Syndication) feeds or blogs

TIP *Past buyers may or may not remember your name. It's important that you remind them of your name, eBay user ID, location, and, if possible, the item they purchased from you. This accomplishes two things: If they had a good experience with you, they may be more receptive to your current offer. Second, if they remember you, they will be less likely to report your e-mail as spam (unsolicited e-mail).*

In 2001, Ron Henderson created AuntiesBeads.com, an e-commerce website catering to hobbyists and professional jewelry designers. He began sending out a monthly e-mail newsletter to encourage repeat business, and in one year, he grew his list to 10,000 names. By April 2003,

Ron had 18,000 customer names in his database, all who chose to receive his free marketing newsletter via e-mail. He reported a high repeat-customer rate as a result of these marketing efforts. These days, his business is still thriving and he speaks at industry conferences about online retailing and the success of his business.

If you are thinking about sending e-mail to your customers, be aware of the risks. People are very sensitive about unsolicited e-mails. You must get permission from people before adding them to your list (they must opt-in to receive e-mails). You must also allow them to unsubscribe (or opt-out) from your list easily.

You must also follow eBay's rules about fee-avoidance and off-eBay transactions. Consult http://pages.ebay.com/help/policies/rfe-spam-non-ebay-sale.html for information.

NOTE   *Some e-mail newsletter services specifically target eBay sellers, for example, AuctionContact and Topica. Look in eBay's Solutions Directory (www.solutions .ebay.com) for the latest eBay-approved vendors. eBay has its own tool called the Email Marketing program (restricted to sellers with eBay Stores); for more information, see http://pages.ebay.com/storefronts/emailmarketing.html.*

Tracking Repeat-Purchase Campaigns

If you are spending money sending e-mails or print marketing material, you want to know if it is working. Knowing your current rate of repeat purchases and tracking it over time is important.

One of the most effective ways of tracking a campaign is to make an offer and require that recipients use a special promotional code to receive the benefits of the offer. For instance, you can include an offer in an e-mail newsletter for $2 off the recipient's next purchase from you if they reference the code accompanying the offer.

You can also measure traffic to your listings immediately after you send out an e-mail or direct-mail piece.

MyStoreCredit (www.mystorecredit.com) offers a service exclusively for eBay sellers that uses a combination of coupon and direct-mail techniques and also encourages first-time buyers to purchase from you. In your current eBay listings, you advertise an offer for a certain discount on the next purchase. Then MyStoreCredit sends monthly newsletters to *all* buyers who have opted in. The monthly mailing reminds the buyers what they purchased from you, tells them the benefits they receive when they purchase from you again (such as a discount), and includes a list of your current listings. This encourages your past buyers to purchase from you again.

MyStoreCredit tracks everything for the seller, so sellers don't have to remember whether a previous customer is eligible for a discount on a current purchase or not. Otherwise, it could be difficult for sellers to keep track. MyStoreCredit uses eBay's API, reviewed in Chapter 3, in addition to its own proprietary system to keep track of data.

TIP   *Remember that if you are trying to offer your own coupons to customers, keep it simple. You don't want to spend hours trying to figure out who gets a discount and who doesn't.*

Once you know whether a current customer has purchased from you before, and what prompted the customer to return, you can judge whether your marketing is paying off.

TIP
Repeat-purchase marketing makes sense only if your customers have had a good experience with you—do everything you can to satisfy your customers. If you don't offer a good customer experience from start to finish, customers may be unhappy and unlikely to come back and buy from you again. If such is the case, you might not want to spend money trying to attract unhappy customers.

Study Repeat Sales Data

As mentioned earlier, you can set up codes to track marketing campaigns, and if you use a coupon, e-mail newsletter, or another type of service, you should have ways to track these campaigns.

If you use an auction-management system (tools that help you manage your auctions), it should be collecting and storing buyer information. When you make a sale, compare the buyer contact information to your list of past customers to keep track of repeat versus new sales.

You can use eBay Sales Report Plus to see what percentage of sales are from repeat customers. Sign in to eBay, go to My eBay, and click Sales Reports. On the Sales Summary page of Sales Reports Plus, under the Sales section, you'll see a list of metrics—the last three are Total Buyers, Total Unique Buyers, and Repeat Buyers % (see Figure 10-3). You can view the current and past two months to see whether the repeat percentage is increasing. Continue to track this metric over time.

10

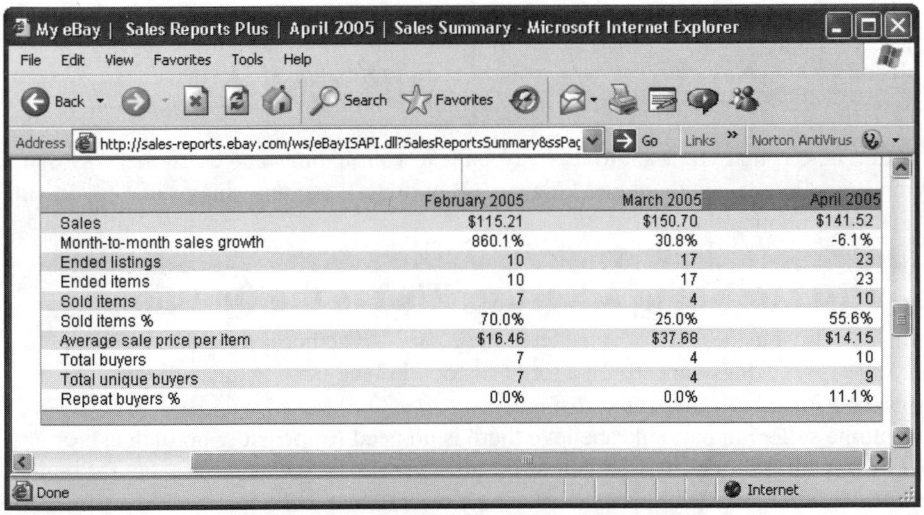

My eBay | Sales Reports Plus | April 2005 | Sales Summary - Microsoft Internet Explorer

	February 2005	March 2005	April 2005
Sales	$115.21	$150.70	$141.52
Month-to-month sales growth	860.1%	30.8%	-6.1%
Ended listings	10	17	23
Ended items	10	17	23
Sold items	7	4	10
Sold items %	70.0%	25.0%	55.6%
Average sale price per item	$16.46	$37.68	$14.15
Total buyers	7	4	10
Total unique buyers	7	4	9
Repeat buyers %	0.0%	0.0%	11.1%

FIGURE 10-3   eBay Sales Reports Plus displays the percentage of repeat buyers. In this report, April saw 11 percent repeat buyers, while previous months' sales were all new buyers for this seller.

Remember that while repeat sales on eBay may be low, your eBay customers could be buying from you on your website on future orders. Make sure you have a system in place for tracking customers and how they originally found you. Your auction-management tool should also be tracking repeat versus new customer data.

#3 Improve Your Advertising and Publicity

In late 2004, an online casino caused an international stir when it won an eBay auction for a grilled-cheese sandwich described as having the image of the Virgin Mary on it. Thus started the beginning of one of the most unique publicity campaigns in recent history. The casino went on a buying spree on eBay, bidding on unusual and strange items to add to its collection. Newspapers, bloggers, and television reporters could not resist writing about the quirky eBay purchases.

This is not to say you should acquire strange items on eBay, or that you should begin selling strange items just for the publicity, but every seller can learn from this the power of mentions in newspapers and magazines and the power of "guerilla marketing" techniques. Some sellers have jumped on the "outlandish auction" method of free publicity. Some do it in hopes of being mentioned in newspapers or on blog sites that specialize in pointing to unusual eBay auctions. Some sellers ask in the auction description that people add a particular auction to their "watched items" list in hopes of making it onto eBay's Most Watched items list on eBay Pulse (www.ebay.com/pulse).

Other sellers take a more sedate approach to public relations and may work with charitable organizations, issuing press releases to announce their good deeds.

> **TIP** *To help build repeat business, be sure to brand your business. Choose a good eBay user ID and a matching eBay Store name, and use a professionally designed logo. Having a distinctive image will differentiate you from the millions of other online sellers.*

The lesson here is that you want to drive eyeballs to your listings and do so in a way that fits in with your brand image—without breaking any eBay rules. For many, this means advertising and old-fashioned public relations.

To Advertise, or Not to Advertise: That Is the Question

Advertising an eBay business is not considered necessary—whether it makes sense to pay to advertise your eBay listings depends on a lot of factors. In fact, posting an auction listing on eBay can be considered a form of advertising.

Low-volume sellers in particular believe there is no need (or possibly no budget) for advertising. eBay has millions of users, all browsing and searching eBay every day for items they want. But as you grow your business, you may want to test some forms of advertising.

A long time ago, Philadelphia department store owner John Wannamaker is said to have remarked, "I know half of my advertising budget is wasted. I just don't know which half." Advertising industry professionals spend lots of time trying to measure the effectiveness of their advertising and marketing efforts. But a lot of advertising involves plain common sense and making sure you are where the shoppers are.

Earlier I mentioned Ron Henderson of AuntiesBeads.com. He told me that each month after he sends out his e-mail newsletter, he sees an immediate spike in traffic in the three to four days following the mailing. This kind of effect can be tracked with counters and analytics tools such as eBay Traffic Reports and Sellathon's ViewTracker, assuming you are running only one campaign or type of ad at a time.

But advertising will get you only so far if you don't have good product offerings, photos and descriptions, and reputation (feedback rating), and if you don't make it easy for shoppers to bid on and buy your items.

It's also impossible to know the effect of a campaign if you haven't measured your "before" baseline metrics. Track your sell-through rates (STRs) and average selling prices (ASPs) by item product line, format (auctions versus stores), and so on. Keep track of dates so you can gauge effects of seasonality and other factors.

You can review reports from your eBay Sales Reports and your auction-management tools, and you can also download them to a spreadsheet program, where you can map out the baseline metrics and follow them as they change. Create columns representing month/year and rows for ASP, sell-through, repeat customers, units sold, and other information related to individual products, product lines, and categories. Add in traffic data and financials, such as gross revenue and margin. Test different advertising methods and see which ones do the most to increase these metrics.

Advertise Auctions or Websites?

Many eBay sellers wonder whether they should be driving traffic to their listings on eBay or whether they want to send traffic to their own unique place on the Internet—be it a storefront, mall store, or website. Whatever your philosophy regarding where to send potential customers, the most important thing you can do before initiating any advertising is to have a clear objective—know what you want to accomplish. Then, when you measure the effect of the campaign, you can determine whether it accomplished what you wanted.

Types of Advertising

What advertising options does an eBay seller have? The most effective advertising for a business on the Internet are banner advertising, text e-mail advertising, and paid searches; all allow those viewing the ads to click a link to be taken to your listings. A postcard in the mail or an ad in a magazine might make an impact, but there's no way to bring that shopper immediately to your eBay listings, since the person reading an ad in a magazine is likely not in front of the computer.

eBay Stores Referral Credit

If you are spending money advertising your eBay Store listings in non-eBay venues, you should sign up for eBay Stores Referral Credit program (http://pages.ebay.com/storefronts/referral-credit-steps.html). eBay will give you credits if shoppers find you from outside of the eBay site and buy something from your eBay Store. Restrictions apply, so be sure to read the program details on the eBay site.

The best advertising format varies widely, depending on the seller and what is being sold, and it can change over time; running small tests can be very helpful to indicate what might work best for your business.

Let's take a quick look at some forms of advertising, and then we'll discuss ways you can use data tools to help you measure the success of an ad campaign.

eBay Auctions

In Chapter 9, we talked about how you can use eBay auction listings as a form of advertising to drive traffic to your store listings. Use eBay auctions to drive traffic to your store. For example, if I were selling children's clothing in my eBay Store, I would list some of the most popular items in an auction format—people browsing or searching the eBay.com site have a much greater chance of seeing my auction listings than my store listings. In the auction description, I would use copy, links, and cross-promotional tools to make sure people who click the listing see that I have many more children's clothing items in my eBay Store.

Offline Advertising

You can advertise in magazines related to your industry. eBay's Co-op Advertising program is designed to help you market your products and services to new and existing buyers via offline advertising efforts. If you follow eBay's advertising guidelines, you will be reimbursed 25 percent of your advertising insertion fees. Restrictions apply, so be sure to read the fine print on eBay's website: www.ebaycoopads.com.

Multi-Channel Selling

While the most compelling reason to sell on a marketplace is to get sales, having a presence on multiple marketplaces also increases your exposure, particularly when you're building a brand and trying to get traffic to your own website. We'll talk more about this technique in "Expand Your Presence" a little later in this chapter.

Marketplace Exposure

One of the ways Overstock.com tried to attract large eBay sellers to its new auction marketplace in 2005 was to offer them a presence on the Overstock.com Auctions home page. This was free advertising for those featured sellers.

The bigger the marketplace, the bigger you have to be to get attention. This is a great reason to try and establish a relationship with your eBay category manager or PowerSeller representative (if you are a large enough volume seller to have one, that is). They want you to succeed, because the better you do, the better their category does, and the better they look to their bosses. They may be able to help you by giving you some added exposure on the category pages on eBay.

Tell your category managers what's in it for them, of course; if you can show them you can increase sales with added exposure, they'll be more inclined to listen. And the best way to make your case is with the data you can gather from your own sales reports. Just remember that they may share the information you give them about your efforts with other sellers in your category to try to boost everybody's sales—so use your best judgment as to the level of detail you give away.

TIP
If you attend industry trade shows, find out if eBay is exhibiting; if so, seek out the category manager at the eBay booth. Another place where you have a chance to talk to category managers is at the eBay Live annual convention. Stop by the eBay booth devoted to the category in which you sell. Even if you are a low-volume seller, at these shows, eBay staff want to talk to you.

Natural Search

A *natural search* gets your listings to show up on the results pages of the search engines. An industry called Search Engine Optimization helps website owners and e-commerce sites get their listings and sites picked up by search engines. Search engines will generally include only fixed-price listings, however.

eBay offers advice to its storeowners to optimize their store inventory to get picked up by search engines. eBay recommends that you have a good store name and make the text in your store listing match the keywords shoppers would enter in search engines when they look for the types of items you're selling. Include these keywords in your store name, custom category names, and the content on your custom pages.

eBay suggests the following to optimize your store for search engines:

- *Choose a store name that describes the products you sell.* For example, let's say you're selling vintage jewelry and jewelry boxes. The store name "Katie's Vintage Jewelry and Jewelry Boxes" is much more effective than "Katie's Vintage Finds."

- *Choose names for your custom categories that include product keywords that you expect buyers to search on.* Even if it proves to be rather repetitive, this will help increase your exposure in natural search. An example: use "Vintage Broaches" and "Vintage Bracelets" rather than "Broaches" and "Bracelets."

- *Include keywords that describe the contents of your store in your store description.* You could include some of the names of your custom categories. Keep in mind that the description appears in the top of your store and is meant to be user-friendly to your buyers, so write one that clearly represents what you sell—too many keywords in the description could look awkward.

TIP
Find more tips in the eBay Stores Discussion Boards within the Community Help Boards online at http://pages.ebay.com/community/boards/.

Paid Search

You can pay for advertising that displays when someone does searches on various search engines. Visit the websites of the paid-search services to learn more:

- **Google AdWords**   http://adwords.google.com
- **Yahoo! Search Marketing (formerly Overture)**   http://searchmarketing.yahoo.com
- **eBay Keywords**   www.ebaykeywords.com

Ad Terminology

You should be familiar with the following terms when advertising on the Internet:

Impressions (hits)   The number of hits an element on your website receives—in this case, banner ads are of particular interest. If a person clicks through the site, each banner he or she looks at receives an impression. If you go to a site and keep clicking the refresh button, you will generate more impressions.

Unique visitors   A more meaningful number than hits, because it represents how many *different* (unique) people came to your site.

Cost per thousand (CPM)   Refers to how a site would charge for advertising. If, for example, you charge $5 CPM, you are charging an advertiser $5 for every 1000 impressions generated on your site (or $5 CPM = $0.005 per impression).

Click-through rate (CTR)   The number of times someone actually clicks an ad, not just views it. This is calculated as a percentage, so, for example, if 200 ad impressions produce 4 click-throughs, the CTR is 2 percent.

Cost-per-click or pay-per-click (PPC)   Refers to advertising rates based on how many clicks an ad receives. For example, if someone sees an ad on a page, the advertiser pays nothing; but if someone clicks the ad, the advertiser pays the cost-per-click rate. Popular sites such as Google use the PPC advertising model; typical rates for a click are 5 to 20 cents or more, depending on how many advertisers are competing for the space.

Conversion rate   The number of orders divided by the number of visitors to your website. (How well you do at turning visitors into buyers.) When you advertise, you want good CTRs to send viewers from the ads to your website, and good conversion rates so that once those visitors arrive at your site, they place orders for your products.

Comparison Shopping Sites

You can send your store inventory listing information to comparison shopping sites, which are search engines for people looking for items to buy online. This does not work for fixed-price and auction listings on the core (non-store) platform. Comparison shopping engines include such sites as Froogle, Shopzilla, and Shop.com.

In the eBay Help files, you can find instructions for "Exporting a File of Your Listings" (http://pages.ebay.com/help/specialtysites/exporting-your-listings.html). The link to export a file is located on the Manage Your Store page.

Affiliate Marketing

You can set up an affiliate marketing program and give a commission of sales price to affiliates who drive buyers to your site. You pay affiliates only when they drive a customer to your site who actually buys something from you. Commission Junction (www.cj.com) and Linkshare (www.linkshare.com) are two services that allow merchants to set up affiliate programs.

Learn from Others: Turning Nickels to Dollars by Advertising

eBay PowerSellers Bobby and Susan Minnich know how to make their listings appeal to coin collectors. If anyone understands eBay marketing, it's Bobby—he spends between 10 and 12 hours a week analyzing reports from eBay and Sellathon to improve his sales and fine tune his listing and marketing strategies.

Bobby uses a variety of marketing techniques, including cross-promoting his listings and advertising through programs like Google AdWords. However, he said he must be careful, because he could easily spend $100 a day on Google AdWords for a generic term like *US Coins*, which would be too much to spend relative to the potential revenue he could bring in with his inventory.

Instead, Bobby uses Google AdWords selectively, such as when he wants to sell a rare coin in good condition. He'll list the coin in his eBay Store and buy a Google AdWord term containing the year and type of coin. For example, he might buy the term *1836 Barber Coin*. If someone types in *1836 Barber Coin* on Google, Bobby's Google ad will appear on the search results page. Bobby pays Google only when someone clicks his ad, and because of the specific terms he uses, it might cost him 5 cents per click. But Bobby is trying to attract a person who would be searching on Google for a specific item that would bring him a big sale—this is extremely targeted marketing.

When purchasing the keyword, Bobby can specify the duration of the ad or cancel it once he has sold a coin. He could also use AdWords to advertise an auction listing; if you do this, remember to set the duration so that the AdWord campaign ends before the auction ends.

Bobby can then look at his Sellathon reports and see where traffic to the coin listing is coming from. In addition, he can review the Google AdWords reports. With auctions for rare items, each additional interested bidder can make a huge impact on the final selling price.

Bobby also uses Sellathon reports to show him which terms shoppers are entering when their searches bring them to his auctions, so he is in tune with the kinds of keywords that might attract good buyers on Google. (This also helps him with Basic Listing Strategy #5: Uncover the most effective keywords, covered in Chapter 8.)

Driving traffic to his listings through 5-cent Google AdWord buys, Bobby literally turns nickels into dollars by achieving higher selling prices for his rare coins.

Study the Advertising-Generated Traffic Data

eBay Traffic Reports and Sellathon ViewTracker tell you where traffic is coming from. Look at the Referrer, or Method of Arrival reports, and track the sources over time.

Figure 10-4 shows an eBay Search Engines Report showing how much traffic is coming from search engines. (Note that this report is a subset of referrer—it does not show all methods of arrival, just the traffic coming from search engines.) This seller's report shows that for the month of April 2005, six visitors came from Yahoo! (75 percent), one visitor came from Google (12.5 percent), and one visitor came from eBay Search (12.5 percent).

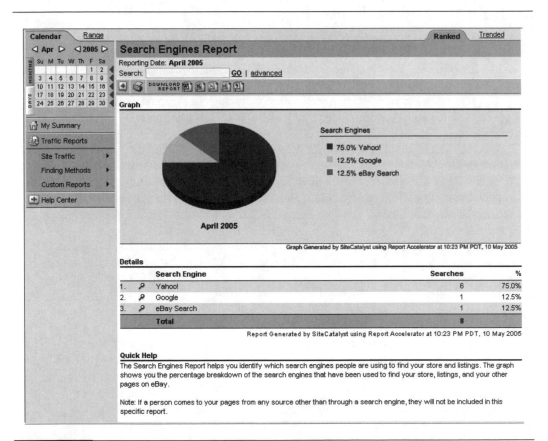

FIGURE 10-4   eBay traffic reports let you see how many people are coming to your listings from search engines (under Finding Methods) so you can measure the success of your advertising and marketing campaigns.

When you spend money on advertising and marketing, you should expect to see an increase in traffic to your listings (or website) and an increase in sales. Sellathon lets you track traffic and the source (Method Of Arrival) of that traffic. Figure 10-5 shows the Highlights page of a report from Sellathon, showing active days and dates and key traffic statistics. If you see an increase in traffic but not sales, you need to investigate why that is and what you can do to improve your listings.

As explained in Chapter 7, you can create custom folders in Sellathon so you can test various approaches to your listings. The Highlights page shows your most active day for all the listings as a whole in this folder. By matching this data with your marketing campaigns, it can tell you whether sending out an e-mail newsletter caused a spike in traffic, or whether a one-day paid search campaign had any effect on traffic. (Naturally you need to compare traffic to your normal level of activity.)

You can also see how many bids and watches this folder has, and you can compare it to another folder to see which group of auctions is doing better. As a seller, you can draw conclusions about the effectiveness of your marketing campaigns based on the traffic and bidding levels you receive during your campaigns.

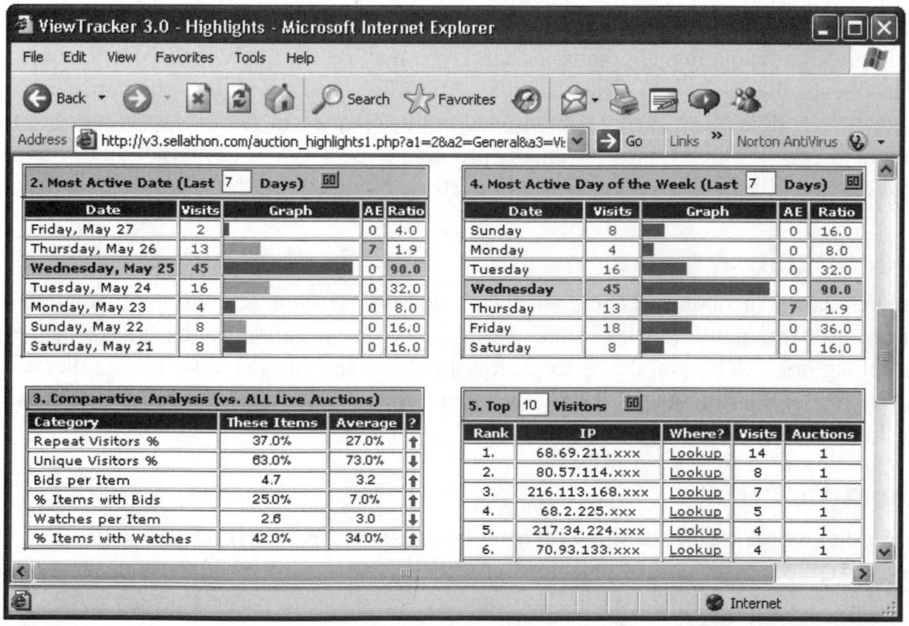

FIGURE 10-5   The Sellathon Highlights page for a folder shows when traffic is coming to your listings (sections 2 and 4), helping you measure the effects of your ad and marketing campaigns.

Unfortunately, tracking the effectiveness of advertising is an inexact science, partly because of the limitations of these tracking tools (as discussed in Chapter 7), and partly because of the limitations inherent in tracking shopper behavior. Someone might see your advertisement in an e-mail newsletter, but she might do a seller search on eBay instead of clicking a traceable link. While challenges do exist, you will grow to be more comfortable with what the data is telling you the more you study it.

NOTE   *A service called ClickThruStats (www.clickthrustats.com) helps businesses track links (URLs) more effectively. You can take advantage of a 30-day free trial by downloading it from the website.*

Some advertising methods have built-in tracking for you, such as Google AdWords. Be sure and spend the time reviewing these reports to see how you can fine-tune your marketing techniques and to make sure it is a good investment of your marketing dollars.

#4 Enhance Your Reputation and Credibility

In 1993, the *New Yorker* magazine published a cartoon by Peter Steiner (no relation) with two dogs sitting in front of a computer. One says to the other, "On the Internet, nobody knows you're a dog." The cartoon illustrates the anonymity the Internet affords users.

When you purchase an item on an online auction site like eBay, you may be dealing with a reputable, professional seller. On the other hand, you may be dealing with an unprofessional or even dishonest seller (a "dog"). The "bad dogs" on eBay spoil it for all of the hardworking sellers, so some vendors, such as those mentioned in this chapter, have developed services for honest sellers to "prove" their honesty. Vendors promote these services as marketing techniques, since they help potential shoppers feel more comfortable buying from the sellers who use them.

eBay Feedback

While research data is inconclusive about whether or not *positive* feedback will improve the selling price of a seller's item, many who have studied eBay *do* believe negative feedback has a negative impact on selling price. Whatever the research, it just seems like common sense that a seller would want positive feedback—and lots of it. It helps if you remind buyers to leave feedback, because many satisfied customers forget to do so.

Your About Me Page

eBay gives you an opportunity to show off your business on a page called About Me. You can include logos, photos, descriptions, links to your website, contact information, your most recent eBay feedback, and your current listings. You can hire a designer to create a professional-looking page. (Look in the eBay Solutions Directory.)

If you create an About Me page, eBay displays an icon next to your user ID. But you can also add a link to your About Me page from your auctions, and sellers who don't have a website may purchase a domain name and redirect it to their About Me page.

You can use traffic reports from eBay or Sellathon to see how many people click to your About Me page. Sellers I've talked to say they hear from customers that when deciding which auctions to bid on from various sellers, the About Me page can be the deciding factor.

Endorsements and Testimonials

If you've had happy customers write you letters, consider asking them if you can use them as testimonials that you can put on your About Me page and website. The same goes for suppliers, or if you've won any awards in your industry. Show off the groups you belong to, such as the Chamber of Commerce or industry associations.

ACityDiscount uses eBay's feedback in creative ways. Going into a listing, you might see a box that says, "What our customers think about this item." Clicking the box brings you to a list of feedback from ACityDiscount customers who purchased the *same* product.

Most sellers link to all of their feedback, but by matching feedback with the type of item sold, it makes for much more effective use of eBay's feedback system. On that page are also links to Feedbacks For This Manufacturer and Feedbacks For This Category. You can test the effectiveness of this strategy by running tests on your own auctions—some using the feature, some without it.

Third-Party Services

You can enhance your reputation on eBay beyond just your feedback rating. ReliableMerchants (www.reliablemerchants.com) was one of the first companies to offer a service to sellers to try and show potential buyers they were legitimate sellers worthy of trust. They were later joined by SquareTrade (www.squaretrade.com), which is eBay's preferred online dispute resolution service. Sellers pay a monthly fee to display seals that show they have been evaluated as trustworthy by the companies. See each service for details of how they work.

buySAFE (www.buysafe.com) took the concept to a whole new level when it launched its services in 2003. It offers bonding that in effect *guarantees* a seller's transaction.

Opinity (www.opinity.com) launched in 2005 to try and combine people's reputations from various websites and make it easier for users to determine a trading partner's reliability.

> NOTE
>
> *College researchers find many aspects of eBay fascinating, especially the feedback mechanism and the concept of an "online reputation." If you are interested in reading about academic research on online auctions, go to the website of the Robert H. Smith School of Business at the University of Maryland, which offers links to some of the reports: www.rhsmith.umd.edu/ceme/statistics/statauctionspapers.htm.*

Study the Test Data

To estimate the effect that a service such as SquareTrade or buySAFE has on your listings, you need to know your track record before you use them to get a baseline with which to make comparisons. You can do tests similar to the buySAFE tests discussed in the following sidebar. Run tests using different user IDs—one using the service, the other not using the service. The two IDs must be comparable, and you should use care in drawing conclusions from the data.

A Model Study: buySAFE's Test

buySAFE conducted a study in 2004 to quantify the effect of its services on eBay auction listings. It's interesting to see how the company structured the test to measure the effect of the buySAFE service on buyer behavior.

You don't have to take buySAFE's word for it; in fact, you shouldn't. Run similar tests yourself for this or other services—so many variables can affect results, like the item being sold, the starting price, titles and descriptions, photos, your feedback rating, and so on. But here's a good example of *how* to conduct such tests.

buySAFE conducted a proprietary test on eBay from August through October 2004. Two eBay user IDs with comparable feedback were used to test items across seven categories, including Art & Antiques, Jewelry & Watches, Clothing, Shoes & Accessories, Toys, Computers & Electronics, Cameras & Photos, and Home & Garden. The price range of items listed was $5 to $200.

Each of the two eBay user IDs listed more than 275 identical items, with titles and descriptions exactly the same for sellers with few exceptions. The listings with buySAFE's seal and that were bonded had the following features:

- The keyword *buySAFE* was used in the title
- The buySAFE seal was displayed in the listings
- The listings and the About Me Page included a paragraph of copy describing buySAFE and how it benefits buyers.

Here are the results of the tests:

- Bonded items had a STR more than 17 percent greater than non-bonded items.
- Bonded items had total sales revenue nearly 15 percent greater than for non-bonded items.

Don't assume you will get results *identical* to those of this study. Shopping behavior varies depending on the item, category, price point, seller, feedback ratio, and other factors. Some sellers of refurbished or used items may not accept returns, making them a less-than-ideal fit for the buySAFE service. But buySAFE's study is a good model for testing third-party services; you can run these tests yourself on your own auctions.

buySAFE says there is a difference between simply posting its seal on a listing and adding descriptive text to help educate shoppers about buySAFE. So if you conduct tests of these services, be sure you are testing the recommended approach to using those services.

#5 Expand Your Presence

If you have found success on eBay, you might be wondering how you can leverage your knowledge of selling on other marketplaces or in other geographic locations. If you have a good system in place for staying organized, it may be worth testing such an expansion. In fact, eBay launched ProStores in recognition of the fact that many of its sellers were looking for their own e-commerce websites. ProStores (www.prostores.com) allows sellers to create a customized e-commerce storefront, independent of the eBay marketplace, for a fee plus commission. However, many services offer e-commerce-enabled websites that don't charge commission fees, so shop around.

Because each marketplace and each country has its own rules and restrictions, you need to create a system to keep track of your orders and policies. A third-party auction-management service that can keep you on track is a good idea to have in place before you jump in.

You can expand your presence in the following ways:

- Broaden your product line.
- Expand internationally. Change your policy so that you will expand outside your domestic market, or sign up and start selling on international eBay sites. You can find links to eBay's international sites on the bottom of the eBay home page.
- Open an eBay Store.
- Open a ProStore.
- Open a storefront. (AuctionBytes has a chart of storefront services in the online-auction industry at http://auctionbytes.com/cab/pages/stores.)
- Open your own e-commerce-enabled website; many services, from GoDaddy (www.godaddy.com) to Interland (www.interland.com) are available.
- Sell on other consumer-to-consumer (C2C) marketplaces and online antique malls from Overstock (http://auctions.overstock.com), to Yahoo! (http://auctions.yahoo.com) and Amazon (http://auctions.amazon.com), to TIAS (www.tias.com) and GoAntiques (www.goantiques.com).

Test the Waters

It's difficult to fulfill orders from multiple marketplaces, even if you are using only two. Dealing with international buyers and postal systems can also be quite challenging. Before you consider *any* expansion strategy or venue, launch some test auctions. Start small—you will learn as you go along, and you want to avoid costly mistakes. You can also do the following.

Research Your Competitors

You should review what your eBay competitors are doing, and you also want to look at the competition you would be facing if you decide to expand your presence. You might be able to identify another auction site or marketplace where ASPs are higher, fees are lower, or STRs are higher, or that provides good exposure to drive traffic back to your own website or eBay listings.

10

Research Discussion Boards

You can learn a lot from community discussion boards. Marketplaces often provide areas for announcements and where sellers gather to discuss the challenges and rewards of selling on that particular venue (or to have plain old gripe sessions).

Amazon.com discussion boards are a good example. Amazon.com places seller announcements at http://forums.prosperotechnologies.com/am-sellannounce/start/?fpi=yes, and if you click Seller Soapbox at the top of the page, you'll be taken to a page where sellers gather to discuss the latest news, policy changes, and glitches.

Seller discussions can be eye-opening if you are thinking about selling on a new venue, and you can ask your own questions of other, experienced sellers.

Go Straight to the Top

If you're thinking about trying a new venue, say a web-hosting service, see if you can get a one- or two-month free trial. If you're a high-volume seller on eBay, you should talk to representatives from other marketplaces to see if they will help you set up tests of their venues. Overstock.com Auctions has been giving large eBay sellers incentives as it tries to scale its auction business. Smaller sellers may not be able to get individualized attention at any marketplace, but being polite and persistent may pay off.

Study the Marketplace Traffic Data

Run tests if you are trying new approaches to your business such as trying another marketplace or a new international site. You will experience a learning curve when using any new marketplace, so you should take that into account when you look at your results. Also take into account that you may not be comparing apples to apples; if you have thousands or hundreds of thousands of feedback on eBay, and no feedback on another marketplace, that may affect buyer behavior. Use analytics tools to measure the results of your test listings.

If you are already selling on multiple marketplaces and your own website, be sure to evaluate the performance of each channel. The tools discussed in earlier chapters are geared toward eBay sellers, but they may add functionality for other marketplaces as they grow. Auction-management services can aid you in evaluating the results of each channel through their reporting features. They also know what their other clients have done and may be able to guide you in the best direction to take.

Having a presence on one channel may be driving traffic to your listings on another venue. Take a big-picture view when you evaluate each channel.

Earlier, you saw how ACityDiscount found non-store fixed-price listings on eBay a failure when measured by itself, but those listings were actually driving traffic to store items. So those listings were actually a success when considering the big picture. The same might be true of other marketplaces; some sellers believe it's best to be everywhere. This works most effectively when the seller has a strong, consistent brand and his or her own website.

Perhaps repeat sales on eBay are low, but your eBay customers are buying more from you on your website. You should try to track this closely. It's important to understand the profitability of each channel and know the "customer acquisition cost." How much are you paying on one channel to get sales on another channel, and are they customers for life or one-time purchasers? All these factors are important to consider when trying to measure and track metrics over time.

While this book focuses on eBay tools, if you have your own website, you should be using an analytics tool to measure traffic and site performance—see Chapter 7 for information about such tools.

How the Tools Stack Up

Tracking marketing campaigns can be tricky, but it's well worth the effort to estimate the revenue they generate and compare it to the costs. You can often use the advertising vehicles' reports to track success—be sure to see what kinds of reports the tool offers before you begin a campaign. You need to anticipate what codes or tracking methods you can use to help you measure the campaign as you go along.

eBay market data is not going to help you figure out the costs of your marketing campaigns. You might use market-data tools to try to help you identify the most successful sellers to see what methods of advertising they are using, but because eBay-approved market data tools do not identify seller by name, using the data is tricky. (You also shouldn't assume that your competitors know the best marketing strategies.)

eBay Reports and Sellathon ViewTracker

On the simplest level, you can review your sales and determine whether they increase or decrease during an ad campaign. This is where eBay market data comes into play. By tracking data at the category or product level, you can also compare your own results with those of other sellers or the category as a whole. While this information can provide only a rough idea, as other sellers may have increased or decreased their own advertising, it can hint to seasonal and other factors that are having an effect beyond your own marketing campaign. Remember to compare year-to-year sales to allow for the seasonal effect of retail sales. (How does this March compare with last March?)

In addition to counting any increases in unit sales, look at the traffic going to your auctions. Be sure and look at the method of arrival and referring domains in Sellathon and eBay Traffic Reports to track how people are coming to your auctions to try and measure the effect of your advertising and marketing campaigns.

Look for International Interest

The Referring Domain report in your eBay Traffic Reports will show you domains from sites outside your country. If you are getting a lot of international eyeballs, this might tell you it's worth exploring selling internationally if you don't already do so, and it may indicate which countries to consider first. You can sell internationally in two ways; open your eBay listings to all buyers by indicating you will ship internationally, and list auctions on international sites.

Figure 10-6 shows the Referring Domain report from eBay Traffic Reports. This report can help you measure your marketing efforts and give you ideas for places you should consider advertising.

NOTE   *When using the Sellathon ViewTracker tool, you can click the question mark next to the IP address to find an indication of the location of the visitor.*

Look for Other Sources of Traffic

If you see a website in the Referring Domain report that you haven't heard of before that seems to be driving traffic to your listings, this might be an opportunity to learn about the site and explore a relationship with it or similar sites.

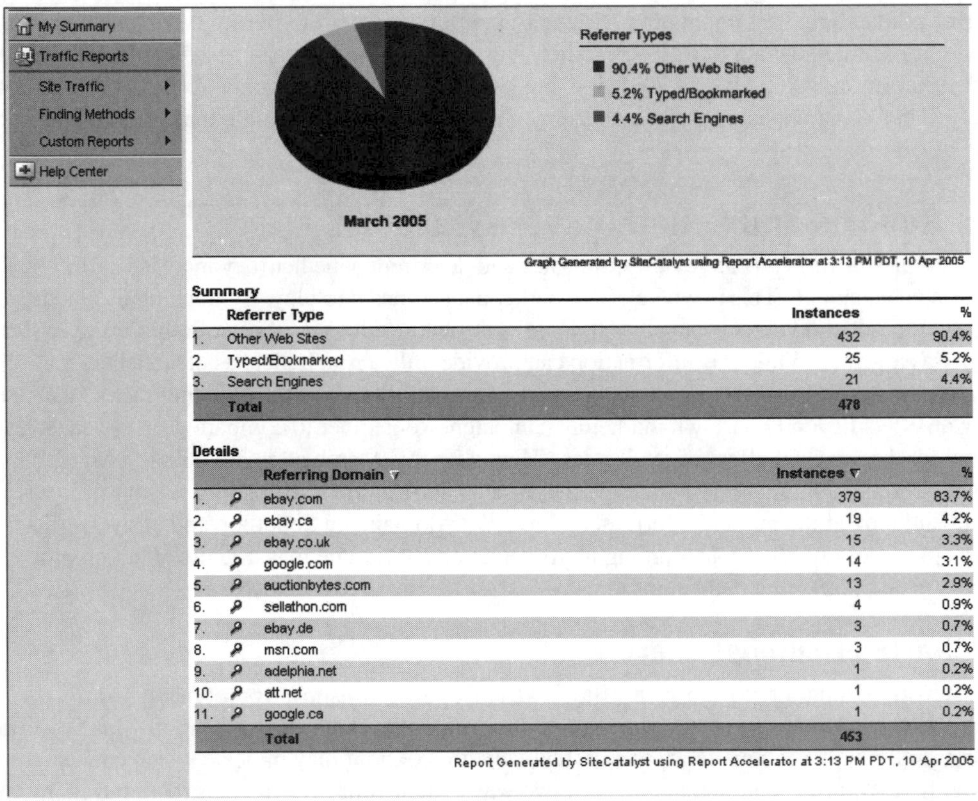

My Summary
Traffic Reports
  Site Traffic
  Finding Methods
  Custom Reports
Help Center

Referrer Types
- 90.4% Other Web Sites
- 5.2% Typed/Bookmarked
- 4.4% Search Engines

March 2005

Graph Generated by SiteCatalyst using Report Accelerator at 3:13 PM PDT, 10 Apr 2005

Summary

	Referrer Type	Instances	%
1.	Other Web Sites	432	90.4%
2.	Typed/Bookmarked	25	5.2%
3.	Search Engines	21	4.4%
	Total	**478**	

Details

	Referring Domain	Instances	%
1.	ebay.com	379	83.7%
2.	ebay.ca	19	4.2%
3.	ebay.co.uk	15	3.3%
4.	google.com	14	3.1%
5.	auctionbytes.com	13	2.9%
6.	sellathon.com	4	0.9%
7.	ebay.de	3	0.7%
8.	msn.com	3	0.7%
9.	adelphia.net	1	0.2%
10.	att.net	1	0.2%
11.	google.ca	1	0.2%
	Total	**453**	

Report Generated by SiteCatalyst using Report Accelerator at 3:13 PM PDT, 10 Apr 2005

FIGURE 10-6   eBay Traffic Reports offers a Referring Domain report to show you what websites people are coming from when they visit your listings.

Wrapping Up

Going from a casual seller on eBay to a business seller means you will start looking for ways to market and promote your listings. Driving traffic to your listings, eBay Store, and your own e-commerce site is key to garnering higher sales and higher profits, and data tools will help you determine which efforts are most effective.

Use data tools to help you test different strategies. Don't be afraid to try new approaches and marketing techniques. eBay Traffic Reports and Sellathon help you measure the effectiveness of your marketing campaigns. What differentiates successful PowerSellers from others is their zeal for collecting, analyzing, and acting upon sales and marketing data.

10

Chapter 11

Staying One Step Ahead of the Competition

An online-auction industry adage says, "eBay is a mile wide but three inches deep." It refers to the fact that you can sell almost anything on eBay (its breadth is wide, from collectibles to business and industrial categories), but you can't sell an unlimited number of items on eBay. When sellers flood the site with *too much* supply of an item, the demand can't keep up, and prices and sell-through rates (STRs) for that item drop. (And no seller wants lower prices and lower sales!)

If your competitors begin flooding the marketplace with supply, this will affect your selling prices. This is just one of the reasons you need to keep track of the competition. While it's challenging to know exactly what your competitors are up to, you can build in early warning systems to alert you to changes that might affect your own business.

Reasons to Monitor Your Competitors

The more information you have, the better decisions you can make in your own business. Here are some reasons why you should be monitoring your competitors:

Watch for New Entrants   If a new seller starts listing items that compete with yours, it may affect your sales and profits. It's much better to know about a new competitor *before* your sales are affected. In some cases, you can react proactively. You may choose to enter a pricing war, you may temporarily adjust the number of items you list, or you may decide to offer a different product line. The key is to anticipate the effect competitors may have on your bottom line.

A seller I know was selling a discontinued line of telephone systems. He had acquired them at a nice price and was getting a good margin on his eBay sales. One day he saw another seller listing the same exact systems at a much lower starting price. He made some calls and found out how the seller had acquired the systems and how many he had acquired. He scaled back his own listings, figuring his prices would nosedive otherwise. He eventually liquidated all of the items on eBay at a good margin, even though it took him longer than he would have liked. If he hadn't been monitoring his competitors, though, their sales might have negatively impacted his profits.

Find Suppliers and Better Sources of Inventory   Your competitors may tip you off to new sources of inventory. Sellers are usually close-mouthed about where they acquire their items, especially if they are getting a great deal. But studying their listings on an ongoing basis may give you some indication of where they are sourcing their inventory. On occasion, a seller will buy something from her competitor in the name of market research to learn more about the product.

Monitoring wholesale sites can also tip you off to possible new competition. For example, if you are selling a special brand of baby clothes on eBay, and you notice several lots of the same brand go up for sale on eBay Wholesale Lots (www.ebay.com/wholesale), you should be concerned that whoever buys those lots—potentially hundreds or thousands of items—could break them into smaller lots or individual items and begin selling them on eBay.com in your category. Knowing this, you might decide to bid on the auctions yourself, or at least prepare for a potential onslaught of supply competing against your listings.

Watch for Better/Cheaper Products   If you are selling a popular item and a competitor comes along with a better model or a less-expensive version, you might consider making adjustments to your sales strategy or considering carrying that product, too.

Watch for Increased Supply   Keeping track of active listings as well as wholesale sources can tip you off to dangerous levels of supply that might bring down everybody's selling price.

Apply "Copycat" Strategies   Reviewing your competitors' offerings on a regular basis can give you ideas for what works—and what doesn't work. You can use what you learn from others to make your listings sell better.

Learn Best Practices   Reviewing other sellers' Terms of Service can help you determine standards about refund policies, shipping and handling charges, and more, and it can help you learn what buyers expect. You can also identify other sellers' marketing strategies and learn from them.

Create Better Listings   Review your competitors' listings and see if you can create more compelling descriptions. Knowing what your buyers have to choose from can help you create a more appealing offer.

Find a Niche That No One Is Filling   Learning about your competitor's product lines can help you identify untapped niches.

Consider Possible Partnerships   Evaluating fellow sellers may lead you to find complementary offerings and possibly even partnership opportunities.

Find Other Marketplaces   Tracking competitors can help you understand the bigger picture about demand for your products. Find out what channels other sellers are using to sell and promote their goods.

Know Your Market Share

Your market share is an important measurement of where you are and can help you determine where you want your business to go. Some of the tools in this book can help you measure eBay categories and allow you to view a category's top (and bottom) sellers.

Compare your sales metrics to those of the category as a whole, and with those of your competitors. Make sure your sales are in line with your market segment. In Chapter 3, we saw how one PowerSeller used eBay Sales Reports to find out that while his gross sales were good, his STR was inferior to that of his competitors. By zeroing in on this problem, he was able to improve sell-through and increase his profits.

With a better understanding of your category, you can create a plan to grow your market share by offering better selection, pricing, service, or some other competitive advantage.

A category leader who notices a new competitor taking away market share might initiate a price war with the new seller, hoping to drive them away. (One Titanium PowerSeller who sells in a lucrative Business & Industrial category told me he does this routinely.) Reaction to new competition differs based on many factors, including whether you are the market leader in your category.

Of course, as your market share grows, more sellers will be studying *your* moves and will be trying some copycat maneuvers on you.

11

Data Tools: Know Your Category

The market-data tools outlined in Chapters 4–6 allow you to do category or keyword searches to get statistics such as average selling price (ASP) and STRs. Andale, Terapeak, and DeepAnalysis all let you review the closed listings making up those search results so you can peruse them and learn more about the sellers, their products, and how they present their offerings.

Andale's Sales Analyzer Pro, reviewed in Chapter 4, lets you compare your performance with the category as a whole.

Studying your category gives you a big picture view of your market, helps you identify your competitors, and gives you metrics to compare your performance against the category as a whole.

How to Monitor Your Competitors

Once you take your eBay selling seriously, it's inevitable that you will be curious about what other sellers are doing to be more profitable. But rather than just having a sense of what other sellers are doing, it pays to do some research and to track changes over time.

Think Like a Buyer

Thinking like a buyer can help you understand your competitors. You should be searching eBay regularly for the items you sell to see how search results come back, find out who is using special features such as Featured and Bold, and other listing strategies those sellers are using (such as starting price and ending day). Of course, just because other sellers are using a particular strategy does not mean it's profitable for them, or would be profitable for you. But it can give you a big-picture view and help you understand what *might* attract buyers to *your* listings.

Use Data Tools to Identify Competitors

Terapeak and DeepAnalysis have seller lists. They don't identify individual sellers, but they do allow you to sort by various criteria, and in some categories, users who study their category in-depth can find patterns that reveal significant information about the top sellers in that category.

The DeepAnalysis Report tab includes a section called Top Sellers (Figure 11-1). This report shows a snapshot of the top 10 and the bottom 10 sellers in a category so you can see their dollar sales and ASPs as a group.

The DeepAnalysis Seller tab (Figure 11-2) lists the sellers and their performance, though it does not reveal the identity of each seller. It does identify them with a unique number, however. You can sort the list by column head to look for specific information—for example, did the number one auction in terms of number of auctions have the lowest or highest ASP? And because the seller is tagged with a unique number (though it's not possible to *search* by that number), you can see whether that seller shows up in other categories you are researching.

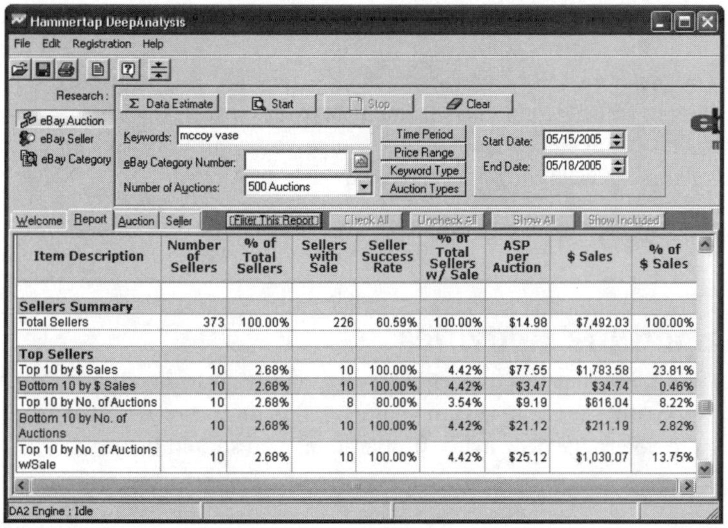

FIGURE 11-1 DeepAnalysis provides a snapshot view of the top 10 and bottom 10 sellers in a category.

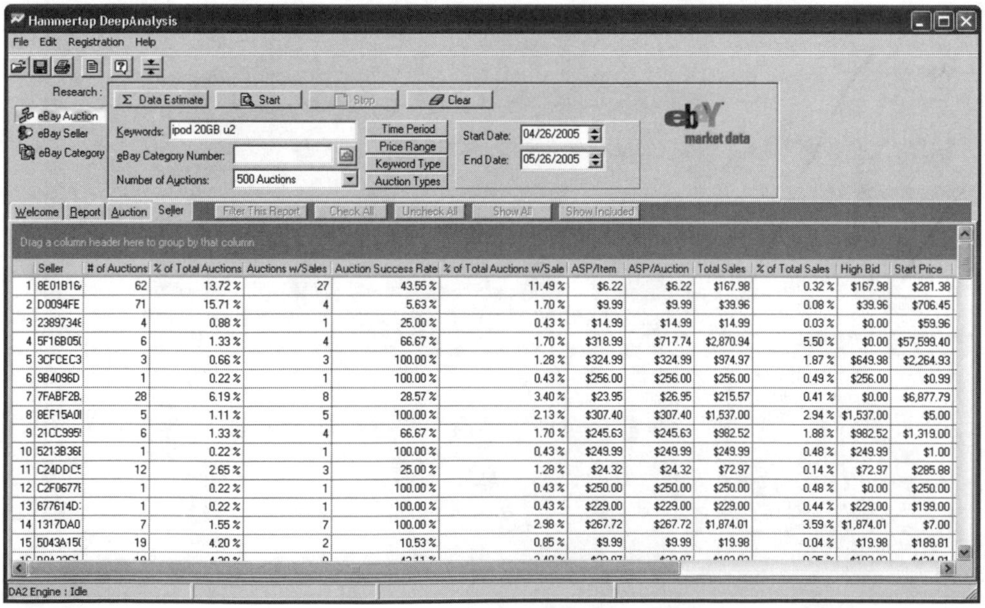

FIGURE 11-2 The DeepAnalysis Seller tab lists the sellers in your search results, allowing you to sort sellers by highest ASP or highest STRs.

Terapeak allows you to view seller lists, too. Browse a category or do a search, and when the results come back, click the Seller icon. Figure 11-3 shows an example of a resulting list, which can be sorted by market share, items sold, successful listings, listings, and bids. At the time of this writing, it does not assign a unique code to each seller due to eBay restrictions, making it more difficult to compare sellers when you sort the lists by criteria.

With all reports, make sure you choose the date range you want to cover and sort by various criteria to dig around and see what the data can reveal.

TIP   *Export (or download) reports and save them so you can track the top sellers in a category over time.*

Monitor Competitors' Activities

To achieve optimal sell-through and selling prices, you don't want to flood the eBay marketplace with items. You have control over your own inventory and listings, but you also need to monitor other sellers' listings to determine how many similar items you should list.

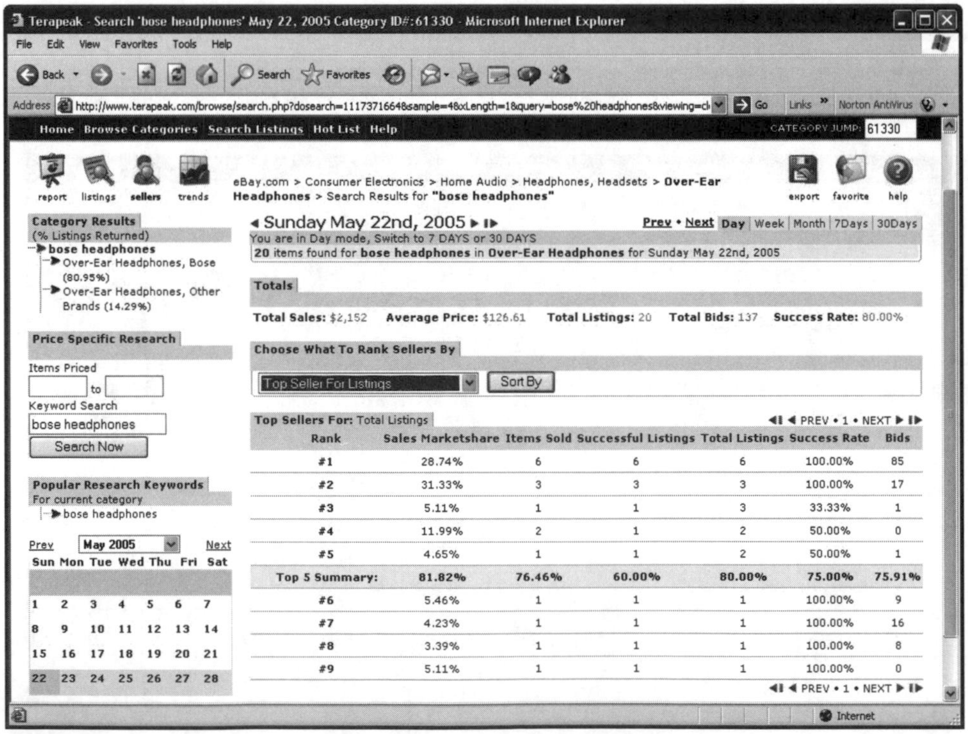

FIGURE 11-3   Terapeak's seller lists give you a top 5 summary, and you can sort the list by market share, items sold, successful listings, listings, and bids.

In addition to searching eBay for current supply (active listings), you should keep track of supply, selling prices, and STRs over time to get a full picture. You can use the tools and techniques in this book to help you track those metrics.

You might want to explore the following about your competitors to help in your thinking:

- What format are they using (auctions/Fixed Price/eBay Stores)?

- What optional eBay features are they using?

- What third-party tools are they using?

- What are their policies and fees?

- What products and models are they selling?

- What overall strategy are they employing?

- Are they selling on multiple marketplaces?

- Where are they getting their inventory?

Don't assume the answers are a guidebook for you to follow. While you might assume that a top seller putting most of her inventory in stores must know stores are the best approach, it also could mean that an opportunity exists for you to do well listing auctions for similar items. Top sellers may also be taking a certain approach to listing and marketing without having a clue whether it's the most profitable approach. Ask the preceding questions with an open mind, and run your own category analysis and tests (as outlined in Chapters 8–10) to see what approach works best for *you*.

Understand the Concept of Shadowing

Most sellers I talk to have multiple user IDs on eBay, some for buying and some for selling. The most common reason cited by sellers for using this tactic is to prevent their competitors from seeing what they are buying from eBay.

In his book *eBay Hacks*, author David Karp talks about the practice of *shadowing* buyers. This occurs when bidders who regularly buy in a particular category start to recognize other regulars who purchase the same types of items. They begin to follow the others' bids in an effort to find good deals.

Some of these buyers are collectors or bargain-hunters, but others are sellers. It's fairly common for sellers to buy poorly listed or poorly described items on eBay and "flip" them for a tidy profit. You can take shadowing one step further: look for those items to appear again on eBay with better descriptions, titles, and photos. If you find them, you can shadow those buyers who are reselling their bargains—they are your competitors. Remember to use a different user ID if you start bidding against them, so they don't know who you are.

Monitor Sourcing for Competitive Information

Monitoring sourcing can help you identify where your competitors are getting their inventory. It can also help you find new suppliers, and it may help you gauge future supply on eBay, allowing you to adjust your inventory levels accordingly.

11

In many categories, sellers buy from liquidation sources, which often include out-of-season stock, irregulars, or reconditioned items. Some popular suppliers among eBay sellers, particularly for "practical" items, include the wholesale-lots category on eBay (www.ebay.com/wholesale), drop-shippers, and supplier sites such as Alibaba (www.alibaba.com). Larger sellers attend trade shows and even travel abroad to meet with suppliers in other countries, and they may be selling new inventory as well as liquidation items.

Ideally, you would like to know exactly what your competitors are buying and in what quantity. This isn't easy to do, but tracking online sources of supply can help you.

As an example, let's say you are selling clothing. Go into eBay's Wholesale Lots category and search for the kinds of items you are selling. If you see the same seller buying regularly, you might be able to spot her listings if she is breaking up the lots into smaller lots and listing them in the regular eBay clothing and accessories categories. (Don't expect her to use the same user ID, though; you'll have to take some educated guesses.) There's no guarantee that Wholesale Lot buyers are selling on eBay, of course.

Know Your Industry

Read trade publications and stay on top of the current trends, styles, and technology. Know what the new lines are, what the top brands are, and what kinds of marketing campaigns manufacturers are running.

Do a search online for *(your item) trade show*. For example, when I did a search on Google (www.google.com) for *clothing trade show*, the first item that came back was a site called Apparel Search (www.apparelsearch.com), which lists all the trade shows in the apparel industry.

Digging around on the Apparel Search website, I found a show called Boston Collective, which has meetings in Massachusetts and Connecticut, where representatives of clothing lines are available to speak to attendees. On the Boston Collective website, I found a link to a magazine called *Daily News Record* (www.dailynewsrecord.com), which bills itself as "the leading news magazine of men's fashion and retail, published every Monday." The site provides information and market reports on men's wear retailing, design trends, apparel, and textiles. It claims that its readership includes retail managers, buyers, merchandisers, designers, and executives in the retail, apparel, textile, fiber, financial, and advertising industries.

In a few minutes, from consulting this single site, I could compile a list of trade shows and trade publications in my category that could help me keep up to date with all the industry news and trends.

If you need help with researching your industry, take a trip to your local public or college library. Talk to the reference librarian, who can help you find resources such as trade publications, directories, websites, industry associations, wholesalers, and other priceless information.

Or, for example, suppose you are selling this year's latest fashions in sneakers on eBay. You notice that another eBay user is bidding on a lot of irregular sneakers in this year's styles in the Wholesale Lots category at a cheap price. If the winner of that lot starts listing those sneakers individually in your category on eBay, the competition can bring down prices for your items. This is especially painful since you paid more for your items because they were not irregulars.

You may consider buying the lot yourself (after doing more research, of course). You continue to monitor your category looking for those items to show up, ready to be proactive in your response to new competition.

Online wholesale sources include Liquidation.com (www.liquidation.com) and Alibaba.com (www.alibaba.com). You might be monitoring sources already as part of your inventory acquisition strategy. Build in a gauge to predict how availability of goods in your category could affect future supply on eBay.

Use Pluck Auction Scout, Prospector, and AuctionSieve

Pluck Auction Scout (www.pluck.com) creates persistent searches that scour eBay around the clock. The tool is geared to help buyers find the best deals before anyone else, but you can use it to keep an eye on active listings in your category. Pluck puts everything you need in a single browser window, so you can slice and dice search results quickly and read them like e-mail. You can use it to search other sites in addition to eBay, to give you a more complete picture of what's available to Internet buyers. An exclusive version is available for eBay members (www.pluck.com/partners/ebay). Pluck Auction Scout continuously searches eBay and uses RSS technology to notify buyers when new listings come online that meet their specific criteria.

Prospector (www.moxieproxy.com) is a search tool that eBay sellers can use as a monitoring tool.

AuctionSieve (www.auctionsieve.com) is geared to eBay shoppers, but sellers can find it useful as well. You can set up automatic searches to keep an eye on your categories. If you are selling a certain line of women's shoes, for example, you can set up searches to alert you when new listings appear on eBay.

eBay's Biggest Sellers

You can consult lists of some of the largest eBay sellers to help you identify large sellers in your category. You may find it useful to look at what the top sellers are doing to get ideas from experienced sellers.

eBay sellers can be measured several ways, but the most commonly accepted form is by sales revenue. Other measurements include unit sales and number of feedback ratings.

Large eBay sellers began organizing in 2003 with the creation of The eBay Elite, which later changed its name to Professional eBay Sellers Alliance (PESA); its website is at www.gopesa.org. They don't make a member list available, however.

Places you can view eBay top sellers—usually ranked by number of feedback (an indicator of how many transactions they've completed)—include the following three lists. These are guideposts only—be sure to check the dates of each list to know how current it is when you access it.

11

Nortica   Nortica used to make available for free a list of the top 500 sellers on eBay. You can view the list from July 2004: www.nortica.com/UserArea/ebay500_15.asp. Today it sells a list of the top 100 sellers for $100 (www.nortica.com/UserArea/Nortica100.asp). This information might prove useful, but the average seller can probably get by without it, since Nortica covers all of eBay, while most sellers are more interested in concentrating their selling efforts in one or a few categories.

X-Titles   X-Titles (http://x-titles.com/top-ebay-sellers-list) makes available an eBay list of top sellers. Check the date to make sure it's current when you read it.

Glinos   Glinos (http://glinos.is-a-geek.com:63125/cgi-bin/total.html) lists the top 20 eBay sellers by feedback.

Wrapping Up

Getting a good competitive picture of your market (or eBay category) can help you take proactive measures to increase your sales over that of your competitors. Analysis will reveal seller best practices and points of weakness that you can capitalize on in your own listings and business strategies.

Use data analysis and market-data tools to look for warning signs that can alert you to negative developments down the line—such as a new competitor who is undercutting your prices, or a top seller who is flooding the marketplace with too many items given the amount of demand. Use your insight and improved understanding of the marketplace to prevent costly inventory-acquisition or listing mistakes and to identify opportunities, such as when a top seller of a particular product has disappeared from eBay.

eBay is careful about protecting the identity of its users. Services that license eBay market data cannot reveal the identities of individual sellers, but remember the ways we reviewed to study data and look for patterns.

As top sellers get more sophisticated about branding themselves, they also make it easier to track them. Study your category's top sellers to anticipate their moves, and see if they have an international presence and if they are selling on multiple marketplaces.

The more information you know about your competitors, the better advantage you will have. Use this knowledge to help you formulate your own strategies on eBay and elsewhere.

An investment in time, some subscriptions to market-data and traffic-tracking tools, and some brain power can set you apart from your competitors and make you a better, more profitable, eBay seller.

NOTE   *eBay launched Marketplace Research as this book was going to press; see Appendix B for information on how its Seller filter can help you research your competitors.*

Appendix A

Data Reports from Auction Management Services

Auction-management services that cater to large, high-volume sellers have developed reports that sellers can use to measure their performance. Use these reports in conjunction with the services from eBay and third-party vendors outlined in this book, and apply them to your listing and marketing strategies in the same way we discussed in Chapters 8–11. These reports provide the following key metrics:

- Fee summaries (including the costs of your payment services)
- Sales summaries (including gross merchandise sales, number of units sold, average selling price (ASP), sell-through rates (STRs), and sales-growth metrics such as month-to-month sales growth, and so on)
- Customer summaries (repeat buyers versus new buyers)
- Sales by SKU or category and profit-and-loss summaries (based on marketplace and payment service fees only)

Find out what reports are available to you and whether your auction-management service provider can help you customize reports for your own usage. If the service does not offer reports, but it offers data you can extract (usually through an export or download function), you can create your own reports using spreadsheet programs.

You can get the latest lists of auction-management services from the following sources:

- **eBay Solutions Directory**   http://solutions.ebay.com
- **Auction Software Review**   auctionsoftwarereview.com
- **AuctionBytes**   auctionbytes.com/cab/pages/ams

Following are some sample reports taken from two services to show you what kinds of reports are available through auction-management services. The first is a report from ChannelAdvisor, which is geared to high-volume, multi-channel sellers, and the second is from MarketBlast, which is a software program geared toward small- to medium-sized sellers on eBay.

ChannelAdvisor Dashboards Example

ChannelAdvisor is an auction-management service that caters to high-volume eBay sellers. Its program features "dashboards" that let sellers view and track their metrics. A review of some of ChannelAdvisor's reports helps gain insight into the big-picture view you should be taking to measure your performance to make sure you stay on track.

TIP   *Read ChannelAdvisor CEO Scot Wingo's book,* eBay Strategies *for helpful information.*

Figure A-1 shows ChannelAdvisor's Closed Listing Profit-Loss report, which allows sellers to see which products were most and least profitable based on the original cost of the item and the marketplace fees. The data appears in spreadsheet format, making it easy to sort reports by SKU and marketplace as well.

Figure A-2 shows the ChannelAdvisor Strategy Dashboard. A chart that tracks a month's performance visually makes it easier for you to see what's going on with your total sales. The Data in Figure A-2 shows a dip in the middle of the month, but things were looking up again by the end of the month.

The Strategy Dashboard looks at sales (Gross Merchandise Volume), total quantity sold, ASP, conversion rate, and gross margin. For sellers who look at reports daily and weekly, these reports mean no surprises at the end of the month, and they let you compare the current month's performance with past months.

Closed Listing Profit-Loss

Monday, September 27, 2004 through Sunday, October 03, 2004 — Executed on 10/7/2004 5:17:54 PM

SKU	Site	Site Listing ID	Title	Insertion Fees	Reserve Fees	Special Fees	Misc Fees	Closing Fees	Featured Fees	Gallery Fees	Total Fees	GMV	Original Cost	Profit/Loss
MEGA CENTERCH	eBay	5721307035	Polk Audio Alpha 2Way Dual 5-1/4" Center Channel Speaker	$0.30	$0.00	$0.20	$0.00	$45.00	$19.95	$0.25	$65.70	$2,125.00	$1,556.02	$503.28
MEGA CENTERCH	eBay	5722371759	Polk Audio Alpha 2Way Dual 5-1/4" Center Channel Speaker	$0.30	$0.00	$0.00	$0.00	$43.50	$0.00	$0.25	$44.05	$2,025.00	$1,559.85	$421.10
MEGA CENTERCH	eBay	5722682140	Polk Audio Alpha 2Way Dual 5-1/4" Center Channel Speaker	$0.30	$0.00	$0.00	$0.00	$42.45	$0.00	$0.25	$43.00	$1,955.00	$1,559.85	$352.15
MEGA CENTERCH	eBay	5722192732	Polk Audio Alpha 2Way Dual 5-1/4" Center Channel Speaker	$0.30	$0.00	$0.00	$0.00	$18.97	$0.00	$0.25	$19.52	$667.00	$338.16	$309.32
MEGA CENTERCH	eBay	5722382596	Polk Audio Alpha 2Way Dual 5-1/4" Center Channel Speaker	$0.30	$0.00	$0.00	$0.00	$41.65	$0.00	$0.25	$42.20	$1,902.00	$1,556.02	$303.78
MEGA CENTERCH	eBay	5723221662	Polk Audio Alpha 2Way Dual 5-1/4" Center Channel Speaker	$0.30	$0.00	$0.00	$0.00	$41.25	$0.00	$0.25	$41.80	$1,875.00	$1,559.85	$273.35
MEGA CENTERCH	eBay	5722382588	Polk Audio Alpha 2Way Dual 5-1/4" Center Channel Speaker	$0.30	$0.00	$0.00	$0.00	$20.84	$0.00	$0.25	$21.39	$735.00	$442.82	$270.79
MEGA CENTERCH	eBay	5722378606	Polk Audio Alpha 2Way Dual 5-1/4" Center Channel Speaker	$0.30	$0.00	$0.00	$0.00	$19.77	$0.00	$0.25	$20.32	$696.03	$424.33	$251.38
MEGA CENTERCH	eBay	5722197165	Polk Audio Alpha 2Way Dual 5-1/4" Center Channel Speaker	$0.30	$0.00	$0.00	$0.00	$13.16	$0.00	$0.25	$13.71	$456.00	$191.70	$250.59
MEGA CENTERCH	eBay	5723441818	Polk Audio Alpha 2Way Dual 5-1/4" Center Channel Speaker	$0.30	$0.00	$0.00	$0.00	$7.64	$0.00	$0.25	$8.19	$255.00	$0.00	$246.81
MEGA1200S BK-Z	eBay	5723783870	Polk Audio ALPHA 1200S 12" 500-Watt Powered Subwoofer Blk	$0.30	$0.00	$0.00	$0.00	$6.88	$0.00	$0.25	$7.43	$227.50	$0.00	$220.07
MEGA20BE	eBay	5723764973	Polk Audio ALPHA 20 2-Way Bookshelf Loudspeakers Speakers	$0.30	$0.00	$0.00	$0.00	$6.74	$0.00	$0.25	$7.29	$222.50	$0.00	$215.21

FIGURE A-1 ChannelAdvisor's Closed Listing Profit-Loss report lets you see how each product performed.

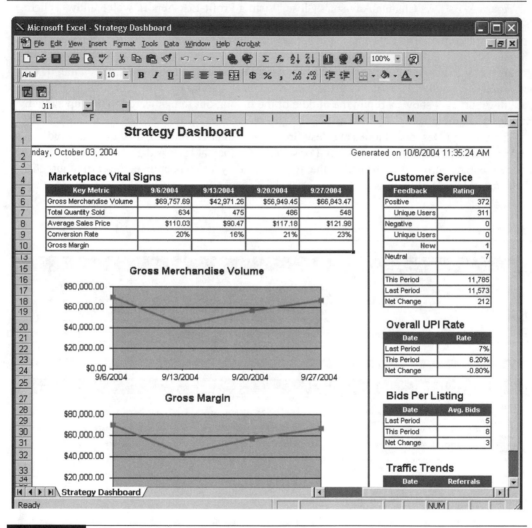

FIGURE A-2 ChannelAdvisor's Strategy Dashboard gives you vital statistics by marketplace.

Figure A-3 shows that some auction-management services also offer the kind of traffic-tracking capabilities discussed in Chapter 7. Managing your marketing budget can be challenging, and analytics (traffic-tracking) tools like Sellathon and those provided by your auction-management service can provide immediate feedback on whether a campaign is working for you.

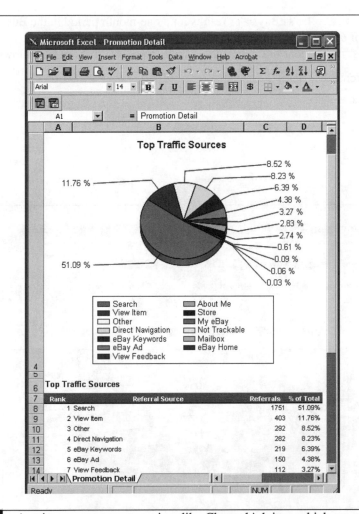

Auction-management services like ChannelAdvisor, which are geared to large, multi-channel sellers, have tools to track traffic, as in this Top Traffic Sources report, helpful in determining the effectiveness of your marketing strategies.

MarketBlast Software Example

MarketBlast is a software program for eBay sellers that is geared to small and mid-level sellers. MarketBlast is not a web-hosted service, like many auction-management tools. Instead, you download the software to your computer for a one-time charge, with no monthly subscription or commission fees. The software is compatible with Windows and Macintosh.

Figure A-4 shows a seller's eBay sales results for a one-month period in the Business Trends report. The week of 6/19/05, the average price of items sold was $162.08.

You can access five sections of the Business Trends report by clicking the following tabs:

- Gross Merchandise Sales
- Average Sales Price
- Listings
- Fees
- Feedback

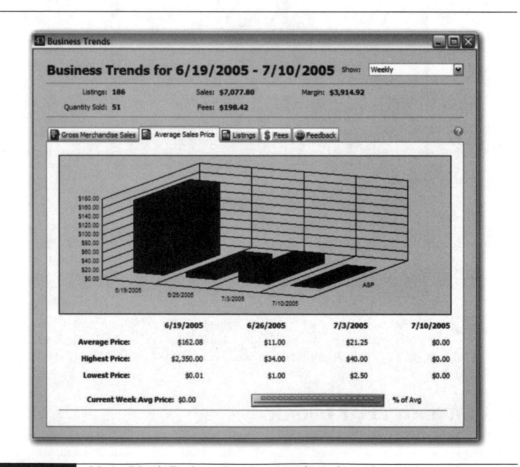

MarketBlast's Business Trends report shows key sales metrics, such as selling-price data.

Figure A-5 shows the Category Trends report, which breaks out sales numbers into categories. This report shows that the Power Mac G5 was the category that contributed the most to this seller's sales ($4700, or 66.81 percent of dollar sales) in the month of June.

You can access four sections of the Category Trends report by clicking the following tabs:

- Sales By Category
- ASP By Category
- Listings By Category
- Fees By Category

Since MarketBlast is based on 4D, a powerful database program, you can customize reports to suit your needs (without needing special programming skills).

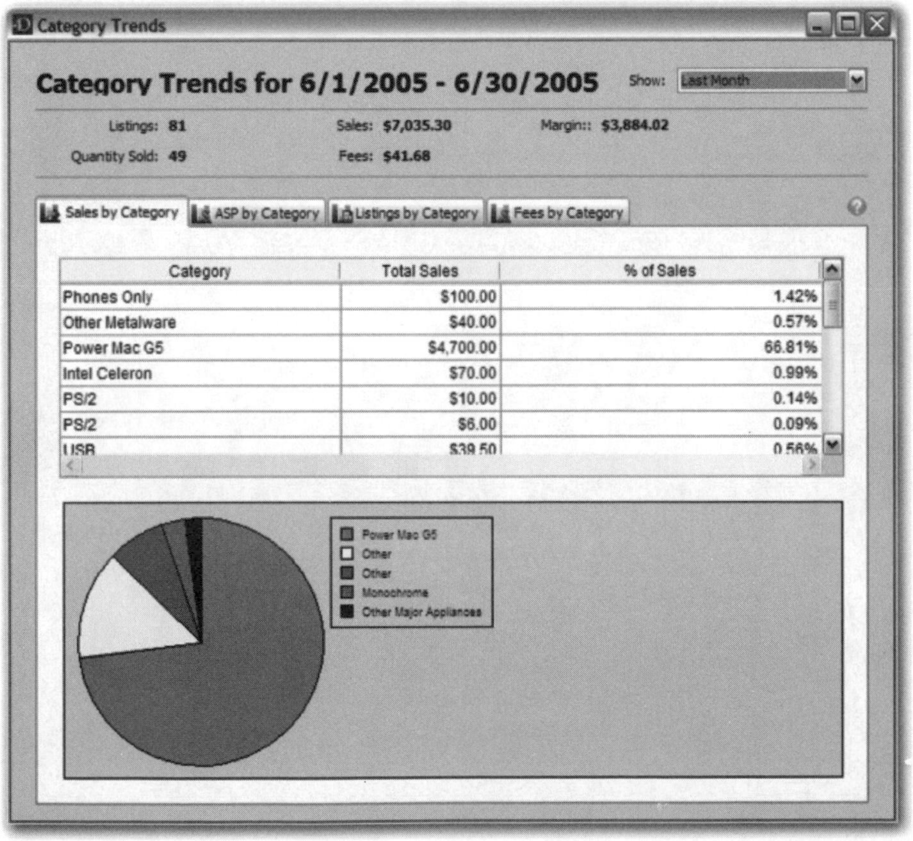

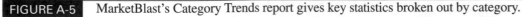

FIGURE A-5 MarketBlast's Category Trends report gives key statistics broken out by category.

Appendix B

eBay MarketPlace Research

eBay introduced Marketplace Research as this book was going to press. This service provides subscribers with data that includes top searches on eBay and metrics such as ASP, average starting price, and average shipping cost.

Accessing eBay Marketplace Research

Sign in to My eBay and in the left navigation bar under My Account, click Subscriptions. Under Available Subscriptions—eBay Marketplace Research, you can sign up for the service you wish to subscribe to:

- **Marketplace Research Fast Pass**   Two-day pass; data contains ASPs but not STRs and goes back only 60 days.
- **Marketplace Research Basic**   Monthly subscription; data contains ASPs and STRs and goes back 60 days.
- **Marketplace Research Pro**   Monthly subscription; data contains not only ASPs and STRs, but it also goes back 90 days and includes international market data.

Once you have signed up for a subscription to Marketplace Research, it will appear under My Subscriptions in My eBay.

Unique Features of eBay Marketplace Research Pro

There are a number of differences between eBay's own data tool and the tools that license data from eBay. You may find it helpful to refer back to the beginning pages of Chapter 4 on evaluating eBay market-data tools.

There is no lag time with eBay Marketplace Research. Keep in mind that vendors like Terapeak and DeepAnalysis "clean up" the eBay data, which adds value. eBay provides metrics on active listings, so you can see the number of active items and the average starting price for listings currently for sale on eBay.com and eBay Stores. Active listing data is useful to understand current market supply and should be used in conjunction with closed-listing data.

Key differences between the eBay Marketplace Research tool and the data tools that license market data from eBay include the following:

- A Seller filter, allowing you to search metrics by an individual eBay seller or Store
- Keyword searches only—no category analysis
- International coverage from all eBay sites worldwide
- Active Listings with zero lag time and 90-day coverage
- Real Estate category
- Top Searches from eBay.com and international sites

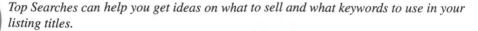

TIP   *Top Searches can help you get ideas on what to sell and what keywords to use in your listing titles.*

Using eBay Marketplace Research Pro—Charts & Metrics

After you sign in, you can enter a keyword search and select a category, then click the Run Research button. Figure B-1 shows the main page for doing keyword research using eBay Marketplace Research Pro. To narrow your search, select All Filters under Add Filters. Figure B-1 also shows the two tabs that let you switch between viewing Completed Items and Active Items.

Figure B-2 shows sections from the reports you will see when you select the Completed Items tab (the screen on the top) and the Active Items tab (the screen on the bottom).

The Seller Filter is extremely valuable because you can now easily compare your performance with your competitors to see if they are getting better ASPs and STRs for a particular product or product line, though not by category or on eBay as a whole.

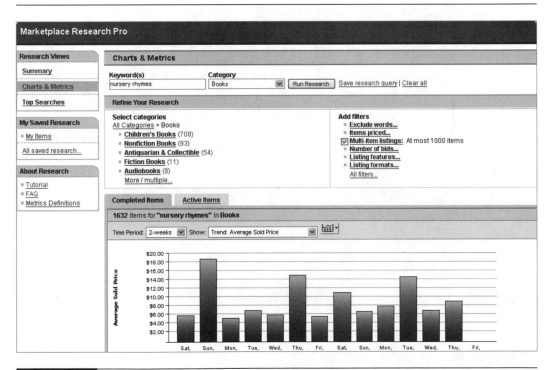

FIGURE B-1   eBay Marketplace Research Pro allows keyword searching on current and completed items going back 90 days.

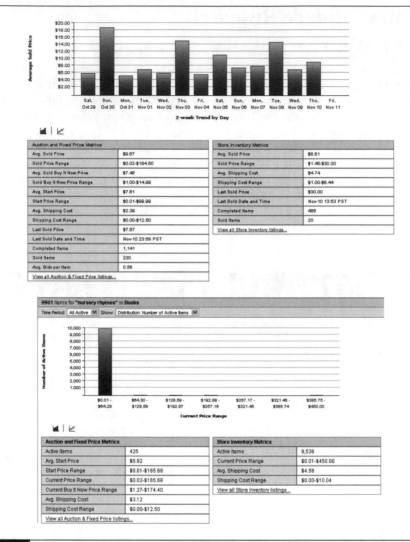

The following metrics tables appear within the figure:

Auction and Fixed Price Metrics (Completed Items)

Auction and Fixed Price Metrics	
Avg. Sold Price	$9.57
Sold Price Range	$0.02-$184.50
Avg. Sold Buy It Now Price	$7.48
Sold Buy It Now Price Range	$1.00-$14.99
Avg. Start Price	$7.81
Start Price Range	$0.01-$99.99
Avg. Shipping Cost	$2.39
Shipping Cost Range	$0.00-$12.50
Last Sold Price	$7.67
Last Sold Date and Time	Nov-10 23:58 PST
Completed Items	1,141
Sold Items	230
Avg. Bids per Item	0.56
View all Auction & Fixed Price listings...	

Store Inventory Metrics (Completed Items)

Store Inventory Metrics	
Avg. Sold Price	$9.51
Sold Price Range	$1.46-$30.00
Avg. Shipping Cost	$4.74
Shipping Cost Range	$1.00-$8.44
Last Sold Price	$30.00
Last Sold Date and Time	Nov-10 13:53 PST
Completed Items	486
Sold Items	20
View all Store Inventory listings...	

9961 items for "nursery rhymes" in Books
Time Period: All Active   Show: Distribution: Number of Active Items

Auction and Fixed Price Metrics (Active Items)

Auction and Fixed Price Metrics	
Active Items	425
Avg. Start Price	$5.92
Start Price Range	$0.01-$165.68
Current Price Range	$0.02-$165.68
Current Buy It Now Price Range	$1.27-$174.40
Avg. Shipping Cost	$3.12
Shipping Cost Range	$0.00-$12.50
View all Auction & Fixed Price listings...	

Store Inventory Metrics (Active Items)

Store Inventory Metrics	
Active Items	9,536
Current Price Range	$0.01-$450.00
Avg. Shipping Cost	$4.58
Shipping Cost Range	$0.00-$10.04
View all Store Inventory listings...	

FIGURE B-2   The top screen shows Completed Items data, and the bottom screen shows Active Items data.

Wrapping Up

eBay Marketplace Research Pro offers some data you can't currently find elsewhere, but market-data tools like Terapeak and DeepAnalysis offer features that eBay Marketplace Research does not. These are truly complementary services, though sellers may not feel they can justify the costs of a subscription to all three services. Become familiar with each service and determine which ones are most useful to you. Keep checking for new features, as things move rapidly in the eBay world.

Index

A

About Me page, 205, 234–235
account hijacking risks, 143
ACityDiscount
    cross-promoting listings
      by, 221
    feedback for, 235
    Fixed Price format used
      by, 205
    for starter prices, 180–181
acquisition costs, 223, 239
active listings, 20
Add To Favorites link, 38
Advanced Analysis option, 66
Advanced Economics Research
    Systems (AERS) Inc. *See*
    Terapeak tools
advanced listing strategies,
    35, 196
    auction-style listings vs.
      Fixed Price format,
      201–203, 205
    competition in, 212
    data for, 206–207
    hot items in, 197
    industry sources for, 197
    for inventory, 200–201
    listing components in,
      210–211
    offers and policies, 210–213
    optional features and
      upgrades, 208–210
    product identification
      in, 204
    product research in, 196,
      198–201

    rare vs. common items, 203
    reserve prices, 207–208
    shipping and handling
      in, 212
    stores effect, 204–205
    summary, 215
    testing in, 211–212
    tools for, 213–215
advertising and publicity, 226
    auctions vs. websites, 227
    data for, 232–234
    terminology for, 230–231
    types of, 227–229
AERS (Advanced Economics
    Research Systems) Inc. *See*
    Terapeak tools
affiliate marketing, 231
Alibaba site, 250
All Categories list, 37
All Methods of Arrival
    section, 156
AMS (auction-management
    services), 254
    ChannelAdvisor dashboards
      example, 254–257
    MarketBlast software
      Example, 257–259
    traffic tracking tools, 166
analytics tools, 5–6, 13, 144
    See also traffic data
Anchor stores, 55, 64
Andale tools, 13, 79
    for advanced listing
      strategies, 213–214
    Counters, 86–87, 174
    for ending time data, 174
    for listing strategies, 190

    Price Finder, 208
    for repeat sales, 225
    Research, 82–85
    Sales Analyzer, 87–88
    Smart Andale analysis
      method, 85–86
    summary, 89
    for timeliness of
      data, 76
    What's Hot, 80–82
AntiqueArts.com site, 199
antiques dealers, 14
Appraisers Association of
    America, 204
archived reports
    DeepAnalysis, 138
    Sales Reports, 52
Arrival Methods tab, 155–156
ASPs (Average Selling
    Prices), 6
    calculating, 7
    comparing, 8–9
    in duration data, 178
    in ending time data,
      174–175
    need for, 9
    studies on, 14–15
Association of Online
    Appraisers, 204
auction-management services
    (AMS), 254
    ChannelAdvisor dashboards
      example, 254–257
    MarketBlast software
      Example, 257–259
    traffic tracking tools, 166
Auction Software Review, 166

Auction tab, 135–136
Auction Type section, 128–130
AuctionBytes
    end day survey by, 172–174
    Forums, 204
    Newsflash article, 26
AuctionBytes-Update
    newsletter, 14
AuctionHelper, 220
AuctionIntelligence program, 158
auctionisle* user, 10
auctions
    for advertising, 227–228
    duration of
        background, 176
        data for, 178–179
        practicals vs.
            collectibles, 177
        search index
            for, 178
    as marketing tools, 204
    unknown services
        for, 143
AuctionSieve tool, 39, 251
Auctiva service, 220
AuntiesBeads.com site, 223
Average Sales Price Per Item By
    Format chart, 49
Average Selling Prices. *See*
    ASPs (Average Selling Prices)

B

Basic stores, 55
Bidding and Buying reports, 55,
    66–67
BidRobot tool, 39
Bids Report, 67
biggest sellers, 251–252
BIN Auction Duration
    section, 133
BIN (Buy It Now) format, 27
    and auction duration, 178
    vs. auction listings, 27
    availability of, 203
    listings, 28–29
BizRate site
    popular products on, 199
    for searches, 186
Bloglines service, 39

Blueberry Boutique
    cross-promoting listings
        by, 221
    on keywords, 188
    sales by, 198
Boston Collective website, 250
brands
    vs. generics, 20
    for repeat business, 226
Bright Builders. *See*
    DeepAnalysis tools
BrilliantShopper.com site, 199
Browsing categories in
    Terapeak, 95, 112–115
Business Trends report, 258
Buy It Now (BIN) format
    and auction duration, 178
    vs. auction listings, 27
    availability of, 203
    listings, 28–29
Buy It Now Report, 67
buyer perspective in monitoring
    competitors, 246
*Buyer's Guide to Web
    Analytics*, 147
Buying Solutions section, 70
buySAFE tests, 235–236

C

C2C (consumer-to-consumer)
    marketplaces, 237
Cano, Jen, 123–124
categories
    browsing, 112–114
    changes in, 27–28, 115
    comparing, 96, 114
    and competitors, 246
    in data analysis tools, 78
    DeepAnalysis searches for,
        139–140
    jumping, 96–97
    in listings, 183
        data for, 185–186
        Item Specifics and
            Product Finder tool,
            183–184
        multiple, 183
    Sales By Category charts,
        50–52

trails for, 95
    viewing, 96–97
Category Trends report, 259
CDI (Consumer Demand
    Index), 199
Certified Providers, 143
Certified Providers Catalog, 70
ChannelAdvisor service, 15
    dashboards, 254
    for repeat sales, 225
chili pepper ranking system, 81
Chris, Sherman, 186
Circuit City chain
    traffic and sales reports
        for, 161
    ViewTracker use by, 158
click-through rate (CTR), 230
ClickThruStats service, 234
client-based programs, 122
Closed Listing Profit-Loss
    reports, 255
Co-op Advertising program, 228
collectibles
    auction duration for, 177
    in early years, 14
Commission Junction service, 231
common items in advanced
    listing strategies, 203
comparison shopping
    sites, 230
comparisons
    of categories, 96, 114
    guidelines for, 20
competitive intelligence tools, 13
competitors
    in advanced listing
        strategies, 212
    copying approach of, 19
    monitoring. *See* monitoring
        competitors
    researching, 237
Complete Paths option, 65
Completed Item Search, 190
Completed Listings searches, 41
    in advanced listing
        strategies, 213
    conducting, 43–45
    features data, 210
completed listings vs. items
    for sale, 20

comprehensiveness of data analysis tools, 78
compressing reports, 64
Consumer Demand Index (CDI), 199
consumer-to-consumer (C2C) marketplaces, 237
conversion rates
  defined, 230
  measuring, 145–146
  vs. sell-through rates, 145
CoreMetrics service, 147
cost of data analysis tools, 13
cost-per-click in advertising, 230
cost per thousand (CPM) in advertising, 230
counterfeits, 21
counters
  Andale, 86–87, 174
  ViewTracker, 148
coverage dates, 78
CPM (cost per thousand) in advertising, 230
credibility and reputation, 234
  data for, 235–236
  feedback for, 234–235
  third-party services for, 235
cross-promoting listings, 218–219
  data, 222
  tools for, 219–220
CTR (click-through rate), 230
custom folders in ViewTracker, 162–163
Custom Reports section, 58
customer costs, 223, 239
customer summary reports, 254

D

Daily News Record, 250
dashboards, ChannelAdvisor, 254–257
data analysis
  applying, 8–9
  ASP calculations, 6–7
  background and definitions, 5–6
  benefits, 8, 10
  caveats and pitfalls, 19–29
  changes in, 14
  for listings, 11–12
  for marketing, 12
  overview, 4–5
  STR calculations, 7–8
  tools for, 5, 12–15
  wise use of, 18–19
Data Licensing Program, 70
data mining, 7, 34–35
  basic strategies, 35–36
  date ranges in, 63–64
  help for, 68–70
  Market Data program, 70–71
  pricing data, 72–73
  for purchase decisions, 45–47
  Sales Reports. *See* Sales Reports
  searches. *See* searches
  Store Traffic Reports. *See* Store Traffic Reports
  working with data from, 60–64
dates
  analysis tool coverage, 78
  in reports, 63–64
  viewing by, 97
DeepAnalysis tools, 13, 122
  for advanced listing strategies, 213, 215
  Auction tab, 135–136
  for competitor identification, 246–247
  data levels in, 28
  for ending time data, 174, 176
  Keyword tab, 138–139
  for listing strategies, 190–192
  navigating, 124–127
  Report tab, 127–128
    Auction Type section, 128–130
    Feature Analysis section, 130–131
    Regular & Dutch Auction Duration and BIN Auction Duration sections, 133
    Sellers Summary and Top Sellers sections, 134–135
    Starting Day and Ending Day sections, 132
  Research Reports, 215
  reserve prices data, 207
  saving reports in, 138
  searching in, 139–140
  Seller tab, 137–138
  for starting price data, 182
  summary, 140
  for timeliness of data, 76
  versions, 123
demand
  CDI, 199
  determining, 36, 41
descriptions
  keywords in, 187–188
  listing information in, 27
Detailed Visitors Log pages, 159–161
Developer program, 68–70
discussion boards, 68, 238
domains, 59
dominant players, 25
downloading
  Store Traffic Reports, 64
  ViewTracker data, 164–165
duration, auction
  background, 176
  data for, 178–179
  practicals vs. collectibles, 177
  search index for, 178
Dutch auctions, 21, 177

E

e-commerce websites, 147
e-mail newsletter services, 224
eBay Auction tool, 139–140
eBay Category tool, 140
eBay Community Hub, 204
eBay Keywords service, 229
eBay lists, 197–198

eBay Pulse
    for high-demand items,
        197–198
    for searches, 39–40
eBay Sales Reports. *See* Sales
    Reports
eBay Seller tool, 140
eBay Stores
    searching, 38
    traffic reports. *See* Store
        Traffic Reports
Efficacy package, 71
Email Marketing program, 224
emetrics, 144
Ending Day section, 132, 174,
    191–193
ending time
    data for, 174–176
    in DeepAnalysis, 132, 174,
        191–193
    selecting, 171–174
endorsements, 235
evaluating
    products, 201
    tools, 77–78, 183–184
excluding keywords, 189
Experienced Users Only:
    Override The Default Folder
    Set option, 162
exporting reports, 78

F

fads, 23–24
fakes, 21
false reports, 22
Fatfingers service, 181
Feature Analysis section
    items tracked in,
        130–131
    for reserve price
        data, 207
Featured stores, 55, 64
features
    in advanced listing
        strategies, 208–210
    tracking use of, 94, 117–118,
        130–131
Features tool, 94, 117–118

feedback
    for reputation and
        credibility, 234–235
    seller, 26
fees
    for STRs, 146
    summary reports, 47, 254
Fees Summary section, 47
Filter feature, 136
finding data. *See* searches
Finding Methods reports, 57–58,
    62–63
Findings tab, 127
5 Most Common Page #s Users
    Found section, 156
Fixed Price format, 27
    in advanced listing
        strategies, 201–203, 205
    starting prices for,
        180–181
folders in Sellathon
    in listing strategies, 233
    managing, 162–164
    purpose of, 149–151
ForeSee Results service, 147
free listing days, 24–25
freezer liquidations, 180
Froogle site, 199
Full Paths section, 64–65
Future Now, Inc., 147

G

Gallery feature, 208
General Announcements
    Board, 115
generics vs. brands, 20
George, Janet, 80
Getting Started tutorial, 38
Glinos site, 252
GMS (Gross Merchandise Sales),
    7, 14
GMV (Gross Merchandise
    Volume), 7
GoAntiques.com, 71
Golf company, 210–211
Google AdWords service,
    229, 231
Google Groups, 204

Google search engine, 186
Green, Andrew Evan, 220–221
Gross Merchandise Sales
    (GMS), 7, 14
Gross Merchandise Volume
    (GMV), 7
Groups for Sellers site, 68

H

HammerTap site, 122
handling charges, 212
Hartsoe, Allison, 53–54, 60–61
help
    for data mining, 68–70
    for searches, 38
Help File for Sales Reports
    Plus, 68
Henderson, Ron, 223, 227
Highlights page in Sellathon, 153
    Arrival Methods tab,
        155–156
    for listing strategies, 192
    Search Terms tab, 156–159
    for traffic data, 233
    Visitor Data tab, 153–154
hits in advertising, 230
Hitwise service, 24, 147
holiday shopping season, 24
hosted vs. desktop system
    tools, 77
Hot Categories report, 42
hot items
    in advanced listing
        strategies, 197, 199
    in Terapeak, 97–98
    What's Hot tool, 80–82
Hot Items By Category tool, 197
Hot List, 42
Hourly Analysis, 105, 190
How to Find Items section, 38
How To Sell feature, 82, 214

I

impressions (hits) in
    advertising, 230
industry sources for advanced
    listing strategies, 197

Infopia service
  for repeat sales, 225
  reports from, 15
international traffic, 239
Internet search engines, 186
inventory
  product evaluation for, 201
  purchase decisions for,
    45–47
  sources of
    competitors, 244,
      249–250
    online, 251
    strategies for, 200
irrelevant keywords, 25
Item Specifics feature
  evaluating, 183
  in searches, 44
  Terapeak use of,
    99–100
  for unstructured data, 27
items for sale vs. completed
  listings, 20
ItemScout.com tool, 39

J

joeleighs user, 210–211
jumping categories, 96–97

K

Karp, David, 249
key ratios, 101
Keyword tab, 138–139
keywords
  data on, 189
  designing, 188–189
  importance of, 187
  irrelevant and
    misleading, 25
  Search Keywords Report,
    62–63
  in searches
    Andale, 86
    DeepAnalysis,
      138–140
    search expansions, 184

strategies for, 186–187
Terapeak, 95
spamming, 26
in title and description
  fields, 187–188
Kovel, Ralph, 199
Kovel, Terry, 199
Kovels.com site, 199

L

lag time, 78
length of visits data, 159
levels of data, 28
licensing options for Market
  Data program, 70–71
Linkshare service, 231
Listing Duration, 107–108
Listing Features, 101–102, 215
listing strategies, 35, 170
  advanced. *See* advanced
    listing strategies
  auction duration,
    176–179
  categories in, 183–186
  data analysis for, 11–12
  ending time, 171–176
  game plans, 170–171
  keywords, 186–189
  quality of listings, 25
  starting prices, 179–182
  summary, 193
  tools for, 189–193
Listing Type Usage vs. Success
  Rate, 104–105, 215
Listings tool, 93, 109–110
Lockergnome service, 39
logos, 226
low starting prices, 179–180

M

Main Report tab, 136
Manage It tool, 72
Manage Your Store page, 230
market and historic sales data
  analysis, 171
market data licenses, 28

Market Data program, 34,
  70–71
market-data tools, 5, 13
market share, 245–246
MarketBlast software, 257–259
marketing strategies, 36, 218
  advertising and
    publicity, 226
    auctions vs.
      websites, 227
    data for, 232–234
    terminology for,
      230–231
    types of, 227–229
  cross-promoting listings,
    218–223
  data analysis for, 12
  presence expansion,
    237–239
  repeat sales, 223–226
  reputation and credibility,
    234–236
  starting prices in, 181
  summary, 241
  tools for, 239–240
marketing tools, auctions as,
  204–205
marketplace exposure, 228
Marketplace Research
  subscription service, 52–53
  accessing, 262
  charts and metrics in,
    263–264
  features of, 262
Marketworks service, 15, 225
Matching Categories list, 37
McGrath, Skip, 209
Medved
  listing data from, 24
  QuoteTracker end day
    survey by, 171, 173
menu bar in ViewTracker, 149
Merchandising Calendar feature,
  42, 197
Method of Arrival reports,
  186, 232
Miller, Jim, 200
mining data. *See* data mining

Minnich, Bobby
  cross-promoting listings
    by, 221
  data analysis by, 171, 231
  on keywords, 188
Minnich, Susan, 231
misleading keywords, 25
misspellings
  in keywords, 25, 188
  in searches, 38
monitoring competitors, 244
  activities, 248–250
  biggest sellers, 251–252
  buyer perspective in, 246
  market share, 245–246
  reasons for, 244–245
  summary, 252
  tools for, 246–248
  trade publications for,
    250–251
Month-To-Month Sales Growth
  item, 52
Most Popular Sorting Methods
  section, 156
multi-channel selling
  for advertising, 228
  tools for, 15
multiple user IDs, folders for, 164
My Summary page, 56
MyStoreCredit, 224

N

names for stores, 229
natural searches, 229
navigation
  DeepAnalysis, 124–127
  Terapeak, 93–95
  ViewTracker, 149–151
Nedungadi, Prashant, 80
new items vs. used items, 20
Next Page Reports, 66
NexTag site, 199
99-cent/no reserve starting-price
  strategy, 181
non-eBay sellers, 15
nonapproved eBay tools, 142–143
  auction-management
    services, 166

risks with, 143
Sellathon. *See* Sellathon
  tools
  summary, 166
Nortica, 252

O

offers, refining, 210–213
offline advertising, 228
Omidyar, Pierre, 201
1-day auctions, 177
online wholesale sources, 251
Opinity service, 235
optional features and upgrades,
  208–210
Other Solutions section, 70
OTWA (Online Traders Web
  Alliance), 204
Overstock
  advertising by, 228
  auctions by, 15

P

Page Views Reports, 58–59
paid searches, 229
passwords for third-party
  services, 143
Path Lengths option, 65
Path reports, 55, 64–66
pay-per-click (PPC), 230
peaks in traffic, 24
Perch feature, 39
PESA (Professional eBay Sellers
  Alliance), 251
phantom listings, 21–22
Playstations, phantom, 22
Pluck Auction Scout search
  tool, 251
policies, refining, 210–213
Popular Listings Report, 63
Popular Pages Report, 63
PPC (pay-per-click), 230
practicals
  auction duration for, 177
  growth of, 14
Price Finder Tool, 190
Price Ranges feature, 106–107

Price Summary feature,
  82–83
PriceMiner service, 71
prices
  data and reports
    for listing
      strategies, 191
    SmartCollector,
      72–73
    studies on, 14
    in Terapeak, 102–104
  for fads, 23
  starting, 179
    99-cent/no reserve, 181
    in auction vs. Fixed
      Price format,
      180–181
    data for, 181–182
    low, 179–180
    in marketing
      campaign, 181
Product Finder tool
  evaluating, 183–184
  for listings strategy, 162
  in searches, 44
products
  in advanced listing
    strategies
      identifying, 204
      researching, 196,
        198–201
  competitor, 244
  evaluating, 201
Professional eBay Sellers
  Alliance (PESA), 251
promotions, 24–25
Prospector search tool, 251
Proxy Bid feature, 161
publicity and advertising, 226
  auctions vs. websites, 227
  data for, 232–234
  terminology for, 230–231
  types of, 227–229
purchase decisions, 45–47

Q

quality of listings, 25
quantity of items, 21

R

ranges
    date
        in data mining, 63–64
        viewing data by, 97
    price, 106–107
rare items
    in advanced listing
        strategies, 203
    issues of, 22
Really Simple Syndication
    (RSS) fees, 39
Referrer report, 232
Referring Domains report, 57,
    59, 68, 239–240
Regular & Dutch Auction
    Duration section, 133
Reilly, Tim, 158, 161
relative numbers and ratios, 28
relevance of data analysis
    tools, 78
repeat buyers, 53
repeat sales, 223–224
    data for, 225–226
    tracking campaigns for,
        224–225
reports
    DeepAnalysis Report tab,
        127–128
        Auction Type section,
            128–130
        Feature Analysis
            section, 130–131
        Regular & Dutch
            Auction Duration
            and BIN Auction
            Duration sections,
            133
        Sellers Summary and
            Top Sellers sections,
            134–135
        Starting Day and
            Ending Day
            sections, 132
    Sales Reports. *See* Sales
        Reports
    Terapeak Report tool, 93,
        100–101
    Traffic Reports. *See* Traffic
        Reports

ViewTracker
    Detailed Visitors Log
        pages, 159–161
    Highlights page,
        153–157
reproductions, 21
reputation and credibility, 234
    data for, 235–236
    feedback for, 234–235
    third-party services for, 235
Reserve Price feature
    in advanced listing
        strategies, 207–208
    operation of, 12
retail cycles, 24
retention costs, 223
Return on Investment
    (ROI), 7
risks with auction services, 143
RSS (Really Simple
    Syndication) fees, 39

S

Sachs, Robert O., 45–46
Sales Analyzer tool, 87–88
Sales By Category charts,
    50–52
Sales By Format section,
    48–51, 53
Sales Marketshare, 112
sales performance
    tools for, 13
    traffic data for, 144–145
Sales Reports, 13, 47
    accessing, 47–48
    archived, 52
    Marketplace Research
        service, 52–53
    Sales By Category charts,
        50–52
    Sales By Format section,
        48–51, 53
    Sales Reports Plus, 48
        for advanced listing
            strategies, 213–214
        for listing strategies,
            190, 201–202
        for marketing, 239
        for repeat sales, 225

Sales Summary section,
    47–48, 53
    for success measures,
        53–54
Sales Reports Discussion
    Board, 68
Sales Reports News Group, 68
sales summary reports, 254
Sales Summary section,
    47–48, 53
saving
    reports
        in DeepAnalysis,
            78, 138
        in Terapeak, 78,
            118–119
    searches, 38
scams, 143
Search Engine Optimization
    industry, 229
search engines for hot lists, 199
Search Engines Report,
    61–62, 232
search expansions feature, 184
search index for auction
    duration, 178
Search Keywords Report, 62–63
Search Listings reports, 95
Search Terms tab
    for listing strategies,
        159, 192
    sections in, 156–157
Search Title And Description
    option, 37
SearchDay search engine,
    186–187
SearchEngineWatch.com search
    engine, 186
searches, 36–37
    for advertising, 229
    Completed Listings, 41,
        43–45
    DeepAnalysis, 139–140
    eBay Pulse for, 39–40
    eBay Stores, 38
    help for, 38
    improving results of, 38
    inferences from, 39–40
    keyword. *See* keywords
    refining, 37–38

searches (cont.)
    saving, 38
    by seller, 212
    Terapeak, 115–117
    tools for, 39
    What's Hot page, 42–43
seasonal factors
    in data analysis, 24
    in Sales Reports, 52
Second Chance Offers, 106
security at auction services, 143
sell-through rates. See STRs
    (sell-through rates)
Sellathon tools, 142–143
    for advanced listing
        strategies, 215
    for advertising, 231
    for auction duration data, 178
    for categories, 185–186
    Details page, 186
    folders in
        in listing strategies, 233
        managing, 162–164
        purpose of, 149–151
    Highlights pages
        Arrival Methods tab,
            155–156
        Search Terms tab,
            156–159
        Visitor Data tab,
            153–154
    keyword spamming study
        by, 26
    for keywords, 189
    for length of visits data, 159
    for listing strategies, 192
    for traffic data, 233
    for unique visits, 146
    ViewTracker service in. See
        ViewTracker service
    Yeager interview, 152
Seller Filter, 263
Seller tab, 137–138
SellerPower service, 157–159
sellers
    biggest, 251–252
    DeepAnalysis data for,
        134–135, 137–138
    discussion boards for, 238

feedback for, 26
    searching by, 212
    Terapeak data for, 94,
        110–112
Sellers Summary section,
    134–135
Seller's Voice service, 209
Selling Solutions section, 70
Senese, Jay, 179
Senese, Marie, 179
shadowing, 249
shill bidding
    defined, 21
    warning signs, 22–23
shipping and handling
    charges, 212
Shopping.com search
    engine, 186
shopping from work, 161
Shopzilla.com search
    engine, 186
site stability of auction
    services, 143
Site Traffic reports, 56–57
SiteCatalyst tool, 147
Smart Andale analysis method,
    85–86
SmartCollector service, 71–73
Snipe bids, 41
Solutions Directory
    for auction-management
        services, 166
    for repeat sales, 224
sorting sellers, 138
sources of inventory
    competitors, 244, 249–250
    online, 251
    strategies for, 200
spamming, keyword, 26
special features in data analysis
    tools, 78
Specific Research area, 99
SquareTrade service, 235
Stack, John, 205–206
Starting Day section, 132
starting prices, 179
    99-cent/no reserve, 181
    in auction vs. Fixed Price
        format, 180–181

data for, 181–182
    low, 179–180
    in marketing campaign, 181
status bar in DeepAnalysis,
    126–127
Steiner, Peter, 234
stickiness, 147
Store Home Page Views
    Report, 63
Store Search Keywords
    Report, 63
Store Traffic Reports, 54
    accessing, 55
    Bidding/Buying Reports,
        66–67
    Custom Reports, 58
    downloading, 64
    Finding Methods reports,
        57–58
    Path Reports, 64–66
    Site Traffic reports, 57
    store types in, 55–56
    types of, 56–57
stores
    in advanced listing
        strategies, 204–205
    for fixed prices, 203
    names for, 229
Stores Referral Credit
    program, 227
Strategy Dashboard,
    255–256
STRs (sell-through rates), 6
    in auction duration data,
        178–179
    calculating, 7–8
    comparing, 8
    vs. conversion rates, 145
    in ending time data,
        174–175
    fees for, 146
    in Sales Reports, 50–51,
        53–54
    studies for, 14–15
Sub-Category Revenue & Seller
    Breakdown report
    data in, 108–109
    for listing strategies, 191
subcategories in Terapeak, 96

Subtitle feature, 189
Success factors statistics, 127
Successful Listing Duration
  Lengths report
    data in, 107–108
    for listing strategies, 191
    for optimal duration,
      178–179
Sukow, Andrew, 92
Sukow, Anthony, 92
Sullivan, Danny, 186
Summary information in
  DeepAnalysis, 127
supplier sources, competitors
  for, 244, 249–250
supply, determining, 36, 41
synonyms in searches, 38

T

Taximarket user, 220–221
Terapeak tools, 13, 92–93
  for advanced listing
    strategies, 213, 215
  for auction duration
    data, 178
  for categories, 95–97,
    112–115
  for competitor
    identification, 246, 248
  data levels in, 28
  for dates and ranges, 97
  for ending time data, 174
  Features tool, 117–118
  Hot List, 97–98
  Hourly Analysis, 105
  Item Specifics, 99–100
  for key ratios, 101
  Listing Duration,
    107–108
  Listing Features,
    101–102, 207
  for listing strategies,
    190–191
  Listing Type Usage vs.
    Success Rate, 104–105
  Listings tool, 109–110
  navigating, 93–95

Price Ranges feature,
  106–107
  for pricing, 102–104
Report tool, 100–101
  for reserve prices, 207
Save Report, 118–119
Second Chance Offers, 106
Sellers tool, 110–112
Sub-Category Sales,
  108–109
timeliness of data in, 76
Trends page
  Browsing Categories,
    112–115
  Searching Listings,
    115–117
Terms Of Service, 211
testimonials, 235
testing
  in advanced listing
    strategies, 211–212
  guidelines for, 18–19
ThinkMetrics articles, 146
third-party services
  passwords for, 143
  for reputation and
    credibility, 235
TIAS.com, 71, 199
Time Spent Per Visit option, 65
timeBLASTER site, 38
timeliness of data tools,
  76, 78
title fields
  keywords in, 187–188
  listing information in, 27
  SellerPower for, 158–159
Top 5 Methods of Arrival
  section, 156
Top 5 Most Popular Categories
  Browsed section, 156
Top 5 Most Popular Categories
  Searched section, 156
Top 10 Search Terms Used
  to Find Your Auction(s)
  section, 156
Top Categories chart, 84
Top Sellers section, 134–135
Total Sales by Format chart, 49

tracking codes in ViewTracker,
  151, 153
trade publications, 250–251
trademark infringement, 26
Trading Circuit Team, 158
traffic data, 5–6, 13, 144
  auction-management
    services for, 166
  conversion rates, 145–146
  e-commerce websites, 147
  pitfalls, 146
  for sales increases,
    144–145
  Sellathon. *See* ViewTracker
    service
  stickiness, 147
Traffic Reports, 6
  for advanced listing
    strategies, 213
  for advertising, 227
  for cross-promoting
    listings, 222–223
  for ending time data,
    174–175
  for keywords, 189
  for listing strategies,
    190–191
  for marketing, 239
  Page Views Reports,
    58–59
  Referring Domains
    Report, 59
  store. *See* Store Traffic
    Reports
  Unique Visitors
    Reports, 58
  Visits Reports, 59
Trend It tool, 72
Trends section
  in Andale, 83, 85
  in Terapeak, 94
    Browsing Categories,
      112–115
    Searching Listings,
      115–117
Truition service, 15
Typed/Bookmark category, 60
typos, 25

U

Ugg boots, 23
unique buyers, 49
unique visitors, 58
    calculating, 146
    defined, 230
Unique Visitors
    Reports, 58
unstructured data, 27
used items vs. new
    items, 20
user IDs, folders for, 164

V

Value Guide package, 71
Value It tool, 72
Vendio tool, 225
ViewTracker service, 6, 13,
    142, 148
    for advanced listing
        strategies, 213
    for advertising, 227
    for categories, 185
    Circuit City use
        of, 158
    for cross-promoting
        listings, 222
    downloading data from,
        164–165
    features data in, 209
    folder management in,
        162–164
    for keyword exclusions, 189
    navigating, 149–151
    overview, 148–149

reports in
    Detailed Visitors Log
        pages, 159–161
    Highlights page,
        153–157
for starting price data, 182
tracking codes in, 151, 153
tracking methodology
    in, 164
for traffic data, 232
Visitor Data tab, 153–154
visitors
    Counters tool for, 86–87
    Detailed Visitors Log
        pages, 159–161
    Highlights page, 153–154
    unique, 58, 146, 230
Visits reports, 59

W

Wagner, George, 10
Wannamaker, John, 226
Web Analytics Association
    site, 147
WebAnalyticsDemystefied.com
    site, 147
WebSideStory service, 147
websites
    vs. auctions, 227
    e-commerce, 147
    usability of, 144
WebTrends tool, 15, 147
Welcome tab, 126
What's Hot list
    in Andale, 80–82, 214
    in DeepAnalysis, 127

What's Hot page,
    42–43
Whitman, Meg, 187
wholesale sources, 251
Wilkinson, Julia, 188
Wingo, Scot, 208
Winning Bid tool, 39
work, shopping from, 161
www.pricegrabber.com
    site, 199

X

X-Titles, 252

Y

Yahoo Groups, 204
Yahoo! search engine, 186
Yahoo! Search Marketing
    service, 229
Yaskulka, David
    cross-promoting listings
        by, 221
    on keywords, 188
    sales by, 198
Yeager, Wayne
    on keyword spam, 26
    on searching vs.
        browsing, 187
    Sellathon development
        by, 148, 152

Z

Zoovy tool, 225